MINNESOTA:
Its People and Culture

MINNESOTA:
Its People and Culture

by
W. E. ROSENFELT
and
HENRY HULL

Publishers
T. S. DENISON & COMPANY, INC.
Minneapolis

T. S. DENISON & COMPANY, INC.

Standard Book Number 513-01736-4
Library of Congress Card Number: 82-70019

Copyright © 1982 by T. S. Denison & Co., Inc.
Minneapolis, Minn. 55431

Introduction

This is a story of Minnesota! Discover the land, the people and the events that have made this state such a wonderful place to live.

Minnesota is often referred to as "The North Star State," or "The Land of 10,000 Lakes." Some prefer "The Land of Sky-Blue Waters," a description related to the early Indian word "Minnesota," which meant "Sky-Tinted Waters." Some people refer to Minnesota as the "Gopher State," and still others prefer to call it "The Bread and Butter State." It is clear then that Minnesota means different things to different people. Which of these meanings or descriptions do you like best?

The land of "sky-tinted water" was the home of the Chippewa and Sioux Indians long before the first white people came to the area. The many lakes and rivers provided a means of transportation for these people, as well as providing food and furs from the many fish and animals living in and around the water. We will try to learn what the land and its people have contributed to our present-day Minnesota. We will also look at these peoples' customs, their problems and actions, and attempt to find out where we fit into this overall picture of present-day "Gopher-land."

Minnesota is waiting for you to discover its many interesting secrets.

ACKNOWLEDGEMENTS

Burlington Northern, Inc.

Deere and Company

Educational Affairs Department, Ford Motor Company

The Greyhound Corporation

Hamline University Library

International Institute

Metropolitan Airports Commission

Minnesota Community College System

Minnesota Department of Agriculture

Minnesota Department of Economic Development

Minnesota Department of Education

Minnesota Department of Natural Resources

Minnesota Department of Transportation

Minnesota Historical Society

Minnesota State Planning Agency

Northwest Orient Airlines

United States Bureau of Mines

United States Department of Commerce, National Climatic Center

United States Department of Interior, Geological Survey

Cover photo, source of Mississippi River, courtesy of Minnesota Energy Department

TABLE OF CONTENTS
Minnesota: Its People and Culture

Unit Five: Minnesota Since 1920

UNIT ONE: GEOGRAPHY OVERVIEW

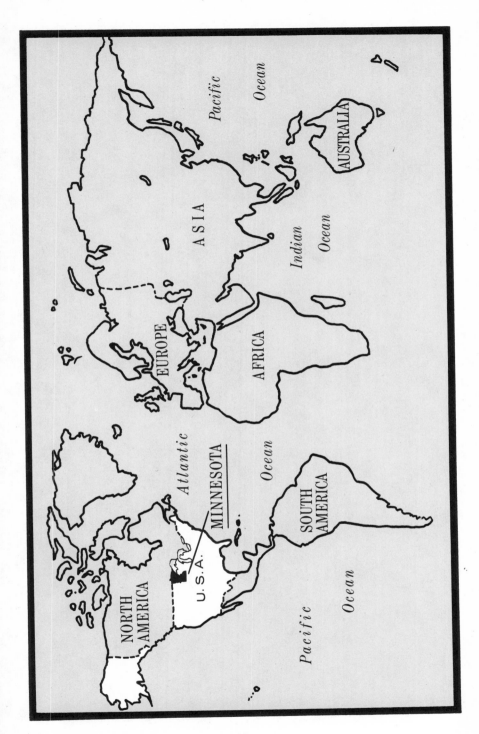

CHAPTER ONE

LOCATION AND CLIMATE

Location

Minnesota is one of the largest states. Of the fifty states, it is twelfth in size, having 84,068 square miles. Suppose you were to walk from east to west across the state, from one border to the other. Do you know how long it would take you? (The distance is approximately 360 miles.) For those who would like to walk across the state from north to south, the distance is about 400 miles. How long would this take?

Minnesota may be one of the largest states, but it is really only a small part of the world we live in, a small area on the continent of North America. The continent of North America is but one of seven continents that make up our global world, so you see, the portion of the globe we call Minnesota is really very small indeed. If all the land area of the world would suddenly disappear, leaving only Minnesota, it would appear as a tiny speck in a vast ocean.

With about four million population, Minnesota ranks nineteenth in that category. Its motto is a French phrase, "L' Etoile du Nord", which means "Star of the North". Until Alaska became a state, Minnesota was the northernmost of the United States. Minnesota is bordered by Canada on the north, Wisconsin on the east, Iowa on the south, and North and South Dakota on the west.

Boundaries

The state of Minnesota is easily recognized on a map because of its shape. The lines on the map that outline the state are called boundaries. These lines are determined usually in two ways:

1. By government survey (artificial boundaries).

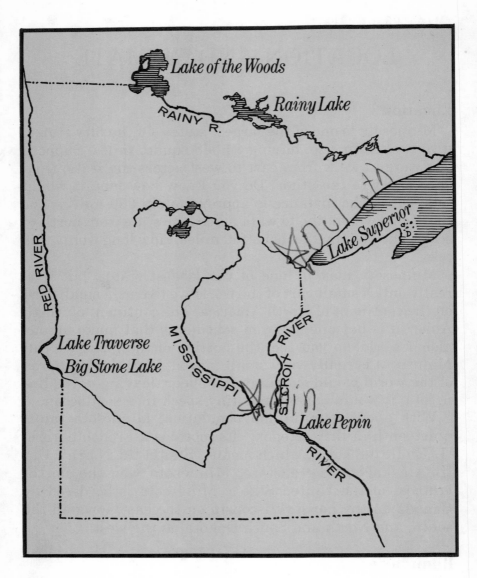

2. By natural terrain features (lakes, rivers, and in
   some states, oceans).

Which of these kinds of boundaries does Minnesota have?

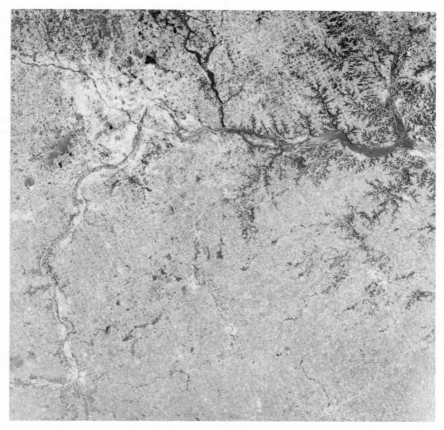

This photograph taken by NASA's Earth Resources Technology Satellite shows the St. Croix, Minnesota and Mississippi Rivers. Compare it to the map of the state to get a better idea of location.

Scales, Symbols and Legends

Mapmakers, in order to place a great deal of information on a map, must use scales and symbols to convey meaning or information in as few words as possible. This group of symbols is referred to as the map legend. Can you suggest why the term "legend" is appropriate? The mapmaker, by using the legend, makes it possible for anyone looking at the map to identify and locate those things that are placed on the map. It is a kind of sign language that everyone can read.

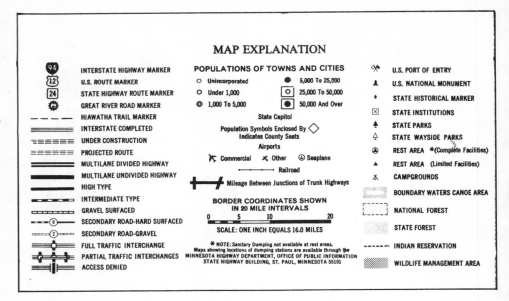

MAP EXPLANATION

94	INTERSTATE HIGHWAY MARKER		
12	U.S. ROUTE MARKER		
24	STATE HIGHWAY ROUTE MARKER		
	GREAT RIVER ROAD MARKER		
	HIAWATHA TRAIL MARKER		
	INTERSTATE COMPLETED		
	UNDER CONSTRUCTION		
	PROJECTED ROUTE		
	MULTILANE DIVIDED HIGHWAY		
	MULTILANE UNDIVIDED HIGHWAY		
	HIGH TYPE		
	INTERMEDIATE TYPE		
	GRAVEL SURFACED		
9	SECONDARY ROAD-HARD SURFACED		
2	SECONDARY ROAD-GRAVEL		
	FULL TRAFFIC INTERCHANGE		
	PARTIAL TRAFFIC INTERCHANGES		
	ACCESS DENIED		

POPULATIONS OF TOWNS AND CITIES

○ Unincorporated   ● 5,000 To 25,000
○ Under 1,000   ▣ 25,000 To 50,000
◉ 1,000 To 5,000   ▣● 50,000 And Over

State Capitol

Population Symbols Enclosed By ◇
Indicates County Seats

Airports

✈ Commercial   ✖ Other   ⊕ Seaplane

Railroad

Mileage Between Junctions of Trunk Highways

**BORDER COORDINATES SHOWN
IN 20 MILE INTERVALS**

0   5   10   20

SCALE: ONE INCH EQUALS 16.0 MILES

✳ NOTE: Sanitary Dumping not available at rest areas.
Maps showing locations of dumping stations are available through the
MINNESOTA HIGHWAY DEPARTMENT, OFFICE OF PUBLIC INFORMATION
STATE HIGHWAY BUILDING, ST. PAUL, MINNESOTA 55101

⚒	U.S. PORT OF ENTRY
⚑	U.S. NATIONAL MONUMENT
♦	STATE HISTORICAL MARKER
⊠	STATE INSTITUTIONS
♣	STATE PARKS
⚘	STATE WAYSIDE PARKS
⊛	REST AREA ✳(Complete Facilities)
▲	REST AREA (Limited Facilities)
⋏	CAMPGROUNDS
	BOUNDARY WATERS CANOE AREA
	NATIONAL FOREST
	STATE FOREST
	INDIAN RESERVATION
	WILDLIFE MANAGEMENT AREA

Elevation

Elevation refers to the distance the land rises above sea level. Mountainous states such as Colorado have some points of land rising as high as 14,000 feet above sea level. Minnesota is not a mountainous state, but the highest point in the state is called a mountain, and rises to 2,301 feet above sea level. Do you think people in Colorado would consider this a mountain?

The Rocky Mountains. Where are they?

Minnesota has chiefly a flat or gently rolling terrain or land surface except for a few areas with rugged depressions and valleys.

Climate

Our state has what is called a humid continental climate. That means that we have from a little over twenty inches of moisture on the western border to well over thirty-three inches a year in the southeast. Some of this comes as rain, and much, especially in the north, comes as snow.

The climate can be classed as cool on the average, although there are differences. If you really want to find out about the climate, go to a local seed corn salesman. You would find out that in some parts of southern Minnesota, you can plant 110-day corn. This means that there are 110 days out of the 365 of the year without frost.

All of Minnesota has a cold winter. Even in the most southern portions, twenty degrees below zero Fahrenheit is recorded each winter, and in the northern third of the state, the temperature sometimes reaches more than forty degrees below zero. The Dakotas to the west of us have a highland known by the geographical term of "steppe". On the Dakota and Canadian steppe, terrible winter storms develop, and sometimes spill over into our generally more gentle land.

Minnesota is often referred to as a climate "theater of seasons", with the scene changing four times each year. Each season of the year is beautiful in its own way, and many people prefer this variety in climate conditions. There are people, however, who dislike one or more of the seasons, or have a season they like best. How do you like the four seasons? Do you have a favorite season?

Words to Know — Define these words and terms. You may need to use a dictionary or encyclopedia to find some of the answers.

Boundaries
Climate
Continent
Elevation
L' Etoile du Nord
Humid continental climate
Map legend
Population
Terrain

Writing Activities

Suppose you have a pen pal in a country in Africa or Europe. With particular emphasis upon the area in which you live, write a letter to your foreign friend describing the terrain and climate of Minnesota.

CHAPTER TWO

PLANT AND ANIMAL LIFE

Plant Life

When the first white people came to North America, they found a hardwood or broad-leafed forest running from the Atlantic shore well into Minnesota. The southeast corner of Minnesota was once partly open country, but it was also covered with such trees as oak, ash, birch, cottonwood, box elder, aspen, hickory, and the hardest of all woods on our continent, ironwood or hop hornbeam. North of this area to the Canadian border was a vast forest of softwood or nee-dle-coniferous trees.

We still have evergreens. They are mostly white and red pine, spruce, cedar and jackpine. The better soils grow broad-leafed trees, including the hard or sugar maple.

After we leave the forested area of the southeast, we find reasonably level open country across southern Minnesota, that was once covered with high grass. Some of this land is poorly drained and hard. It still has many swamps and lakes, although not so many as northern Minnesota — the land of 10,000 lakes. Much of central Minnesota is open country. The Red River Valley of the North, an area of very rich soil, was and still is open country.

23

Hardwood forest in southern Minnesota

■ VEGETATION AT TIME OF EARLIEST WHITE SETTLEMENT

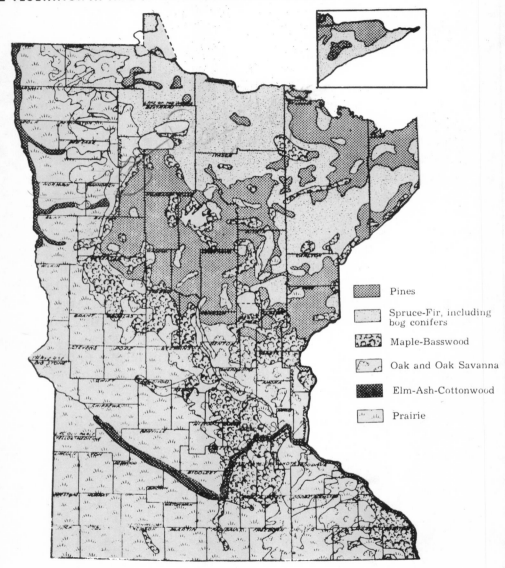

Pines

Spruce-Fir, including bog conifers

Maple-Basswood

Oak and Oak Savanna

Elm-Ash-Cottonwood

Prairie

From USDA-SCS 1965 map after F. J. Marschner, USDA 1930.

24

Superior National Forest in northern Minnesota

Animal Life

Before the white people came, Minnesota was a land rich in wild birds and game. Passenger pigeons, now extinct, ranged all over the hardwood region and beyond. The early pioneers of Goodhue, Winona and Fillmore Counties told of flocks of many thousands of these gray-green birds. Wild geese and ducks were here in great numbers, as were the smaller birds we see today. The loon, our state bird, screamed in lonely lakes. Bank swallows and purple martins cruised with open mouths, looking for insects. Hawks with nearly motionless wings hung in the sky, looking for striped gophers and meadow mice.

In the area of the Mississippi River, great white-headed eagles dropped with incredible speed to grab a buffalo fish, a red horse sucker, a gizzard shad or a dog fish in their black talons. Today the rivers and lakes of Minnesota are filled with many fish, ranging from primitive armor-plated sturgeon and crude, bewhiskered catfish, to silvery minnows not as long as a child's finger.

In the early days, Minnesota had many large wild animals. Two varieties which are found only in zoos today are the mighty bison and the woodland caribou of the north forest. We still have a few elk in the north, and many

Buffalo (Bison) once lived in Minnesota.

Minnesota wildlife—the moose

moose and white-tailed deer. The grizzly bear has been gone for many years, but there are still many black bears and wolves in what remains of the northern forest.

Going down in the scale of size, we have brush wolves or coyotes. Minnesota has predators with fine fur coats: martens and fishers, wolverines, badgers, foxes and white weasels that speed almost invisibly across the winter snow. Mink and otters swim and run along the water courses looking for anything they can catch.

Minnesota wildlife—the black bear

Minnesota wildlife—the wolf

The sleek brown muskrat often sits on top of its grass house at sunset and emits its thin, squeaky call over the swamp land. In the north and south of Minnesota, if you listen you can hear the "splat" of a beaver's tail on the water. There are raccoons in Minnesota and recently a visitor from the South, the oppossum, has established its home in Minnesota. The oppossum is one of the world's most primitive mammals; it is a small, gray animal with a bare tail and sharp teeth.

Our state has three types of rabbits. Actually, only the cottontail is a true rabbit, a small gray-brown animal that may be seen on the edge of the forest, morning or evening. The other two are "varying hares". Varying means that the animal varies its color with the season so that it will more easily blend in with its surroundings.

One of the varying hares is the white-tailed jackrabbit that lives in the open country of western Minnesota. It is brownish-gray in summer and turns to snow-white in winter. These are big hares, weighing up to twelve or more pounds. They look much like Bugs Bunny of the famous Hollywood movies.

The other varying hare of Minnesota is the snowshoe rabbit, which is about half the size of the jackrabbit, and lives in the forests of the north. It also varies its color from gray-brown to snow-white with the coming of the snow. The "snowshoe" name comes from its large feet which grow long, stiff hairs in the winter so that the rabbit can run silently on top of the deep snow.

Words to Know — Define these words and terms. You may need to use a dictionary or encyclopedia to find some of the answers.

Coniferous trees

Extinct

Varying hare

Writing Activities

Describe what you think the area around your house looked like before any white people came to Minnesota. (The vegetation map on page 24 can help to give you some ideas.

CHAPTER THREE

THE GEOLOGIC PAST
OF MINNESOTA

We use the term "Geologic Past" to tell us about very early Minnesota. Geology is the study of the earth's structure, and tells us of prehistoric times when the earth cooled off from a flaming mass of gas, and solidified. Ancient rocks, called igneous, that remain unchanged from these prehistoric times, can still be found in the Duluth area.

An Ancient Sea

After the earth cooled off and air formed, life came, and water covered much of Minnesota so that it looked like a shallow sea. Millions of shellfish or mollusks lived in this sea. They were enclosed in shells of lime, and lived for millions of years. After they died, their shells eventually settled to the bottom. These shells formed the beds of limestone at Winona and Mankato.

In modern times, we have used this limestone for constructing buildings and sidewalks. In the Mankato area, the many buildings faced with yellowish stone are made of limestone. In the very old city of Winona, the pale gray sidewalks are made of this stone, and the compacted shells of these sea creatures who lived in Minnesota millions of years ago are a part of Sugar Loaf Mountain.

Animals in Early Minnesota

After the ancient sea dried up, our area was still far from dry. Great fern forests grew out of many swamps between firmer land. The neighboring states of the Dakotas and Iowa had even more luxuriant fern forests. Many fern forests decomposed and in time they formed thick beds of peat, decayed plant matter that can be used as a fuel.

In Minnesota there was enough vegetation to support an abundance of reptiles. Huge egg-laying beasts, called dino-

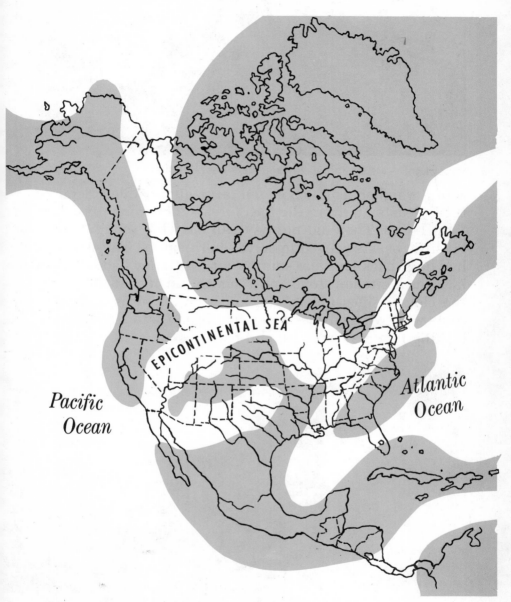

Pacific
Ocean

EPICONTINENTAL SEA

Atlantic
Ocean

Map showing the sea that covered part of Minnesota in ancient times

"Sugar Loaf"—Mississippi Valley landmark near Winona

saurs, weighed as much as ten large automobiles. Some of these beasts ate from the fern forests all through the daylight hours. They did not have an easy life though; other gigantic beasts preyed upon the herb eaters. These beasts had huge back legs and small front legs. They had heads as large as a kitchen stove and a mouth full of sharp teeth. In the cloudy skies above, the ancestors of birds and bats, some with wings over sixteen feet from tip to tip, hovered, looking for small reptiles and fish.

Dinosaur

The dinosaur age ended and dry land emerged. The climate changed significantly. The reptiles survived only in the form of snakes and smaller reptiles. The mammal became the dominating animal. Remember, a mammal is a warm-blooded animal.

There were a variety of mammals in Minnesota. There were forms of animals you would not recognize, like the giant sloth, and mammoths which looked like huge elephants. Camels and horses, and bison twice as large as the modern type roamed widely. There were three-hundred pound beavers with gigantic teeth able to cut down any tree, and hogs over five feet high at the shoulder. Dire wolves, the size of modern tigers, roamed in packs and huge cats with foot-long sabre teeth preyed upon many animals. A change in the animal population came with the glaciers. While some mammals survived by fleeing to the south, many became extinct.

Mammoth

Skull of giant beaver, twice the size of present day beaver

Glaciers

The weather grew colder and colder and snow fell most of the time. The weather was not warm enough to melt the snow, so over centuries the snow accumulated and the bottom layers turned to ice from the weight of the snow. The ice built up possibly as thick as five thousand feet or more.

These great masses of ice, called glaciers, moved toward the south and carried much soil with them. They carved up the surface of our state. There were three phases of the glaciers, lasting for periods of thousands of years. The last one, the Wisconsin Glacier, finished melting about twelve thousand years ago.

The extreme southeastern corner of Minnesota did not feel the bite of the ice; it is believed that the Wisconsin Glacier did not cover this part of Minnesota. This region is called the "driftless area". It comprises the south part of Winona County, most of Fillmore County, and all of Houston County. Most of this area has very rough terrain. The

Map showing glaciers that covered Minnesota in ancient times

water of millions of years has cut it into deep valleys and the ancient limestone formations and sandstone can still be seen.

Here too, are many caves. Underground water, running for an incredible length of time, has dissolved the stone and left great hollow spaces under the hills. Doubtless there were limestone caves at one time in other parts of Minnesota but the terrible weight of the glaciers crushed them.

Lakes caused by glaciers

The glaciers have left their mark in many ways. Northeastern and north central Minnesota had thousands of low places that filled with water. This resulted in the thousands of lakes of that region. Much of the good soil of northern Minnesota was mixed with the ice. When the last

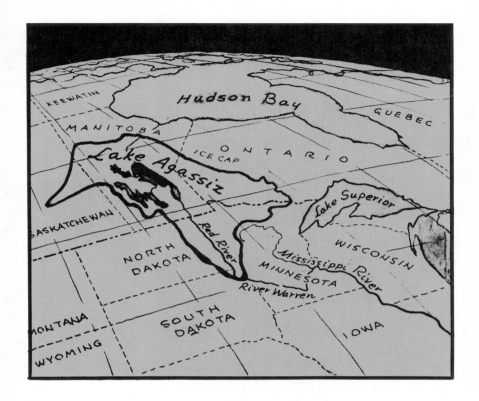

Melting glaciers formed a gigantic lake, called Lake Agassiz.

glacier finally melted, the water, laden with the silt, ran west. A gigantic lake formed, Lake Agassiz, covering what is today the great Red River Valley of the North. The soil settled to the bottom. The water, blocked by the ice to the north, ran in a great torrent down the Minnesota River Valley and the Mississippi River Valley. Both of these valleys have great flood plains and show the effects of the old glacial rivers.

In time, the Canadian ice melted and what was Lake Agassiz became the Red River Valley — one of the richest agricultural districts on earth, because the glacier left soil over twenty feet thick. After the melting of the last glacier, Minnesota watersheds or draining basins were formed.

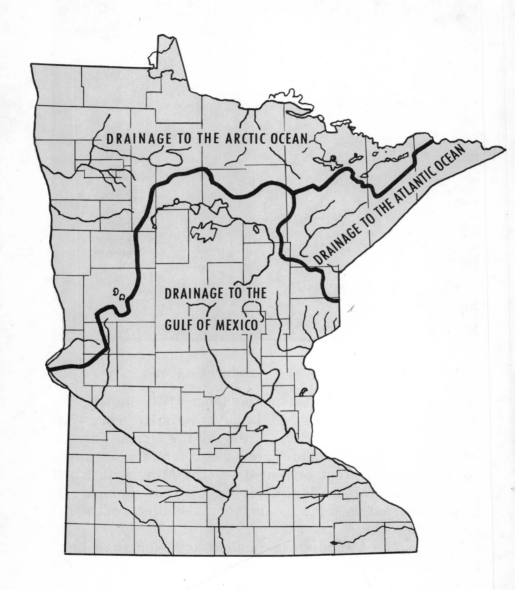

Minnesota's waters drain in three directions.

The Mississippi watershed that drains much of the state is the largest. The northeast area drains into Lake Superior and eventually through the other Great Lakes and St. Lawrence River into the Atlantic Ocean. The Red River Valley area drains north into Canada and finally into the Arctic Ocean.

About twelve thousand years ago, the recognizable form of our state had been established, with most of the wild animals, birds and plants we know today. The weather pattern that we are familiar with had been formed.

Words to Know — Define these words and terms. You may need to use a dictionary or encyclopedia to find some of the answers.

Dinosaurs –
Driftless Area
Geology
Glaciers
Igneous
Mammal
Mollusks
Peat
Red River Valley
Reptiles
Silt
Watershed

Writing Activities

Write brief answers to the following questions:

1. What effect did the glaciers have on the geography of Minnesota?
2. Where did the peat beds come from?
3. What caused the rough terrain and caverns in the southeastern corner of Minnesota?
4. What caused the beds of limestone that can be found at Winona and Mankato?

CHAPTER FOUR

THE LAND AND ITS RESOURCES

The Minnesota Wilderness

Adventurous explorers and pioneers found the frontier land we call Minnesota to be a vast expanse of beautiful wilderness. There were no roads in those days and often only blazed trails through the timber enabled people to get from place to place. The many rivers and lakes helped early travelers greatly as they provided the means for developing water travel routes.

The only inhabitants of this huge, unspoiled wilderness were the Sioux and the Chippewa Indian nations, and the great numbers of wild animals such as the bison, deer, mink, beaver and muskrat.

Tales of the beauty of this land and of the riches to be gained in furs and lumber spread far and wide, and soon people began to come into the area in search of their fortunes. At first, only small numbers came to brave the wilderness hardships, but soon wave after wave of immigrants arrived, searching for their promised land or new life. Timber was cleared from much of the land, crops were planted, towns and settlements came into being and roads were built, linking communities to the outside world. The wilderness was soon conquered by the adventurous people of the frontier.

Natural Resources

The land and water of Minnesota have provided a rich variety of natural resources without which industry and manufacturing would not have prospered as they have over the years. Some states have been blessed with mineral deposits such as gold and silver. (Can you name them?) Others have their rich oil deposits. (Can you name some of these states?) Minnesota offered a different kind of gold. It

Minnesota wildlife—the beaver

Minnesota wildlife—the deer

was called "iron ore" and most recently "taconite." (What is the difference?) This "Minnesota Gold" has provided the foundation upon which a good share of the state's industrial growth has been built.

Other resources that the earth has released for important use in the state are granite, sandstone, limestone and a type of clay ideally suited for pottery making. Granite from Minnesota has been recognized nationally as an outstanding building stone and has been used in such buildings as the Louisiana State Capitol building, the Chicago Tribune Tower building, and the Federal Courthouse in New York City. In Minnesota this native stone was used in the building of the St. Paul Cathedral and in several college buildings around the state.

The forests of Minnesota have been another valuable resource. The timber logged during the colorful lumbering era provided jobs for many immigrants and money for many lumbering industries. Greed and lack of conservation practices nearly used up all of this great natural resource and today only smaller-scale industrial use is made of the remaining timber supply. Wiser conservation practices have taken over where early greed and waste ruled, and today much of Minnesota's forest areas are protected as either State or National forests.

The waters of Minnesota have proved to be valuable as a resource. In early days they served as a means of transportation and a home for fur-bearing animals which brought the fur traders and their companies into the area. Water has also made it possible to run the mills of early industry and to serve as a transportation route, bringing both people and products into and out of the state. These waters also provide fish both for commercial fishing and for sport, and, as a resource, bring in thousands of vacationers each year, making the tourist business an important part of the state's economy.

The rich soil of the agricultural regions of Minnesota has made it possible to grow a variety of crops and to provide feed for large numbers of livestock. The resource of soil has made agriculture a main industry of the state. Meat products and dairy products are also made possible by the benefits of soil.

The people of Minnesota may also be looked upon as a natural resource. The industrious qualities and dependable work habits of Minnesota people have been important factors in the success of both business and industry in the state.

Minnesotans have provided the state and the nation with leadership in nearly every type of business and industry, as well as in education, government, labor movements and many other areas of importance.

Recreation in Minnesota

The land of 10,000 lakes has been a favorite sport and recreation area for people from all over the world. People were spending summer vacations here as far back as the 1800's. The lakes and streams provide the setting for fishing, boating, swimming and water skiing. The many forest areas offer campers a retreat from busy daily routine and a chance to appreciate the wonders of nature much like the early voyageurs viewed it. Hundreds of resorts scattered over the many miles of lakeshore are a home away from home for thousands of tourists each year, and tourism has become a major part of the state's economy. Winter also provides recreational activity. Ice skating, skiing and snowmobiling are very popular with all age groups. It was once thought by many that Minnesota's frigid winters were something to be avoided, and to counteract this belief some enterprising state "boosters" influenced many doctors across the country to prescribe Minnesota's winter climate as a cure for tuberculosis!

Swimming at a State Park

Camping at a State Park

In the fall, when the forests are arrayed in their brilliant colors, hunting is a major sport. Grouse, pheasants and ducks have long been favorite targets of the hunter in Minnesota. Other hunters seek out the deer and the black bear. All of these forms of wildlife have become smaller in num-

Minnesota's lakes and rivers are popular at vacation time.

Hunting is a popular fall sport in Minnesota.

ber over the years due to the growing number of hunters, and the clearing of forest lands and draining of swamp areas. The Minnesota Department of Natural Resources is concerned with protecting many forms of wildlife from extinction. Some people predict that by the year 2000, the deer and bear, and such birds as the grouse, duck and pheasant, will no longer be with us due to hunting pressure and the destruction of a natural habitat. How can we save these forms of wildlife from becoming extinct?

Special Land Use

Much of Minnesota's land area has been designated by the State and Federal governments to serve special purposes. The Red Lake Reservation was set aside as a home for many of the Chippewa people. The White Earth Reservation is another example of land being used or set aside for the Chippewa. How do you think these people felt when they were directed to live in such a small area? Remember, the Indians had once called all of Minnesota their home before the white people came. How would you feel in this situation?

Land has also been set aside to serve as state and national park areas. In this way, the natural beauty of a region can be preserved in its natural state for all to enjoy. We might consider these park areas as one of our most valuable heritages, and pause to say thank you to those people in our state's history who had the foresight to see that wise land conservation practices were established.

Military bases have been still another example of special land use. Fort Snelling is one example of this type of land use. Throughout Minnesota history Fort Snelling has stood as a majestic sentinel, perched on a high cliff overlooking the point at which the Minnesota River joins the Mississippi. There have been other forts in Minnesota's past. Perhaps you can find the names of some of them.

Early Fort Snelling

Fort Snelling Round Tower

Other examples of special land use are agricultural experiment stations for both crops and animals, and prisons and reformatories. Can you think of other ways in which land is set aside for special use?

Words to Know — Define these words and terms. You may need to use a dictionary or encyclopedia to find some of the answers.

Conservation

Heritage

Immigrants

Industrious

Iron ore

Minnesota Department of Natural Resources

Natural resources

Taconite

Tourists

Wilderness

Writing Activities

Write brief answers to the following questions:

1. What provided the first travel routes used by the pioneers in Minnesota?
2. Name some of Minnesota's natural resources.
3. What might cause some species of Minnesota wildlife to become extinct?
4. Name some of the ways that Minnesota land is set aside by the government for special use.

UNIT TWO: SYMBOLS OF THE PAST

CHAPTER FIVE

PEOPLE OF PREHISTORIC TIMES

We have books and other written records of much that has happened in the past, but these written accounts do not go back far enough into the past to tell us about people who lived in Minnesota long ago. We call this period of time "prehistoric" because we have no written history that tells about the people who lived then. How then do we know about these early people? Their story is like a puzzle to which we can find only some of the pieces. By studying these pieces, we can make some guesses about how these people lived.

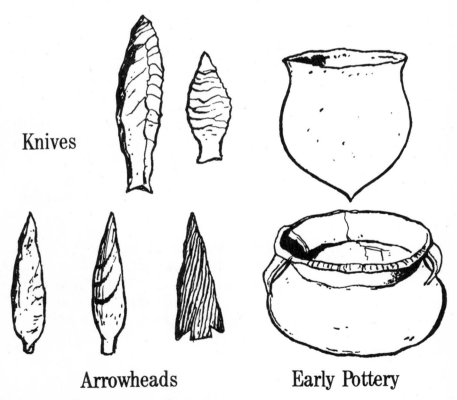

Knives

Arrowheads   Early Pottery

Remnants from another culture

51

Archaeologists have found many relics or artifacts used in these bygone days, such as stone tools and dishes, arrow and spear points, and skeletal remains of animals used for food. The great majority of Minnesota's archaeological relics have come from the thousands of Indian mounds and village sites that dot the state. Although the mounds are more obvious than the village sites, the latter are particularly rich in relics. Even hammered copper implements have been found in Minnesota, suggesting that prehistoric races may have mined this workable metal in the region of Lake Superior.

Sometimes the skeletons of some of these early people have been found, and by studying these, scientists have drawn conclusions as to what they looked like. Several years ago, a crew of road builders near Pelican Rapids dug into the silt of an old lake bed and found well-preserved remains of a young girl. The fossil skeleton was judged to be about twenty thousand years old. The Brown's Valley Man, another famous Minnesota skeleton, found a few years later, is of a more recent time.

It is now believed that these early people came to North America by the narrow ice bridge across the frozen Bering Sea from Asia, well over 25,000 years ago. Possibly many waves of these migrants came through the following centuries. In time, they spread over North and South America.

The Mound Builders

Most Americans have grown up believing that the people who occupied the United States before the coming of the white people were nothing more than savages. Americans think of primitive people who hunted, fished and wandered about the country, carrying their skin teepees with them from place to place. It seems impossible to imagine that they could have built a great city, and from it operate a vast trading system, but this is exactly what they did, nearly six hundred years before Columbus ever sailed.

In recent years, archaeologists have made some amazing discoveries that fit some of the pieces of the puzzle together, and now we can be fairly sure of how these early people lived and what they accomplished. These ancient inhabitants of North America, now generally known as the Mound Builders, have left numerous traces of their existence, mainly in the form of Indian mounds scattered over the United States from the South to the North. Perhaps the greatest concentration of these can still be seen in southern Illinois near St. Louis, along the Mississippi River in an area where other rivers join or empty into it.

Two early Minnesotans, Alfred H. Hill and Theodore Lewis, located almost eight thousand mounds in Minnesota before 1895. Many other mounds have since been charted, most located near rivers and lakes. Mounds have been found along the upper Mississippi from Point Douglas to the Anoka area north of St. Paul, and along the St. Croix River Valley.

Series of early mounds, photographed about 1906. Hundreds of mounds like these have been destroyed through cultivation and road building in Minnesota.

The Grand Mound, Itasca County. This is the largest mound ever discovered in Minnesota. Compare its size to the people in the picture. Originally, there were no trees or vegetation on this mound. Why do you think it was built, and by whom?

The Lake Minnetonka area was also the site of a great mound complex, and a city on that lake bears the name Mound. Mounds View is yet another indication of a local area named for these early mounds. The Point Douglas area and the Grey Cloud area in Washington County seem to have been a major location for such mounds. Mounds are scattered throughout the state, even as far north as International Falls, although weathering, farming, road building and relic hunting have reduced their number.

Although usually knob-like and symetrical, some were shaped to resemble birds, turtles, fish or other animals. Some of these mounds have been opened and found to contain skeletons of human beings as well as various relics of the past, and many that seem empty now may have contained decomposed human remains. A sufficient number contain preserved skeletal remains to make it clear that their primary use was for burial.

This practice had to spread through culture contact among various tribes and it would seem that it all started at the early culture center in southern Illinois, at what we call the Cahokia site. It was here that these amazing early people built an enormous city of over forty thousand inhabitants, and provided most of the services that our cities of today provide. This city, which we now call Cahokia, was a sort of kingdom by itself, and from it the ruling class of people exerted great influence for thousands of miles in all directions. Cahokia was the largest city ever to appear in what is now the United States until Philadelphia reached a population of forty thousand by the 1830's. These early people developed a religious belief, an agricultural system, and were highly advanced in several areas of mathematics and science. They also developed a vast transportation system using a series of canals to navigate all of the major rivers in central North America.

Cahokia Mounds

To try to understand these early people better, we might study some of these areas in which they were the leaders of their time. The sun was at the very center of their religious practices. Whether they worshipped the sun as a god, or as a visible symbol of a Supreme Being, we cannot be certain.

By examining their art we find that the sun was a major influence. They made the rising and the setting of the sun an important point in their every action and they probably made sacrifices to the sun in the form of crops, animals, and even human lives on occasion.

Their leader was feared and respected as an earthly representative of the sun. His every wish was carried out in all matters of the kingdom. It is probable that the powers and knowledge that this ruler possessed were handed down from one select group to another, just as the powers and knowledge of later American Indian medicine men were passed from one generation of chosen men to another, and the secrets carefully guarded lest they become common tribal knowledge.

Where this knowledge came from we can only guess. One theory is that when an ancient kingdom in Central America broke up, some of these people migrated up into the present day United States, and probably settled in the Cahokia area. Here the civilization again began to flourish. They utilized at least parts of the old civilization, especially those of sun worship, agriculture, and leadership qualifications. It is likely that some parts of the culture found their way up the Mississippi River to present day Minnesota, and then up the St. Croix and the other tributaries of these rivers.

When the first white people came into our area, they found only the Sioux and the Chippewa. Although there is some indication that the mounds were still in use when the first explorers arrived, it is thought that most were built in the centuries immediately preceding the coming of the white people. The early settlers in the 1800's questioned the Indians in regard to these mounds, but they denied all knowledge of their origin. The Indians did, however, sometimes use the mounds as burial places for their own dead.

The Indian skeletons are not difficult to distinguish from those of the Mound Builders, as they are usually not deeply buried and are frequently accompanied by trinkets or old gun barrels, indicating trade with white people.

The idea that the Mounds Builders were of the same race as the Indians seems to be gaining ground, but it is evident that their way of life was totally different from that of the great majority of Indians existing in the United States at the time the white people came. We can do little more than guess how the Mound Builders, without any beast of burden or knowledge of wheelbarrows, heaped up the earth, toiling up the slope with baskets on their backs. We don't know what rites they celebrated upon the summit to worship the gods of the lake or stream; or what quantities of the corn they tilled were taken from them by a ruling class; or how at last the gathering tribes of the wilderness brought this civilization to its downfall.

The Mound Builder at work

Grey Cloud Island Tells Its Story

(Grey Cloud Island is located on the Mississippi River between the present-day cities of St. Paul and Hastings. See if you can find it on a map.)

Nearly ringing five-mile long Grey Cloud Island is a series of earth mounds, many of them flattened now by roads or cultivation. They bear silent testimony to the fact that at one time, probably from 1000 B.C. to 1700 A.D., the island was home to groups of Mound Builders. From the other Minnesota mounds that have been excavated (the Grey Cloud mounds have been surveyed, but not extensively excavated) it can be assumed that the Grey Cloud Island mounds were used for similar purposes. Tools and ornaments were frequently buried in this grave type. Usually fairly small, the height of the Grey Cloud mounds varied from one foot to nearly eight feet.

Archaeologists have been long interested in Grey Cloud's potential, particularly in the mounds. The first surveys of mound groups were made in the late 1800's. A total of 102 mounds, more than exist today, was then recorded. Most recently, state archaeologists excavated a large area of the eastern tip of the lower island in 1958. The site yielded many riches for the scientists, establishing through carbon dating that Woodland Indians, a group of Mound Builders, had once camped there. Carefully sifting through the soil, inches at a time, they compared soil types and artifacts, and concluded that the area had been used by Indians back to the Early Woodland period, from 1000 B.C., down to the late prehistoric Indians, whose culture existed from about 900 A.D. to 1700 A.D.

The greatest amount of artifacts was deposited during the Middle Woodland period, 600 B.C. to 600 A.D., and consisted of distinctive pottery ware. These tribes had developed their own outstanding kinds of pottery, different

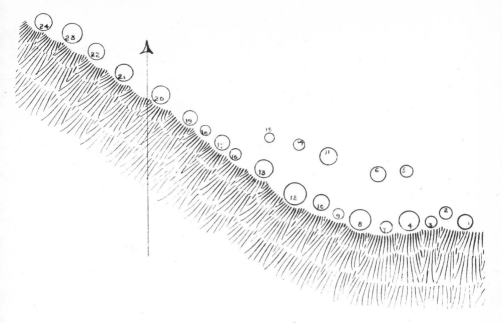

Mounds at lower end of Grey Cloud Island, Washington County. Archaeologist's sketch, made in 1887. Note how the mounds are situated along a ridge or brow of hill.

Woodland pottery

Woodland pottery

from that used by other cultures. Woodland pottery was often stamped on the outside with a paddle that had been wrapped in sinew or plant fibers, leaving a striped pattern. Through the discovery of these cord-marked pieces of pottery at the Grey Cloud site, along with arrow or spear points, it was established as one of the two earliest Woodland sites yet excavated in Minnesota.

According to a report stemming from an Historical Society survey made in 1971, it was no accident that all the known Indian sites on Grey Cloud lie near natural waterways and along the rim of the island, as the early people were heavily dependent on water for travel, drinking purposes, and a source of food in fish.

Gradually, the Woodland Indians were replaced by another culture called the Mississippian, dating from about 800 A.D. to 1700 A.D. The Mississippians cultivated patches of corn, beans, squash, sunflowers, and tobacco, in addition to hunting and fishing as their Woodland ancestors had done. They continued the practice of burial mounds, which usually contained primary burials with grave goods, or tools and ornaments.

The remains of an ancient Mississippian camp were discovered by accident during the 1971 survey, when the mounds themselves were not excavated, but nearby areas were. One trench was placed by accident directly over an ancient fire hearth. The surveyors found that many of the nested stones there were cracked by fire. A fragment of pottery was also discovered and found to belong to the Upper Minnesota or Oneota culture, centered along the Mississippi and Minnesota Rivers.

This exploration of the Grey Cloud area probably marked the end of mound excavation on the island. A member of the 1971 survey team said that finding early building sites would be more revealing than further mound excavation. Archaeologists now do not favor the idea of digging into burial mounds. Why?

By 1776, when Captain Jonathan Carver arrived at the mouth of the St. Croix River, he found three large groups of Sioux (Dakota) Indians. In late prehistoric and early historic times, the Mississippians had been supplanted by the Eastern or Santee division of the Sioux.

Words to Know — Define these words and terms. You may need to use a dictionary or encyclopedia to find some of the answers.

Archaeologist
Cahokia
Carbon dating
Fossils
Migrated
Mississippian Indians
Mound Builders
Prehistoric
Relics and artifacts

Supreme Being

Woodland Indians

Writing Activities

Write brief answers to the following questions:

1. Where might the first people in North America have come from?
2. What culture do some people think led to the Cahokia Mound Builders culture?
3. What Mound Builder groups lived on Grey Cloud Island?
4. What kinds of relics and artifacts have helped us to learn about the Mound Builders?

CHAPTER SIX

THE SIOUX AND THE CHIPPEWA

Our written history begins with the Indians who were in this area when the first white people came, during the late 1600's and the early 1700's. By the seventeenth century, when the first Frenchmen arrived, there were several groups of Indians living in Minnesota.

The Sioux (also called Dakota) occupied part of the open land and quite a bit of the northern forest. A tribe known as the Cheyenne lived both in South Dakota and in the Minnesota region of the upper Minnesota River Valley, but when they obtained horses from the continuing trade and the migration of European and African horses from the Southwest, they left Minnesota. The third group were forest Indians of the Algonquian language group, known as the Chippewa. This can be confusing, because they were also known as the Anishabe and the Ojibwa. For purposes of simplification, they will be called Chippewa in this book.

63

Buffalo robe (skin) on which many Indian tribes portrayed their tribal history using a kind of picture writing.

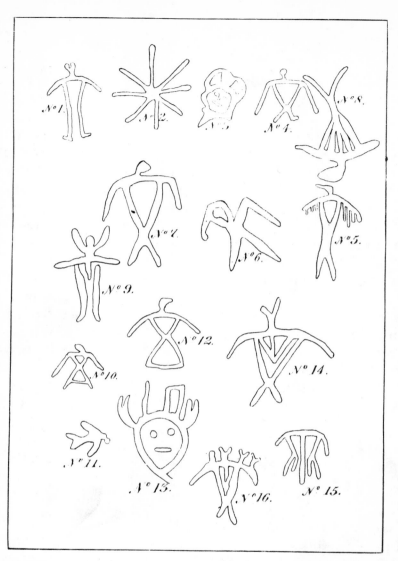

Early Sioux pictographs as observed in the 1800's on the high embankments of the St. Croix River near Stillwater.

The Sioux

The Minnesota Sioux were only one group of a large family or nation that once occupied all of the Midwest. Other tribes in the family were the Omaha, the Crow and the Winnebago. The Mdewakanton Sioux, one of the seven great tribes or council fires of the Sioux nation, inhabited this area. This tribe was divided into several smaller bands, each with its own chiefs. Among these early leaders were Little Crow, Wabasha and Shakopee.

Sioux Chief Little Crow

Little Crow's village, called Kaposia, was located at various places along the Mississippi from present day St. Paul to the South St. Paul-Newport area. Here the Sioux lived and hunted for hundreds of years before the coming of the white settlers.

Perhaps an Indian youth killed his first deer in the Afton hills and proudly hurried back to Little Crow's village at Kaposia to receive words of praise and admiration from his elders, and to accept the long-awaited invitation to join one of the warrior societies of the tribe. If you listen, you can almost imagine that you hear the beat of the skin drums and the singing and shouting of the tribe up the river as they might have celebrated the joyous occasion with a special deer dance, or a social round dance, to honor the young hunter.

The Minnesota Sioux had customs and habits common to both forest and prairie. They cultivated crops, but were skilled hunters; their arrows resembled those of the West, their bows those of the East. They had large permanent villages on many of Minnesota's thousands of lakes. They used the rivers for highways as did the fur traders. They even attempted cultivation of the rice crop, although their simple methods of harvesting usually scattered sufficient kernels for the repeated seeding of the swamps.

Sioux woman dressing buffalo hide.

They had to travel far to hunt bison, but nearby were bear, deer, moose and many smaller animals. They, of all the great Indian tribes, were most like the Wild West Indian of movies and story books. Their deerskin shirts and leggings, fringes and embroidered trimmings, leather moccasins and elaborate headdress became the almost classic Indian costume. They rode horses, hunted with bows and arrows or spears, covered their dome-shaped wigwams with skins, and crossed the lakes in awkward round boats. These boats were shaped like washtubs, with a wood framework covered by skins.

The Minnesota Sioux were forest dwellers and thus differed in many ways from the prairie Sioux farther west. Their food included wild rice and swamp roots — staples scarcely known to the Plains people.

The Sioux of Minnesota apparently got their first horses in the eighteenth century. The horse changed their way of life almost completely. Now they had a better means of travel. Lodge poles could be lashed on the sides of the saddle and a much larger version of the old dog sleds could be used. In the summer time the buffalo hunters, mounted on horses, could gallop right into a herd and select the buffalo they wanted. Life became richer and more exciting.

Buffalo hunt

The Chippewa

The Chippewa spring from another Indian line, the Algonquian family, who, with most of the Iroquoian peoples, occupied a region near the upper Atlantic Coast. Also of Algonquian stock were the Ottawa, Cree, Blackfeet and Kickapoo.

Chippewa Chief Hole in the Day

It was customary for several Chippewa tribes to hunt together, exchange weapons and patterns for clothing, and even borrow embroidery designs. Intermarriage helped still more to mix tribal customs.

Another factor was the white people's custom of coining tribal names. In this fashion many Chippewa tribes came to be known by disparaging or flattering names, several by their geographic locations, others for characteristic activities. Thus the Potawatami were "council fire makers", the Kemisteno were "killers", the Menominee were "wild rice gatherers", the Nopeming were "inlanders" (located farther from the Lakes), the Muskego were "swamp dwellers", and the Mukkundwa were "pillagers", or more literally "takers".

This last band had established itself in Minnesota near Leech Lake, when one day a sick trader, one of the first white people in the area, stopped at their encampment with a huge load of furs. They gave the suffering man a night's lodging but took from him his valuable cargo because he had sold firearms to the Sioux. From that time they were known as pillagers. The cause given for their taking of the furs typifies the hostility that existed for two centuries between the Chippewa and the Sioux.

Conflict Between the Chippewa and the Sioux

The Chippewa and the Sioux were bitter enemies and many battles were fought between the two nations. The great contest between the Chippewa and the Sioux for the lands of Minnesota began in the seventeenth century and was not concluded until after the historic Sioux outbreak against the white people in 1862.

The Sioux were living both in the forest and the open country in the seventeenth century, but were forced out of the forest by the Chippewa. It happened this way. Early in the seventeenth century, Dutch traders supplied the Iroquois with guns and steel weapons. The Iroquois pushed west into the Great Lakes country, driving other Indians further west. Some of these displaced Indians were the Chippewa. The western Great Lakes Indians, including the Chippewa, started trading with the French who came over the river routes from Canada. The Chippewa acquired firearms and steel weapons from the French to protect their interests and drive the Sioux out of northern Minnesota.

The first major battle in the St. Croix Valley between the Sioux and Chippewa is thought to have occurred about 1755. It was often told that a great massacre occurred at Point Prescott, near where the St. Croix joins the Mississippi. Here the Chippewa, despite a peace pipe ceremony, fell upon the Sioux and took over three hundred scalps. Many more of the Sioux were said to have perished in an attempt to escape by canoe to the opposite shore.

Other major battles occurred over the years. One, near the end of the 1700's, about 1790–1795, took place among the rocky palisades high above the river at the Dalles, near present day Taylors Falls. A band of Fox Indians, who had been earlier pushed out of Wisconsin by the Chippewa, persuaded a Sioux war party to join them in a fight to gain back part of their country from the Chippewa. The famed Chippewa chief, "Waub-O-Jeeg" (White Fisher), heard of this in advance and led some three hundred of his warriors south from Lake Superior to do battle. The Fox at first attempted to win the fight by themselves, telling the Sioux to watch, but it soon became evident that the Chippewa were gaining the upper hand, and the Sioux then pitched in to help.

The combined Fox and Sioux had almost managed to turn the battle in their favor when another band of Chippewa braves arrived to reinforce their comrades. The Fox and Sioux were driven from the heights to the roaring water's edge and were slaughtered in every gorge and crevice to the last man. For years after, this place was referred to as the "Valley of Bones". Sporadic fighting took place for years as both the Sioux and Chippewa came to consider each other as bitter enemies. Each took advantage of the slightest opportunity to seek revenge for past deeds.

The Coming of the White People

The coming of the white people had its effect on both Sioux and Chippewa, and land was taken from both, usually through treaties that the Indian never fully understood. Sometimes the Indians resisted the advance of the white people, but usually the white people, supported by United States Army troops, gained control of the land. The Sioux either migrated farther north and west or were forced onto reservations to live.

The Chippewa were also relieved of their land and forced onto reservations. Through force, trickery and broken treaty agreements, these two proud nations were removed from the land they called home.

The Indians' Contributions

What did these two great nations, the Sioux and the Chippewa, contribute to our present day culture? Can you think of anything? You have only to look at a map of Minnesota for some clues.

The name Minnesota itself comes to us from the Sioux. Winona was a name given by the Sioux to an eldest child if it was a daughter. Red Wing was named after several chiefs of the Sioux who lived near the present day city of that name. Mahtomedi means "White Bear" and is located on the lake of the same name translated into English. Mah-Kah-to, translated to English Mankato, means "Blue Earth". Chaska is named after the eldest son of a Sioux chief. Wabasha means "Red Leaf" and Isanti in Sioux meant "Long Knife," referring to the long swords carried by American soldiers. Anoka meant "On Both Sides," as it was located on both sides of the Rum River. Can you find these names on your map of Minnesota?

The Chippewa gave us many names also. Bemidji means "Cross Lake," because the head stream of the Mississippi

Indian Artifacts

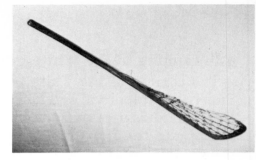

Lacrosse stick

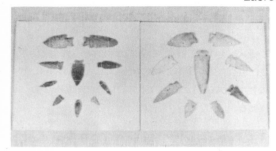

Arrowheads

Drum

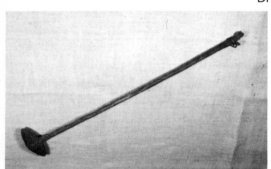

War club

72

Tomahawk

River crosses it and comes out on the opposite side. Mesabi to the Chippewa meant "Giant Range." Mahnomen meant "Wild Rice" and Kanabec was the Chippewa word for river or snake. The words "Powwow," "Bar-be-cue," "Canoe," "Moccasin" and "Toboggan" are words that we use often in our language and all come from the Chippewa.

The Indians' love of and appreciation for the many bounties of nature have given us many beautiful legends. These legends were often a part of the Indian religious belief. They explained the origin of corn or "maize" by the following story:

The Origin of Indian Corn

Mondamin was the son of a chief, and when it came time for his trial of fasting, he made up his mind that he would try to learn something which would help his people. He was a very earnest young man, very kindhearted, and it hurt him year by year to see his tribe almost starve toward the end of the winter, for they had nothing to live on but fish and game, and these never lasted into springtime.

So he went away to his little lodge where he was to be all alone for seven days, or until dreams came to him. After he had been alone one day, he walked in the evening and looked at plants and pulled them up by the roots, trying to find something that would feed his people all winter. On the third day of his fast, a beautiful spirit, dressed in a rustling robe of all shades of vivid green with plumes above his head and a face like the sunshine, came and wanted to wrestle with him and encouraged him by telling Mondamin that he would finally throw him. Mondamin was very weary, but as he wrestled, he seemed to get strong, and although the spirit overcame him, he lay down that night and dreamed again of the beautiful vision. Mondamin wrestled with the spirit three times, each time getting stronger, although he had nothing to eat all the while.

On the evening of the sixth day, the stranger told him that on the morrow Mondamin would overcome him, and said that he must plant him where he fell, keep the ground soft, and not let any weeds grow above him. All this happened, and Mondamin kept it all a secret, going every few days to keep the earth soft and the weeds away. One day late in summer, he took his father to see the beautiful green dress of the tall Indian corn with its nodding plumes, which has ever since been a blessing to the Indians in the long, hard winter.

If Mondamin could visit Minnesota today he might be happy to see field after field of our modern hybrid corn. From Indian "maize" to hybrid corn, we can thank the Indian for giving us this life giving food, perhaps the most important grain in American agriculture today.

The Indian ways have been replaced by the white people's culture, but our culture is richer for the contributions these earlier people made. The Sioux and the Chippewa are a part of our cultural heritage.

Words to Know — Define these words and terms. You may need to use a dictionary or encyclopedia to find some of the answers.

Chippewa

Kaposia

Maize

Sioux

Treaties

Names to Know — Identify these people.

Little Crow

Waub-O-Jeeg

Writing Activities

Imagine that you are one of the first white people to make contact with the Sioux and the Chippewa in Minnesota. Write an account describing the Indians and their customs.

Imagine that you are a member of the Sioux or the Chippewa and have just met white people for the first time. Write an account of how you think the Indians described the white people.

CHAPTER SEVEN

EXPLORATION AND DISCOVERY

The New World

The first people in North America probably came across the Bering Strait from Asia. The coming of Europeans to North America is related to the voyages of discovery and exploration made by early sea-going adventurers.

The first Europeans to come were Norwegians. They sailed to Iceland, and by the year 1000 came to Greenland. Some of these people had a settlement on the island of Newfoundland. Without doubt, they touched on the North American continent too. Some of the records of these people tell of a place called Wineland, the mainland of North America. Due to causes we still do not understand, the settlements died out.

A major controversy in Minnesota history is whether or not the Norwegians (also called Vikings) were the first Europeans to explore this region. It centers on the discovery of a mysterious stone, called the Kensington Runestone.

Early in this century, a farmer near Kensington, Minnesota, which is not far from Alexandria, found a stone with writing on it. Experts in language translated this writing, which was in medieval Norwegian letters called runes. The text of the stone said that the Norwegians, with some Swedes, had been in the area in the 1300's. Some men have written books defending this idea. European scholars who are specialists in this language have said that the stone is a fake. One fact remains: whether Scandinavians were here or not in that century, their explorations were not followed by a permanent, lasting settlement in North America.

Runestone monument

Later explorers were hired by the kings and queens of European countries to find a new route to the Orient and to find new lands to claim for their country.

The British based their claim to the New World (the continent of North America) on the voyages of the Cabots. John Cabot and his son Sebastian were Italian sailors, hired to explore by England's King Henry VII. They reached the grim, foggy coast of Labrador in the late 1400's and claimed the land for England. "We discovered it, it is ours" said the British.

"No, we discovered it, it belongs to us" said the French. They based their claim on the voyages of Verrazano, the Italian navigator whom they had hired to explore the New World. He sailed along the Atlantic coast from North Carolina to Newfoundland, claiming the new land for France.

77

Further French claim was based on the explorations of Jacques Cartier of St. Malo, France. He came to Canada and claimed the land for France in 1534. He returned later on two occasions, spending time in the areas that are now Montreal and Quebec.

Spain had already laid claim to the New World because they said, "Our Italian sailor was there first". Christopher Columbus had been outfitted for a voyage of discovery by Queen Isabella. In 1492 he landed in the Bahamas, which he thought was the East Indies, and he promptly named the natives "Indians", a name that has stuck with native Americans over the centuries.

Other Spaniards and Italians followed Columbus. One of them, Amerigo Vespucci, published an essay saying that this new world was not part of Asia as Columbus thought, but a new land. German publishers named the new land "America". This is the name "Amerigo" in the German language of the early 1500's.

All of the European powers claimed the New World; now it would be seen which one would profit from their claim.

French Exploration

French exploration and settlement began in the 1600's. Soldier-explorer Samuel de Champlain established the colony of Quebec in the St. Lawrence River Valley in 1608. Farming was the main occupation but soon many settlers found that there was profit to be made by trading with the Indians for furs. Some of the French fur traders learned enough of the Indians' language to converse, and they hired Indians from Canada to go with them and explore. These men were generally known as voyageurs, or travelers.

Two men, Radisson and Groseilliers, between the years of 1654 and 1660, went farther west in the Minnesota

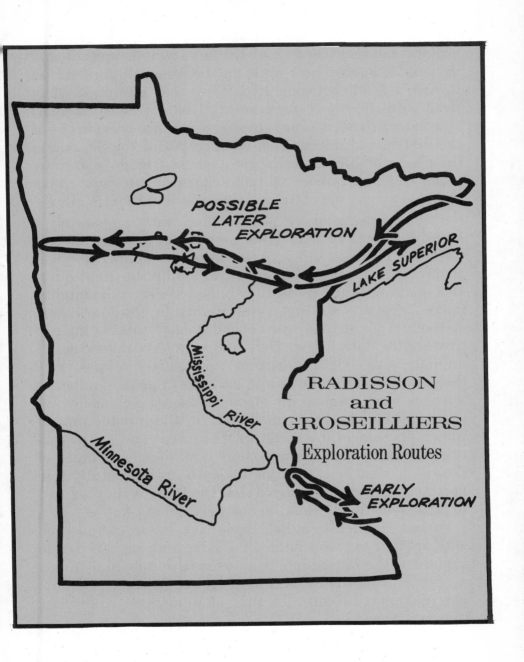

POSSIBLE
LATER
EXPLORATION

LAKE SUPERIOR

Mississippi River

Minnesota River

RADISSON
and
GROSEILLIERS

Exploration Routes

EARLY
EXPLORATION

Territory than any white people had before. On an early exploration they came into the area where present day Winona is located and went up the Mississippi as far as Prairie Island, between Red Wing and Hastings. They lived with the Sioux (or were captives) for nearly a year, and their written accounts of the experience provide one of the first bits of information we have about the Sioux and their way of life. Later, these two men made a journey along the north shore of Lake Superior, and may have traveled across the state as far as the Red River Valley.

Think of these brave people! They were pioneering a route into country that white people had not seen before. Carefully picking their way, watching the wonderful blush of spring in the primitive forest, watching the great numbers of animals and birds, they must have seen the mighty moose, greedily eating water plants in shallow lakes. Without a doubt they saw beautiful deer stalking quietly through the dark forest. They could not have missed small animals with bright eyes that watched them pass. Yes, there were fish and birds and animals in great numbers.

There were unpleasant elements too; the clouds of insects and flies that swarmed and bit, the terrible roar of rapids just ahead in the rivers, the sweat and toil of carrying trade goods. Always there was danger: danger of drowning, danger of freezing to death in the brutally cold northern winter. They hoped that the Indians they wanted to trade with were friendly, but they did not know.

Father Hennepin, a Recollect friar, came to the area with another explorer named La Salle, and was directed to explore up the Mississippi. He was sure that he could find a way to go from the Mississippi River to Japan and China, not realizing the vast expanse of unmapped wilderness that was ahead.

In his travels, Hennepin provided much valuable information concerning the geography of the area. He was the first white person to see the great falls in the Mississippi where the city of Minneapolis is now located. He named them the Falls of St. Anthony. He traveled above the falls and looked over the streams that fed into the area north of what is now Minneapolis. He saw dark pine forests and sky blue water. When he returned to Europe, he wrote about the lovely land that he had seen, and said it was wild, remote and primitive.

Hennepin was captured by the Sioux and remained their prisoner in the Mille Lacs area for many months, until he was found and freed by another explorer, named Du Luth. The adventurous Du Luth appeared on the scene in 1679. One of his first acts was to lay claim to the whole area in the name of his king. For eleven years he traveled up and down the shores of Lake Superior and explored the triangle between the Mississippi and St. Croix Rivers.

Perrot, for some twenty years a leading fur trader in the region, established himself for a while near the foot of Lake Pepin, and in 1689 claimed the area in the name of his monarch. Le Sueur, a companion of Perrot, built a fort on Grey Cloud Island in 1695. Five years later he erected another near the site of Mankato, to which he came not by the usual Great Lakes route, but by boldly ascending the Mississippi from the Gulf of Mexico. It was from this post that he transported to France two tons of blue-colored earth, supposing it to be copper ore, only to discover that it was worthless clay.

In the early eighteenth century, the French built the settlement of New Orleans. Soon they made others, and by 1740 the French had a chain of forts and settlements all the way from Quebec to New Orleans. These settlements followed the Great Lakes and the Mississippi River for the most part. In Minnesota, the French had a permanent post at Grand Portage, which is at the extreme northeast corner of Minnesota, and a post on Lake of the Woods. The French also had some short term trading and mission posts. Stockades occupied intermittently at Fort Beauharnois (later called Frontenac) from 1727 to 1754, brought De Gonnor and Guignas, who opened the first mission in the upper Mississippi basin, and Captain St. Pierre, long prominent as a leader in New France.

In the north, De Noyon discovered the Lake of the Woods about 1688. Between 1731 and 1749 La Verendrye and his sons established the canoe route from Lake Superior to Lake Winnipeg, built a line of forts reaching as far as the present site of Calgary on the upper Saskatchewan in Alberta, crossed the upper Missouri, and probably sighted the Black Hills.

Eventually however, French influence began to wane. Traders and Indians were negotiating with English buyers on Hudson Bay and with merchants in Albany and New York. With the outbreak of the French and Indian War, loyal Frenchmen withdrew from the region and hurried east to the scene of the conflict. They had explored and opened the way to the Minnesota area; they had quieted the suspicions of the Indians and taught them the uses of firearms and brandy; they had established the beginnings of the fur trade. There remained, as evidence of their passing, hundreds of colorful place names and a scattering of half-breed descendants.

The British in Minnesota

The British also played a part in the formation of Minnesota. In the last half of the 1700's, English and Scottish proprietors, whose headquarters were in Canada, now took over the French and half-breed traders, who continued to act as intermediaries with the Indians. A half century of British domination of the fur trade followed.

It was during this period of British trade dominance that Jonathan Carver, a New Englander approved by British officials, made his famous journey. Carver spent the winter of 1766–1767 with the Indians of the Minnesota country. During that time he ascended the Mississippi a short distance above the Falls of St. Anthony and made one trip up the Minnesota River. In the spring, he visited an Indian burial ground, now the site of St. Paul, and entered the cavern since known as Carver's Cave. Carver published a book about his travels in 1778, when Europe's attention was drawn to the revolt of the American colonies. Much of it was plagiarized from earlier accounts, yet it became a best seller. The book was translated into several languages and aroused widespread interest in England's Minnesota domains.

Portrait of Jonathan Carver

St. Anthony Falls as seen by Carver in 1766

Minnesota Becomes Part of the United States

The area between the Great Lakes and the Mississippi passed into the possession of the newly established United States in 1783, and twenty years later, through the Louisiana Purchase, the young nation acquired the land west of the river. Even after the Louisiana Purchase, British companies continued to occupy their posts and Indians followed their leadership well into the next century.

Words to Know — Define these words and terms. You may need to use a dictionary or encyclopedia to find some of the answers.

Kensington Runestone

Runes

Voyageurs

Wineland

Names to Know — Identify these people.

John and Sebastian Cabot

Jacques Cartier

Jonathan Carver

Samuel de Champlain

Christopher Columbus

Du Luth

Father Hennepin

Le Sueur

Radisson and Groseilliers

Verrazano

Amerigo Vespucci

Writing Activities

Making a Time Line: Arrange the following events in the correct order in which they took place.

Le Sueur builds a fort on Grey Cloud Island.
Du Luth explores Minnesota.
The Norwegians settle on the island of Newfoundland.
A French colony is established at Quebec.
Radisson and Groseilliers explore Minnesota.
Jonathan Carver's book about his travels in Minnesota is published.
Columbus lands in the Bahamas.

CHAPTER EIGHT

THE FUR TRADE ERA

The Northwest Fur Company

The French had started the fur trade. By 1800 the Scotsmen came to Canada, hired the Frenchmen as guides, and formed the Northwest Fur Company. This was based in the Canadian city of Montreal, and Simon McTavish was the main organizer of the company. The "norwesters", as they were called, plunged into the wilderness. They spread out and set up major bases at places like Grand Portage, Big Sandy Lake, and Leech Lake, all in Minnesota territory.

When the ice went out of the St. Lawrence River in the spring of the year, the "norwesters" would load their forty foot canoes, called "Canots du Maitre", or "Master Canoes", and hire strong French-Canadians called "Mangeurs du Lard", or "Pork Eaters", to paddle the canoes to far away Minnesota. A group of canoes moving west was called a brigade. The French had already found the way west, up the St. Lawrence, up the Ottawa River, and then up the smaller Mattawa River, finally going ashore. After that they had to carry their packs and canoes to the French River, over the rocks and mud of the trails. Carrying the canoes overland was called a portage.

Portaging a canoe

The voyageurs—trail blazers of the North

The Witch Tree—voyageurs' North Shore
monument

These men were the voyageurs you have heard about. They saw Lake Superior, dark blue, and great flights of bald eagles and geese in the air. They sang songs like "Jolly Allouette" to pass the time.

At Grand Portage, in the northeastern tip of Minnesota territory, the canoes were unloaded, and the Chippewa came to the trading post to trade their furs for gunpowder, knives, needles, muskets and cloth. There were men who stayed in the post all year around.

Many bales of trade goods were put into canoes called "Canots du Nord", thirty feet in length. They carried over a ton of goods and were easier to handle on the inner rivers. Crews picked up the heavy loads, ninety pounds each, adjusted the headstraps and started to walk over the Grand Portage trail. They proceeded up the Pigeon River and up the water path known as the Voyageur's Highway.

In the interior of the territory at places like Big Sandy Lake and Leech Lake, regular fort posts were built. There were fields and gardens in the summer, inside a rectangle

Restoration of fur fort at Grand Portage

88

made of tall, weathered and pointed stockade posts. Two-story buildings stood at the corner of the stockade. In the center were big log buildings that served as stores, warehouses and places to live. Here the traders, under the watchful eye of the manager, traded with the Indians year round. Furs were sorted, and there were dark beavers and shining mink, glistening marten and ermine that was white from weasel trapped in winter. They also had skins of the fisher, otter, wolf and fox. All were made ready for the voyage to Britain and Europe.

There were small trading posts between the larger stockade posts too. A daring trader who did not mind the cold and loneliness would build a two-room cabin for himself and use one room for the trade store, where he could trade with Indians from remote areas. In the winter, if he ran out of trade goods, he could hook up a dog team and travel over the forest trail to the larger posts for supplies. This was difficult. Thick snow fell and it was always miserably cold. Most of the time the dogs would behave, but sometimes they would snap at each other. The trader would have to use the whip to straighten them out. At night he built a spruce bough windbreak, and slept wrapped in fur robes near a fire. It was a hard life.

The Fur Trade War

The Northwest Fur Company had spread to the north and northwest, and it was giving the older Hudson's Bay Company much competition. Lord Selkirk, who was in charge of the Hudson's Bay Company, figured out a way to stop the Northwest Fur Company.

Lord Selkirk got a huge grant of land from the British, located in the valley of the Red River. He brought Scottish settlers from the Hebrides, foggy islands off the west coast of Scotland. These settlers came to Hudson Bay in Canada, then traveled by boat to Fort Garry, where Winnipeg,

Manitoba is now. In the summer of 1811 they moved on to the area where Pembina, North Dakota and St. Vincent, Minnesota are located today. These early Minnesota pioneers were tough, determined people who built cabins and hoped to farm.

Trouble started right away. The Northwest Company had moved its main northwest base from Grand Portage to Fort William, a short distance into Canada. The man in charge of this area for the Northwest Company was a hard-headed Scot, Angus McGillvary, and he did not like what was going on. He got over a thousand of his "Metis" (people of mixed French and Indian ancestry) and some Chippewa Indians to attack the Red River settlement. The settlers were badly outnumbered, and those who were not killed were driven back to Fort Garry.

Selkirk now imported a larger group of Scots, the Sutherland Highlanders. They and the surviving Hebrideans went south and again occupied the Pembina-St. Vincent area. McGillvary's half-breeds and Indians attacked the colony again, this time in great force. The Scots fought back, but Governor Semple and a number of his men were killed at the battle of Fair Oaks. Again the surviving Scots had to return to Fort Garry.

Even this did not stop the resourceful Lord Selkirk. In eastern Canada there was a group of professional soldiers, mercenaries called the DeMeurons. They were Swiss, and had been brought to Canada to take part in an invasion of the U.S. that never came off. Selkirk hired a company of these, about two hundred men, to help him win the Fur Trade War. They were tough fighters with experience in many bloody battles. They knew everything that was to be known about soldiering and killing. You can judge their attitude and determined valor by the words of their marching song: "Our life is a voyage through darkness and night. We search for our courage in a sky without light".

The DeMeurons won the Fur Trade War in a few months. They took the fur trade canoe route to Fort William and arrested McGillvary like a common criminal. They then moved west over the Voyageur's Highway. The Metis who had fought for McGillvary stopped fighting when they faced the calm and efficient Swiss mercenaries.

The Red River settlement was now occupied permanently. Most of the Swiss soldiers stayed as civilian settlers. The colony received more immigrants from Switzerland and a people known as the "Brules" developed. Their ancestry was a mixture of Indian, Swiss, Scot, French and the Metis. This colony was the first real settlement in Minnesota.

The Louisiana Purchase

The Americans, even if they officially owned part of Minnesota, had very little contact with the area. Until 1789, Americans were busy developing their land further east and south. The eastern forest Indians were pushed back and settlers were pouring into western Pennsylvania, Ohio, Kentucky and Tennessee. Farmers from these new areas shipped their goods, ranging from whisky to salt pork, down the Mississippi River. There were hard goods like barrel staves and hides to go to New Orleans. For a while this worked out, and the Americans had a trade treaty with the Spaniards, but trouble erupted.

Napoleon, the dictator of France, forced Spain to give back the land of Louisiana, and stopped trade down the Mississippi. The Louisiana territory stretched from the west bank of the Mississippi to the Rocky Mountains. France had been fighting most of Europe, but now they were at peace and wanted a new American empire for themselves. To do this, they needed their base in the West Indies to protect their supply lines to Louisiana. Then there was a revolt on the French colony of Haiti in the West Indies, and Napoleon had so much trouble with the area that he became discouraged and sold the territory of Louisiana to the Americans for fifteen million dollars in 1803.

Not much was known about the new area, so President Thomas Jefferson sent an American army officer, Lieutenant Zebulon Pike, to explore what is now Minnesota. To Pike was entrusted the duty of extending federal authority over the newly acquired United States territory. From St. Louis he set out in 1805 with twenty soldiers and spent the winter on the upper Mississippi River. He explored the banks as far north as Leech and Cass Lakes. For sixty gallons of whisky and two hundred dollars worth of trinkets, he acquired military sites at the mouths of the St. Croix and the Minnesota Rivers. (The latter site included most of the area now occupied by the Twin Cities.)

Pike and his men managed to get above the Falls of St. Anthony in dugout canoes made out of large trees. In the fall of 1805, they used hand drawn toboggans to move their equipment, and even managed to cross Minnesota on foot in the winter. Pike made notes about the trees, animals, people and weather. It's hard to realize that what we know as towns and cities were then only wilderness. There were Norway pine, black spruce, cedars and many more. If they wanted to eat meat they only had to kill a deer or moose. Snowshoe rabbits flitted ahead of them and they could hear wolves howling at night. They saw lakes of all sizes. Now and then they saw some Indians dressed in furs, hunting or tending trap lines, but they were never attacked.

Well down on United States territory, they found fur trade posts of the Northwest Fur Company. These British fellows treated Pike and his men well, but made it plain that even if they were on American territory, they had no intention of leaving. The Pike expedition went back to the Falls of St. Anthony in the spring, and keelboated back to St. Louis.

In Pike's official report, he noticed something that was especially important. The Northwest Fur Company people were raising grain and vegetables, even in the remote northern areas. This would be important later on, because it would show that food could be grown even with a short growing season.

Later the United States government sent Major Stephen Long and a party of soldiers to explore and survey the Pike territory. Long traveled up the Minnesota River and down the Red River. He also made it to the headwaters of the Minnesota River at Big Stone Lake, which is now on the South Dakota border.

Fort Snelling

As the fur trade grew, the United States government established forts. The government wanted to build a fort near where the Minnesota and Mississippi Rivers meet. They sent Colonel Henry Leavenworth with a detail of men to this spot, and in 1819 the soldiers built a camp beneath the bluffs. They called it Camp Coldwater. Supplies were few and it was a cold winter. Some soldiers died. Colonel Josiah Snelling replaced Leavenworth and in the 1820's Fort Snelling was built. The soldiers quarried native limestone for the buildings.

Some of this stone was put up in the form of walls, towers and supply buildings. From this strong base, mounted patrols went out to try to force the warring Sioux and Chippewa Indians into peace. Officials like the Indian agent Major Lawrence Taliaferro tried to keep the fur trade under control by forbidding the use of liquor. Companies like the American Fur Company brought it in anyway. They used cheap, tobacco juice-colored alcohol in their fur trade, and

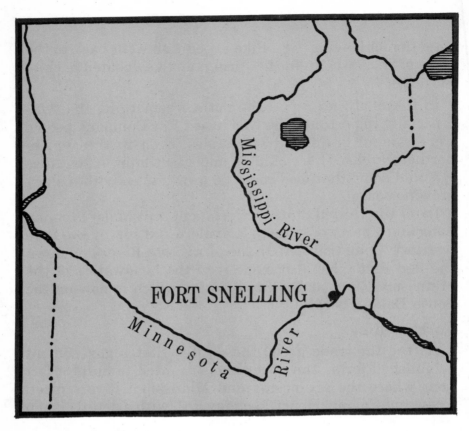
Location of Fort Snelling

had only one intention. The idea was to cheat the Indians by getting the most profit for the least money. Taliaferro and his followers could not stop the demoralizing liquor trade with the Indians.

Even in the officer's quarters, the married women had a hard time. They were isolated from the outside world, and they didn't get to see people very often. They were able to get wheat flour from the local store, ground at Minnesota's first flour mill. This was located at the Falls of St. Anthony. A small sawmill, driven by water power was used to supply the fort with lumber. The enlisted men received fifteen dollars a month or less for pay. Some of them were foreigners who had recently come to America, and some were men looking for adventure. Some farmed and worked in the mills, cut logs and quarried stone, besides acting as soldiers. They rode with the officers to check on the Indians. These people were fairly well fed, and dressed in uniforms that looked like high school band uniforms of today.

After Fort Snelling was established, a small number of settlers began to come to the area. Two of these men, Mike McDonald and Pierre Parrant (who only had one eye, and that looked more like a pig's eye) built saloons or liquor shops under the bluffs below Fort Snelling. On payday the soldiers had a place to spend their money and get drunk on bad liquor. When they staggered up the bluff again, some fell and broke their necks. Parrant and McDonald got the blame for their deaths and were forced to leave Fort Snelling. They both established saloons across the river. Eventually, the army forced the other settlers to move over to the other side of the river, and they built cabins around the saloons and worked for the fur company.

Fort Snelling

FORT SNELLING

This view shows the fort as it looked after completion, but before major alterations were made in the 1840's; it also shows the fort as it will look when the planned restoration is complete.

1. Round Tower	13. Commandant's House
2. Pentagonal Tower	14. Officers' Quarters
3. Semicircular Battery	15. Commissary Warehouse
4. Hexagonal Tower	16. Hospital
5. Shops	17. School/Chapel
6. Gate House	18. Stable
7. Guard House	19. Root Cellars
8. Magazine	20. Cemetery
9. Well	21. Gardens
10. Sutler's Store	22. Fields
11. Short Barrack	23. Landing
12. Long Barrack	24. Wash House

25. St. Anthony Falls — Sawmill, Gristmill

For a while this settlement was known as Pig's Eye, but a Roman Catholic priest, Father Galtier, built a mission at the settlement, and called it the Mission of St. Paul to the Wilderness. When the village was turned into a chartered town, the town fathers decided to call the settlement St. Paul. Minnesota almost had a capital named Pig's Eye, but thanks to Father Galtier, it was named St. Paul instead.

The American Fur Company

Congress passed a law denying fur trading privileges to all but United States citizens, and after 1816 the Northwest Fur Company was entirely replaced in the area by the American Fur Company. Most of the fur traders in the area transferred their allegiance to the Americans.

The American Fur Company was a big business. The company had trading posts all across the continent, in Oregon as well as in Minnesota. The home of the company was New York, where it was led by John Jacob Astor. Its western headquarters were at Mackinac and St. Louis. The Minnesota region was divided into two areas — the Northern, or Fond du Lac, for the trade with the Chippewa, and the Western, or Sioux, for the trade with the Sioux Indians.

The American Fur Company owned and sold land; it raised produce for its employees; it had fisheries on Lake Superior; it made maple sugar; it sold cranberries; it mined lead and copper; and it served as a bank, even issuing paper money redeemable in supplies. It manufactured many of the articles that it sold to the Indians; and it was a transportation agent, carrying goods into the fur country and furs out. All the time it competed fiercely with rival companies and independent traders, trying to crush them by reducing prices.

It was the American Fur Company that sent a young man named Henry Hastings Sibley to Minnesota in 1834 to manage its business here. He had been a clerk in Detroit for the company and was sent to Mendota to take charge of what was called the "Sioux Outfit". This was a branch of the business with fur traders scattered over a wide area north of Lake Pepin, extending as far northwest as Pembina and as far west as the Missouri River. In partnership with Sibley was a famous trader at Prairie du Chien in Wisconsin whose name was Hercules Dousman.

With Mendota as his trading center, Sibley soon developed a thriving fur business. Working under his direction were traders at Lac qui Parle, Lake Traverse, the Cannon River, Traverse des Sioux, and other places. They brought to Mendota the furs that they collected each year. There the furs were sorted, prepared, and packed for reshipment to Prairie du Chien and Mackinac. In 1835

The trading store

Sibley handled the pelts of 389,000 muskrats, 3230 minks, 3200 deer, 2500 muskrat kittens, 2000 raccoons, more than a thousand otters and buffaloes, and hundreds of beavers, fishers, martens and foxes. His traders, in securing these pelts, gave the Indians blankets, scarlet cloth, calico, black silk handkerchiefs, thread, yarn, guns, powder, knives, clay pipes, flint, rings, awls, beads, flour, pork, beef, ham, wine and whisky. Sibley himself did not approve of the use of liquor in the trade, but some of the traders felt that unless they sold it to the Indians they could not get many furs.

Sibley's home at Mendota, built in 1835, was not the rude frontier cabin of the wilderness. It was a well-built stone mansion, furnished in the best of taste. It is still standing, preserved now as a museum.

Sibley was one of the most notable men in the history of Minnesota. After his career as a fur trader, he became one of the makers of Minnesota Territory, the first delegate of the territory in Congress, and one of the framers of the state constitution of Minnesota. He was also the first governor of the North Star State, one of the founders of the University of Minnesota and a general in the war against the Sioux in 1862.

There were other fur traders besides Sibley who became important figures in the early history of Minnesota. Joseph R. Brown, at Lake Traverse, was a lumberman, land speculator and politician as well as a fur trader. Joseph Renville was the son of a French father and a Sioux mother. He lived at Lac qui Parle and had much influence among the Sioux Indians.

After 1837 the Minnesota fur trade began to decline. In that year the Sioux and the Chippewa made their first big cessions of land to the whites, and settlers began to come in. In return for the land cessions, the Indians were given annual payments of money by the United States government. These annuities, as they were called, caused many Indians to give up their hunting, for they could now pay their debts to the traders in money instead of with furs.

There were other difficulties too. All America suffered from the great panic of 1837. The price of furs went down. In the European markets furs imported from South America were competing with the beaver. And in the forests of Minnesota, fur-bearing animals were getting scarcer. All in all, it was hard for the American Fur Company to continue its business, and in 1842 it went bankrupt. Minnesota was nearing the end of the fur-trading era, and the age of settlement was beginning.

Words to Know — Define these words and terms. You may need to use a dictionary or encyclopedia to find some of the answers.

Annuities
Brigade
Canots du maitre
Canots du nord
Land cessions
Louisiana Territory
Mangeurs du lard
Norwesters
Pelts
Portage
Voyageur's Highway

Names to Know — Identify these people.

Father Galtier
Colonel Henry Leavenworth
Major Stephen Long
Pierre Parrant
Lieutenant Zebulon Pike
Lord Selkirk
Henry Sibley
Colonel Josiah Snelling
Major Lawrence Taliaferro

Writing Activities

Write brief answers to the following questions:

1. What caused the decline in the fur trade after 1837?
2. How did the settlement at St. Paul come about?
3. What animals were trapped by the Indians to sell to the fur traders?
4. Why did Napoleon sell the Louisiana Territory to the United States?

UNIT THREE: FROM WILDERNESS TO STATEHOOD

CHAPTER NINE
INDIAN LANDS AND TREATIES

The history of Minnesota would normally move from the era of discovery and exploration into a period of immigration and settlement. Before reading about settlement it is important to realize that the land was not immediately available for immigrants to settle on. All of present day Minnesota was inhabited by the Sioux and Chippewa, and they owned it because they had been here first. In order for the white people to move into the area, mainly for lumbering and farming, it was first necessary to get the land from the Indian nations.

The United States government had devised a unique way to do this, by drawing up treaties with the Indians. These treaties were actually legal documents (at least in the white people's way of thinking) since they were based on the idea that the Indians would give up their land for payments of money and goods. This method for obtaining land was used in Minnesota as well as other states.

As settlers spread westward across the country, the question of the Indian lands became important and more treaties were made to acquire more and more of the choice Indian lands. These one-sided agreements during the years 1826 to 1863 took nearly all of the land in Minnesota away from the two Indian nations. As the Indians were displaced they were either pushed onto reservations or moved further west across the Missouri River and forced to settle elsewhere.

The Indians had trouble understanding these treaties, because their culture had a different view of private property. They thought that the land belonged to all the people. They did not believe that land could be owned by one person or tribe, and sold. When a treaty was made, with a

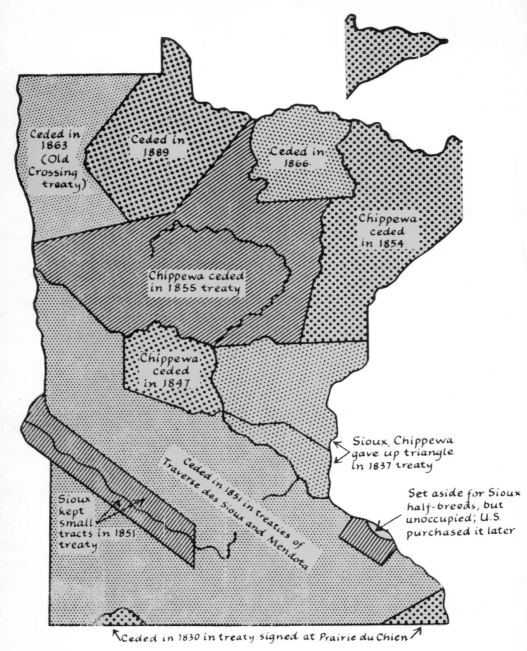

Ceded in 1863 (Old Crossing treaty)

Ceded in 1889

Ceded in 1866.

Chippewa ceded in 1854

Chippewa ceded in 1855 treaty

Chippewa ceded in 1847

Sioux, Chippewa gave up triangle in 1837 treaty

Set aside for Sioux half-breeds, but unoccupied; U.S. purchased it later

Ceded in 1851 in treaties of Traverse des Sioux and Mendota

Sioux kept small tracts in 1851 treaty

Ceded in 1830 in treaty signed at Prairie du Chien

THE LAND CESSIONS BY THE INDIANS IN MINNESOTA

(adapted from Poatgieter and Dunn's *Gopher Reader*).

payment made for the land, the Indians did not understand that they were to leave that land forever.

The following are brief descriptions of some of the treaties made with the Sioux and Chippewa to open the land for "legal" white settlement. Study them carefully before going into your study of early settlement and immigration. This will provide you with some understanding of when the people came, why they came, and how they got their land.

Fond du Lac Treaty of 1826

The Sioux and Chippewa had disagreements about the land where both wanted to fish and hunt. The United States government decided to help both tribes by making dividing lines between their hunting grounds. A meeting was held at Fond du Lac, near Duluth, which historical accounts describe as a major production.

The government agents brought with them a band, and the stirring notes of "Hail Columbia" were rendered periodically as a sort of council theme song. The agents' boat was gaily decorated with flags and red, white, and blue streamers, truly indicative of the importance of the "great white father".

There were seven tribes represented and there was much speech-making and feasting. This continued for five days, and in an effort to speed up negotiations, the agents suggested that the many gifts they had brought would not be given out until the council was over. This technique worked so well that it appears to have been adopted as a standard procedure for negotiating treaties thereafter.

The Chippewa promised not to wage war against the Sioux and to hunt only in certain areas. They promised to give up their allegiance to the British, and to surrender four of their number to the government, for their part in the killing of four white people at Lake Pepin earlier.

Treaty negotiations

This treaty did much to hold down trouble between the two nations at least for a short time, but more important, it established the United States government as the power with whom both tribes should be concerned from that time on.

Fort Snelling Treaty of 1837

A council was held at Fort Snelling in 1837 involving the United States government and the Chippewa. After the usual council proceedings and merrymaking, the results of the treaty gave the United States all the pine forests on the St. Croix River and all rivers that flowed into it. This immense tract of land and unknown wealth was bought for less than two cents an acre. It represented the first major attempt to obtain land from the Chippewa for the white people's benefit.

Sioux Land Cession of 1837

The same year the Chippewa were giving up vast expanses of northeast Minnesota, the Sioux were invited to send representatives to Washington to discuss the status of their land east of the Mississippi. Many white people were eager and waiting to settle this area, but were fearful of what the Sioux reaction might be. This meeting must have been very impressive to the Sioux leaders for they were persuaded to give up all their land east of the Mississippi. Within twenty-four hours, most of this land was staked out in claims by white settlers.

Traverse des Sioux Treaty of 1851

Pioneers in early Minnesota wanted the Sioux land west of the Mississippi River, for farms and timber. They wanted cheap land and the Sioux stood between them and their goal. Much pressure was brought to bear on the government, until territorial governor Alexander Ramsey and Luke Lea were appointed by the Commissioner of Indian Affairs to act as agents in buying this land from the Sioux. They made two treaties, one with the Upper Sioux tribes at Traverse des Sioux, and another with the Lower Sioux tribes at Mendota.

Ramsey and Lea arrived at Traverse des Sioux on June 30, 1851. Many Sioux chiefs were at this meeting. The Sioux, as was their custom, brought many of their people with them. The encampment took on the appearance of a giant campground, and the people enjoyed games, races and tribal dancing. Discussion and debate over the sale of the land dragged on for several days.

The chiefs were finally enticed to sign the treaty, and by doing so gave up all their land in Iowa and Minnesota east of a line drawn from the Red River, Lake Traverse and the Big Sioux. They retained possession of a strip of land extending ten miles on either side of the Minnesota River from Lake Traverse to the Yellow Medicine River. This narrow remnant of land was to be preserved for their home. For the sale of their land the Sioux were promised payment of $1,665,000. Only $305,000 was to be paid at once, and the balance was to be paid to them in yearly payments of $68,000. There were strings attached to this agreement, however, for part of this money was to be paid back to the government for building schools, farms, and mills, and for other things such as equipment to be used on the farms.

At the same time, the Indian chiefs were tricked into signing another agreement which gave most of their money to the fur traders present at the meeting. The traders said that they had sold goods to the tribes on credit, in trade for furs which were to be brought in at the close of the season. They said many of these debts had not been paid, and claimed the Sioux money. The government agents supported this claim to the treaty money, and the Sioux went from the meeting unaware of what had taken place.

Mendota Treaty of 1851

Ramsey and Lea, returning from their successful treaty encounter at Traverse des Sioux with the Upper Sioux tribes, wasted no time in pressing for a similar agreement with the chiefs of the Lower Sioux tribes. They met with these chiefs, one of whom was Little Crow, at Mendota two weeks later, and used much the same procedure that had worked for them earlier.

The fur traders were in attendance again, and again the chiefs signed agreements with the traders, authorizing the government to deduct debt payments from the land-sale money. The same sort of cash and annuity payments were given to the Lower Sioux as had been given to the Upper Sioux tribes. When the chiefs signed, they were paid $30,000 which had been promised them from a previous treaty in 1837. This money had been held back for fear that if the Sioux had all that money, they would not sign future treaties. History tells us that most of this $30,000 was spent in St. Paul over the next few days as the Sioux went on a gigantic shopping spree. Thus the white settlers not only got the land from the Sioux, but the money came back too, in a strange turn of economic events.

The two treaties, Traverse des Sioux and Mendota, both negotiated within a two-week period, managed to obtain for the white settlers all the land that had been used by the Sioux for hundreds of years.

Later Treaties

The treaties of 1854 and 1855 reserved lands for Indian occupancy at certain cherished Chippewa spots, including Sandy, Mille Lacs, Cass, Leech and other lakes over which the Chippewa had won control only a century or so before. The treaties also provided to pay amounts of money regularly to the Chippewa, coverage of Indian debts to the traders, distribute lands to half-breeds, and assurances of land rights for teachers, missionaries and other white people who inhabited the region.

The land remaining in northern Minnesota was taken from the Chippewa by later treaties in 1866 and again in 1889.

Speculators and Indian Lands

The Chippewa treaty of 1854 had appeased the half-breeds of that tribe by giving each adult title to eighty acres of land. The Indian Bureau ruled that a relative of any Chippewa tribe member was eligible to receive the eighty acres of land. Soon ambitious land speculators saw that this was a chance for them to get land, and they set out to search for half-breeds who might otherwise have been overlooked. Twelve hundred were soon discovered. These half-breeds applied for their land title certificates, and the white people promptly offered to buy them. Soon Chippewa half-breeds were being rounded up, paid a small fee for their land, and the bundles of applications forwarded to Washington.

The government tried to stop this practice, but it continued despite their efforts. Optimistic lumber speculators continued to value the applications, and bankers accepted them as valuable investments.

In 1872 Congress was prevailed upon to pass an "Act to quiet certain land titles". Persons who had bought the land certificates in "good faith" would be allowed to make good their claims and purchase the land at not less than $1.25 an acre. In a short time the "innocent parties," whom Congress termed victims of a fraudulent system, had acquired for about $2.00 an acre almost 20,000 acres of Minnesota's richest timber.

The Sioux half-breed tract on the Mississippi had been guarded until 1840 by the honest agent Taliaferro, but in 1854 the President was given power to issue certificates to the mixed-blood Sioux who owned it, whereby they could take up land in any unappropriated territory. Four-hundred-eighty acres was the share for each. As with the Chippewa, speculators fought for these land certificates. White men who had married Indian women rejoiced, and since ten children were worth 4800 acres, their delight is easily understood. Land speculators hastened to prospected town sites, took up the choice lots before the surveys were made, reaped a quick fortune and hunted for new bonanzas. The more adventurous hastened to California with a pocketful of paper to grab rich mineral and timber lands.

The story of the Indian is the sad narrative of the conquest by war and trickery of a proud people. Everywhere the native culture was pushed to destruction. Minnesota's Chippewa and Sioux by 1865 had been stripped of most of their land by a succession of treaties. Their hunting grounds had been turned into cultivated acres by settlers' plows. Wild game such as deer, bear and buffalo was growing scarce. White traders, speaking with forked tongues

Fur trader visiting the Indians

and enforcing their lies with whisky, again and again had taken what rightfully belonged to the Indians. Even government annuities were slow.

The Sioux, realizing that they had been tricked at the treaty table, and literally starving as a result of the failure of the government to deliver their food and annuities on time, went on the warpath in 1862, when they launched attacks on settlers and towns all up and down the Minnesota River Valley.

Words to Know — Define these words and terms. You may need to use a dictionary or encyclopedia to find some of the answers.

Annuities

Fond du Lac Treaty of 1826

Fort Snelling Treaty of 1837

Land cessions

Mendota Treaty of 1851
Sioux Land Cession of 1837
Traverse des Sioux Treaty of 1851
Treaties

Names to Know — Identify these people.

Luke Lea
Alexander Ramsey

Writing Activities

Write an essay in which you take a stand either for or against the use of treaties to gain lands from the Indians. Give reasons for your position.

CHAPTER TEN

THE HOW AND WHY OF EARLY SETTLEMENT

In the early 19th century, Minnesota had only a few tiny white settlements, but it was being prepared for more. Government surveyors like Albert Lea and Joseph Nicollet led their survey parties across the land of Minnesota. They worked spring, summer and fall. Their job was to set down locations and draw maps showing the topography (what the land looked like). They told where rivers, creeks, lakes, forests and open land lay. They left written descriptions of plants, animals, soils and water, and prepared the way for the final surveyors who mapped Minnesota into square-mile sections, each divided into four quarter-sections of 160 acres each, ready for the settler.

More settlements began to spring up. With the cession of the triangle between the St. Croix and the Mississippi in 1837, lumber towns sprang up along the St. Croix. In 1847, settlement began on the east side of the Falls of St. Anthony. Two years later the first of a group of dwellings on the west side was erected. Bridges were to spring from these two hamlets and merge them into the city of Minneapolis.

Early St. Paul in 1855

In the closing days of the pre-territorial period, St. Paul, the river town; St. Anthony, the sawmill town; and the smaller trading settlement, Mendota; were grouped within a few miles of the Minnesota-Mississippi junction. The majority of the other settlers were living at isolated points along the lower St. Croix River, where the biggest town was Stillwater, only fifteen miles downstream from the sawmill village of Marine. French-Canadian voyageurs lived at Wabasha and Traverse des Sioux; at Lac qui Parle the half-breed Joseph Renville lived on a huge estate with his relatives and friends.

A few fur traders maintained scattered posts in the wilderness, with the families of their employees as more or less permanent residents. The more populous were at Fond du Lac (Duluth), Crow Wing, Sauk Rapids, Elk River, Swan River, Long Prairie, and Lake Traverse. Missionaries and agents were still living with the Indian bands.

Far to the north at Pembina the Brules were engaged in trapping and trading furs. They farmed to produce their own food. The Brules also killed many bison in what is now North Dakota, and using both hides and meat made packaged pemmican (bison meat that was dried, finely ground, and mixed with tallow and dried fruit) for sale.

The only strictly agricultural life was at Red Rock, Cottage Grove, Lakeland and Afton in the Mississippi-St. Croix triangle and in the nearby settlements stretching northward from St. Paul to Little Canada.

Winona, Red Wing, Wabasha, Lake City, Read s Landing, Shakopee, Hastings, Stillwater, Mankato, New Ulm and Chaska all got their beginnings as riverside market towns.

In this period none of the points of settlement was self-sustaining. Aside from wild game and fruits, and the little produce raised on the few small farms and in family gar-

Early Winona in the 1860's

dens, everything required by the white people — even most of the food for their livestock — was brought from the outside by steamboat. The dwellings were mostly of logs, some surrounded by stockades. Fallen trees provided the bridges, roads were mere trails, stores were housed in one-room buildings, schools and churches had made scarcely a beginning. From December to April the hamlets were often without mail for weeks at a time, and isolated settlers received none at all.

The opening of the land office at St. Croix Falls in 1848 brought the first great wave of settlers. The majority of these pioneers were lumbermen from Maine, farmers from the mid-Atlantic states, and tradesmen and craftsmen from the cities. They were an independent lot and had grown up in an atmosphere charged with politics. When their numbers approached five thousand, they began to ask for a local government.

Minnesota Becomes a Territory

A convention called to meet at Stillwater on August 26, 1848 took preliminary steps toward the organization of

Minnesota Territory. To aid his Minnesota friends, John
Catlin, recently secretary of the Territory of Wisconsin,
established his "capital" at Stillwater and issued a call for
an election to choose a territorial delegate to Congress.
Henry H. Sibley was named by the convention. At
Washington, after considerable debate, Sibley was seated,
January 15, 1849, officially as a delegate from the Territory of Wisconsin, in reality the representative of the people of Minnesota.

Henry Hastings Sibley

Stephen A. Douglas helped Sibley pilot the bill through
Congress and on March 3, 1849, the Territory of Minnesota
was formally created. Its boundaries to the north, south,
and east were those of today, and the western line was the
Missouri and White Earth Rivers.

In 1948, a plaque was dedicated and placed on the building on the corner of Main and Myrtle Streets in Stillwater
where the Convention Hall stood. The plaque reads as follows:

BIRTHPLACE OF MINNESOTA

On this site, in the frontier river settlement of Stillwater, sixty-one delegates from the vast unorganized wilderness west of the St. Croix assembled on August 26, 1848 to hold the Minnesota Territorial Convention. In this convention the name of Minnesota was selected and the spelling agreed upon. A petition was drawn, memorializing Congress to set up a territorial government, and H. H. Sibley was dispatched to Washington as the delegate of the convention bearing the petition.

This tablet erected by the
Stillwater Territorial Centennial Committee
August 26, 1948

The first territorial legislature assembled in the dining room of a St. Paul hotel on September 3, 1849, summoned by the new governor, Alexander Ramsey, whom President Zachary Taylor had appointed from among his eastern supporters.

Settlers Come to Minnesota Territory

Soon it was evident that the settlers could not be restricted to their comparatively small portion of the vast area included within the territory's boundaries. Already they were turning eager eyes toward the rich timber and prairie lands of the Indians, and were held back with increasing difficulty.

In 1851, through the treaties of Traverse des Sioux and Mendota, more than twenty-eight million acres, some of the richest farm land in the world, became open to the settlers. By later negotiations, the Chippewa relinquished their claims to lands in the north central areas, tracts greatly coveted for lumbering operations.

After the treaties, a great tide of immigration began to flow into the southwestern part of the territory. Pioneer homes began to dot the wilderness, chiefly near lakes and rivers. Villages sprang up almost overnight. The clatter of grist mills was heard on a dozen streams. Merchant milling had its first substantial beginnings in the St. Anthony vicinity in 1854, and soon Mississippi River traffic began to swell with shipments of wheat and flour to eastern and southern markets.

Early grist mill on the Vermillion River, Hastings

Sawmills were overtaxed to supply required building materials. Lumbering emerged as a major industry that choked the rivers with logs. From the Red River Valley there poured into St. Paul an ever increasing quantity of furs and thousands of tons of pemmican. Land offices, hotels, and livery stables were crowded with patrons. Post offices opened so rapidly that by 1856 they numbered 253. Railroads were chartered and endowed with extensive land grants. A capitol, erected with federal funds at a cost of $32,000, was occupied in 1853.

Cultural life followed the pattern of the eastern tradition. The pioneers established churches, public schools and academies. They organized reading circles and singing classes, and concerts and lecture courses brought to the wilderness many a distinguished visitor.

The growing tension between Indians and whites became more and more evident during territorial days. Two trifling quarrels, involving the Sioux and Chippewa, led to minor outbreaks and, although promptly quelled, left in their wake apprehension and unrest.

Financial straits, Indian scares, and threat of the Civil War could not dampen the enthusiasm and self confidence of the territory. The population grew by leaps and bounds as European peasants continued to pour into the land. Representation in Congress was essential to many plans, but now especially to the success of the longed-for railroad to the Pacific. The time was ripe to demand statehood.

Words to Know — Define these words and terms. You may need to use a dictionary or encyclopedia to find some of the answers.

Grist mills

Pemmican

Self-sustaining

Topography

Names to Know — Identify these people.

Albert Lea

Joseph Nicollet

Writing Activities

Write brief answers to the following questions:

1. What led to Minnesota officially becoming a territory?
2. What were the duties of the government surveyors?
3. Name some of the early businesses and industries in the Minnesota territory.

CHAPTER ELEVEN

PIONEER LIFE IN EARLY MINNESOTA

Early settlers were faced with many obstacles in their attempts to put down roots in the wild new country. The natural environment, which seemed so promising at first view, proved to be the most difficult obstacle of all. Those who survived the pioneer hardships earned their reward of a better life and left a heritage for future generations to build on. Those who could not overcome the trials and hardships either moved on to other frontiers or returned east to homes and relatives where life was not so difficult. Many remained behind, buried in crudely marked pioneer graves.

Pioneer Homes

Early homesteaders often came to frontier settlements with very little money and not much in the way of material possessions. In their crude log cabins or sod huts, living conditions were pretty bleak. The women made most of the family's clothing and since cloth was so expensive, they learned to spin yarn and weave it into homemade cloth. Early homes were lighted by wax or tallow candles, and candle making was an important art to learn.

Log house

123

Inside view of a pioneer's cabin

Food was mostly what they could manage to grow on the land, and if they were fortunate enough to raise a few chickens or hogs, some of these were used for food. Ducks, deer, passenger pigeons, and fish were utilized, and corn, "taters", and homemade bread were staples. They picked wild berries and hunted wild game when it could be found, and they made pemmican. Many had only milk and cornbread to eat.

Pioneers hunted deer in the forests for meat.

In winter the freezing temperatures and blizzards would make life nearly unbearable. The families had to gather around the fire in their cabin and try to keep warm. Many stories were told during the long winter evenings. Young men who had once gone north to work in the lumber camps told many strange and wonderful tales of the north country to younger brothers and sisters.

Early day farmers were often snowbound.

Pioneer Farms

The early farmers had only wooden plows at first, and all the farm work was done by oxen. Fences were made of willow or poplar poles when available, or split logs or rails. On most of these early farms the women and children worked alongside the men in the fields.

There were hardships of many kinds for the farmers. Sometimes it rained so much and so often that the crops would be covered with mud. One of the more serious problems was that of the "grasshopper plague". The grass-

Grasshoppers . . . they often ate every green plant.

hopper, or Rocky Mountain locust, had been a nuisance since the 1820's, and had destroyed many crops, but during the years between 1870 and 1877 it became a scourge of the area.

These insects ate everything, the bark on trees, clothes on the line, leather and every blade of grass or crop that appeared above the ground. People even said that they ate saddles and boots.

All sorts of plans were undertaken to rid the land of these pests. They were burned, tarred and buried but still they came in relentless hordes. The plight of the settlers was so bad that bounties were offered to farmers for each bushel of the "hoppers" they could kill off. The governor proclaimed a day of prayer in April of 1878, and overnight as if by some divine answer to the prayers, the weather turned cold and the entire hopper population was killed by freezing. Little trouble with the pests was encountered from that time on.

Illness in the Pioneer Homes

Illness was common to early pioneer homes. Epidemics of measles, typhoid, mumps, scarlet fever, and sometimes smallpox took their toll. Some years saw the frightful scourge of diphtheria come and wipe out all the children in some families. Tuberculosis was also common, as was pneumonia, and sometimes cholera found its way to the area, carried by those coming up the Mississippi by steamboat from the South. Medical treatment was limited and crude. The few horse and buggy doctors had very little in the way of drugs and their meager supplies were only slightly effective.

In sickness and in childbirth, neighbor helped neighbor, since doctors were usually too far away to be called on. Newspapers of the day carried scores of ads for "cure-all" patent medicines. These were called "antibilious, cathartic, vegetable and ague pills", and there were great varieties of syrups, bitters, pitch, liniment, pain extractors, Indian cures, and balms. Opium and cocaine were used without restriction, and many people were drug addicts. The two most important books in the pioneer home were the Bible and the doctor book, and both were read often and carefully.

Many settlers survived all these hardships, however. Life was hard in early Minnesota but it had its pleasant side, too. Families were bound together by love, work and sharing, and many of the settlers shared both work and social activities.

Butchering Day

One of the ways the early pioneers shared work was to set up their own "do-it-yourself" meat markets, usually in the fall in order to store up a supply of meat to last through the long winter months.

These occasions usually had two or more families working together. This provided more hands for the job and enabled them to butcher several animals (usually hogs) in less time than if they worked individually.

First, the animals were killed and bled, then strung up on a makeshift hoist from which they were "scalded" or

Butchering day on the farm

lowered into a barrel of boiling hot water. This process helped in scraping the hair from the skin of the animal.

The next process involved cutting the carcass into quarters and cutting the meat into the desired cuts. Tenderloin cuts were put on the cookstove soon after they were cut, and by evening the entire group sat down to one of the most delicious meals imaginable.

Much of the meat was ground and seasoned for sausage, which was stuffed into the cleaned intestine casings of the animal. The hams or shoulders were later hung in a "smokehouse" where they were heavily salted and smoked over a hickory fire. This preserved the meat and added a taste quality that would appeal to all appetites.

Nearly every part of the animal was utilized, and very little went to waste. Fresh liver, tongue and "head cheese" were considered delicacies, and, of course, pickled pig's feet became an item of considerable importance.

Husking and Quilting Bees

Whenever there was a death in a family, or the man of the house was ill, injured or away at war, neighbors would all gather at that particular farm on a designated day, bringing their own horses and wagons, and proceed to "husk" the entire field of corn in one day.

The women would usually go along on these special occasions and cook up quantities of food to feed the workers. Often each woman would bring some item of food, and by pooling their resources they would prepare a meal equal to the finest smorgasbord ever seen.

During the day, when not busy preparing food, the women would work at what was known as a "quilting bee." The purpose of this was to make a quilt or comforter for adding to the family's bedding supply. A wooden frame was set up and a plain cloth was stretched across it. Some "batting" was placed on top of this, and then a more decorative piece for the top of the quilt. This might be made up of many small pieces of various patterns and colors sewn together, or of larger squares consisting of decorative and colorful needlework. When all these sections were sewn together, a beautiful and useful article of bedding was the result. Each quilter would embroider her name or initials onto her section, and sometimes there might have been a little unspoken competition among them to see whose work stood out above all the rest.

The family receiving the help on these special occasions were usually not embarrassed nor their pride damaged, for they knew they would be helping someone else at some other time in just the same way.

Box Socials

One of the pioneer's social events was the box social. This was usually held in February, close to Valentine's Day, perhaps because of the romantic influence of Cupid at that particular time. The social was usually held at the one-room school in the area, and a program planned for the evening would include plays, skits, readings, and special music.

Each of the women, from teen-ager on up, would bring a beautifully decorated box containing chicken, cake or cookies and other taste tempters. These boxes were to be assembled in secrecy so that no one knew to whom they belonged.

After the program, an auctioneer would be designated to sell each box to the highest bidder, the money usually going to some community or charitable cause. Many young men tried to get advance knowledge of what a certain young woman's Valentine box would look like, and in some instances, the young women would provide a clue to guide the bidding of someone they favored.

You can imagine the excitement on occasion when two or more young men ended up trying to outbid each other for a particular box.

All boxes had to be sold, and when the bidding was over, the man would step forward and pay for the box. Then the owner of the box would be identified, and the two would sit together and eat the contents, while either enjoying or enduring the other's company for the balance of the evening.

Words to Know — Define these words and terms. You may need to use a dictionary or encyclopedia to find some of the answers.

Grasshopper plague

Patent medicines

Smokehouse

Writing Activities

Imagine that you are a member of a pioneer family living in the Territory of Minnesota. Write a letter to a friend of yours in a distant part of the country, describing what pioneer life on the frontier is like.

CHAPTER TWELVE

POPULATION DENSITY

By 1860, Minnesota had grown from a wilderness frontier to a populous state. There were fewer than 5,000 people in Minnesota in 1849, but by the year 1860 this figure had grown to 172,000. Why do you think the population grew so rapidly during this ten-year period?

The magnet was land, which meant people, farms, towns, lumbering, business, industry. Public lands had to be surveyed, land offices established, and public sales announced under presidential authority. Under the pre-emption act of 1841, actual settlers who had established claims could legalize their ownership by appearing at an appropriate office and paying the official price of $1.25 an acre. This plan applied only to surveyed land at first, but from 1849 on, Minnesotans, led by Alexander Ramsey, made every effort to persuade Congress to extend the pre-emption privilege to unsurveyed lands. "The tide of emigration is always in advance of surveys and land sales authorized by the government," wrote a St. Paul editor. The squatters are the "true pioneers", and their acts should be "legalized and the benefits resulting from their hardy enterprise more firmly secured to them."

The governor voiced the frontier doctrine that the squatter deserved first rights of purchase, whether public lands were surveyed or not. In 1854 Congress extended for Minnesota the pre-emption privilege to unsurveyed tracts of public land. This action led to the rush for lands in 1854–57.

By 1855 there were six land offices in Minnesota (Minneapolis, Stillwater, Winona, Red Wing, Sauk Rapids and Brownsville). Actual sales of public lands for the four years from 1854 to 1857 totaled 5,250,119 acres. In the decade

1850–1860 about twenty million acres in Minnesota were surveyed.

Every effort was made to promote the new area. In 1853 the territorial legislature authorized a special exhibit at the Crystal Palace World's Fair held in New York, and William G. Le Duc went there with grains (from the Cottage Grove area), furs, wild rice, a birchbark canoe, photographs, and even a live buffalo. The farm products won favorable editorial notice from Horace Greeley in the *New York Tribune,* and Le Duc believed that this endorsement started the tide of immigration to Minnesota. More important were the efforts of a "commissioner of emigration", authorized in 1855, who went to New York to urge newly arrived immigrants to choose Minnesota as their destination. He distributed pamphlets packed with information about the territory and inserted advertisements about Minnesota in several European newspapers.

Guidebooks like this one encouraged immigrants to come to Minnesota.

Minnesota's rise in the 1850's was also helped by changes in American life, including transportation. Once slow and cumbersome, it was undergoing a revolution, improved by canals, steamboats on the Great Lakes, roads and railroads, and fleets of vessels on the Mississippi River. Steamboats on the Mississippi, the Minnesota and the St. Croix were crowded with passengers and cargo. All the river landings bustled with colorful activity, as with every boat new arrivals disembarked and departed on stagecoaches over the newly constructed government roads. Many boarded the boats down river at Galena, Dunleith, or St. Louis. Others made the tedious journey overland in prairie schooners, driving their cattle, fording streams, and camping by the way.

By 1854 it became possible to travel all the way from New York to Rock Island, Illinois by railroad, with transfers to steamboats headed for St. Paul. Steamboat arrivals at St. Paul, in excess of one hundred in 1855, rose to nearly three hundred two years later, and to more than one thousand in 1858. Settlers poured onto the landing at St. Paul. One packet company alone brought in more than thirty thousand people in the summer of 1855. Settlement was a matter of individual and family action, and a few groups of people banded together in colonization plans, migrating as communities, hunting for lands favorable to farming and to the building of towns of their own.

The pioneers dreamed of great cities at the head of steamboat navigation on "the river", around the Falls of St. Anthony, and in the valley of the St. Croix. Promoters of the 1850's planned villages and cities with room enough for more than eight times the population of Minnesota in 1860. Townsite speculation was the order of the day. Evidence shows that many towns existed only on paper and in dreams. Many of the towns were real, even though some became "ghost towns".

Enthusiasts of the 1850's predicted that Nininger, Ignatius Donnelly's dream city near Hastings, would blossom into the New York of the West. The Nininger townsite was divided into 3800 lots; advertisements promised a great hotel, a ferryboat, and a library. Prices mounted, and Nininger had some five hundred inhabitants before the financial panic of 1857 collapsed its hopes like a punctured balloon.

Early Duluth in 1882

Settlement had started at the west end of Lake Superior where a trading post and mission known as Fond du Lac had long been located. As early as 1853 a road was cut through the pines from Superior on the Wisconsin side to the lumber camps on the St. Croix. When in 1855 a canal was built around Sault Ste. Marie Falls in Michigan, the "Head of the Lakes" was in direct water communication with the ports of Europe through the St. Lawrence River, and with New York City through the Erie Canal. Soon after the Chippewa treaties were signed in 1854–1855, several villages were laid out on the Minnesota shore of Lake Superior. Duluth was platted (mapped out) in 1856.

More than four hundred Minnesota towns, villages and cities were tabulated in the 1860 census, but only eleven reported populations above a thousand. The capital city of St. Paul had 10,401, St. Anthony, 3258 (and its rising neighbor, Minneapolis, on the west side of the river, 2564); Winona, 2464; and Stillwater, 2380. Other cities having more than a thousand were Mankato, Faribault, Rochester, Chatfield, Red Wing, and Shakopee. Duluth, destined to be the third ranking city of Minnesota, made only a faint bow, with eighty residents.

Other early population centers were established in what we now know as the following counties: Brown, Stearns, Swift, Big Stone, Lyon, Murray, Nobles, Cottonwood, McLeod and Fillmore. The early Minneapolis-St. Paul area had the heaviest concentration of people, and the Stillwater area also had become a population center.

The population of Minnesota in 1980 was 4,077,148, composed of many races and nationalities from all over the world. The major population center today is the Twin Cities area, which has about two million people, fifty percent of the state's population living in a five-county area. Can you name other area population centers in Minnesota today?

Cities and Towns: Population Symbols

Did you ever consider a road map to be anything but a highway location device? It is really a book of information and there are many things you can learn by being able to read this book. It is not an ordinary book, for instead of having pages of words, it makes use of a system of symbols to give information. If all the information contained on a common road map were to be put into writing, it would probably contain more pages than the book you are reading now.

Do you know what kinds of information you can get from a road map? What have you learned about map scales and symbols? Most official highway maps have a legend or symbol explanation box to tell you what each symbol represents.

The official highway map of Minnesota is issued by the Minnesota Department of Transportation (try to obtain a copy for your study) and uses the following symbols to give information about cities and towns:

○ Small unincorporated town or village.

◯ Small town under 1,000 population.

◎ Town or city with population between 1,000 and 5,000.

◉ City with population between 5,000 and 25,000.

▢ City with population between 25,000 and 50,000.

▣ City with more than 50,000 population.

✪ State capital city.

◇ This symbol placed around any of the above symbols indicates a county seat city or town.

Look at the following examples:

Hastings, Minnesota, is indicated with this symbol ◈ The diamond outer symbol indicates that Hastings is a county seat. Can you find the name of the county? The inner symbol tells us that Hastings has a population between 5,000 and 25,000. Can you find the exact population of Hastings by looking at the Minnesota index to towns on your map?

Maple Lake, Minnesota, is indicated by this symbol ◎ What does it tell you? Grand Marais has this symbol ◈ What does this tell you? What symbol does your city or town have (or one close to you if you live in a rural area)?

The map also tells us how to quickly locate any city or town in the state. The Minnesota index to towns is arranged alphabetically and shows the latest population figures after each name. Following this, a number and a letter are given. Do you know what they mean? Notice that across the top and bottom of the map are the letters A to T, at one-inch intervals. From top to bottom on both sides of the map are the numbers 1 to 22, also spaced one inch apart. This gives you a grid location system that may be used to locate any city or town listed in the map index. What county seat town in Minnesota is located by the grids 15B? What county is this located in? Locate your own city or town with the grids given in the map index.

Where the People Came From

Earlier we learned that Minnesota was once a wilderness and that many people came here to make their homes. Let us now review where these people came from (or their parents or grandparents). Where did they live before and why did they choose to come to Minnesota?

Minnesota is often referred to as a "melting pot", which means that many different races and nationalities came into the state, became neighbors and friends, and shared common interests and goals so that they all became known as "Minnesotans". Remember, the Sioux and the Chippewa were the original Minnesotans. The Sioux were forced from their land into other areas further north and west. The Chippewa were also forced from most of their land, but are still to be considered a part of Minnesota's population. Do you know where most of the Chippewa live today?

Earlier we learned that the first wave of immigrants came into the area in 1848, and that many of these people came from other states: 30,075 from New York and other middle states, 24,640 from the Middle West and West, and 18,822 from New England. Others from Pennsylvania,

Ohio, Indiana, Michigan and Illinois were similarly of New England background and tradition. They built farms, started towns, opened business places, invested money, speculated, pioneered professions, launched newspapers, schools and churches, engaged in politics and government, and left the imprints of their leadership on numerous institutions.

Then the Indian treaties opened up more land for settlement, and railroads were built, making travel easier. Workers were needed in lumbering and for railroad building, and the demand for crop and livestock products grew rapidly. Agents for the state traveled to the East and to Europe, encouraging people to move to Minnesota. Germans, Belgians, Scandinavians, French, and Swiss families responded in great numbers. Irish and Canadian families also came in great numbers, and Irish colonies were established through the promotion of land by Archbishop Ireland and the railroad builders.

The exploration of the Iron Range brought various groups of people of all nationalities to Minnesota, looking for jobs. In the late 19th and early 20th century, people from Europe were moving to the United States at a great rate. Many came to the Iron Range to mine the iron ore. There were Baltic people from northeastern Europe such as Finns, Estonians, Latvians and Lithuanians. Poles, Russians, Bohemians, Slovaks and Hungarians came.

Southeastern Europe had recently allowed emigration, and people from the Balkan countries, now grouped together in Yugoslavia, came to Minnesota. They were from Serbia, Croatia, Bosnia, Montenegro, Dalmatia, Roumania, Bulgaria, Herzegovinia, Ruthenia. There were also some Turks, Macedonians from northern Greece, Albanians and others.

The congregating of these diverse ethnic groups is an interesting phase of Minnesota history. These various people brought a multitude of dialects and languages to our state. They also brought different life styles, cultural traditions and political ideas. This made the Iron Range one of the most cosmopolitan areas in our state.

At the same time that so many nationalities were pouring into the Iron Range, still other ethnic groups were coming to other parts of Minnesota. There were the English, French, Germans, Finns and others.

The Dutch, or Netherlanders, came from the low-lying area of western Europe. In the 19th century, they came to Michigan, Illinois and Iowa. Some of these, and new immigrants as well, came to our state. Probably no other people on earth knew intensive farming, grading and gardening better than the Dutch. They settled in communities in Minnesota like Prinsburg, Edgerton, Chandler and Hollandale. People from Belgium and Luxembourg also came to Minnesota.

Others who found refuge in Minnesota were the Jews. Probably no people on earth can match their record for being persecuted. Most of those who came would not accept conversion to other religions and because of this were persecuted in Europe. They came to Minnesota even before Minnesota was a state. Most were German Jews. Since then, Polish, Lithuanian, Austrian and Russian Jews have come to Minnesota. There are even a few Spanish Jews in the state whose ancestors were driven out of other countries.

Minnesota also has a number of black people. After the Civil War, the freed men came to many northern areas, including Minnesota. They have worked hard in our state. We also have a sprinkling of West Asians, Syrians, Persians, Lebanese and others. There are a few Chinese, Koreans, Japanese and now quite a few Southeast Asian refugees in Minnesota also.

Someone has said that if you were to stick a pin into any country on the globe, there would be some people from that country (or their descendants) in Minnesota. Red, yellow, black or white, Minnesota has taken all and produced a culture rich from the contributions of all.

Where did the people come from? They came from all over the world. Where did your family originally come from?

Special Customs and Celebrations

Culture is made from custom and tradition, and passed from one generation to the next. Language, clothing, religious belief, games, recreation, festivals, food and many other things go into the making of a culture, and when people leave one area and settle in another, they take these things with them.

What happens when people from many culture backgrounds all move into the same geographic area? Some parts of their old culture die out and they adopt some new characteristics in their place. For example, the English language has almost replaced all other languages brought by different nationalities to Minnesota. Clothing style has changed to reflect the views of the new area.

Some cultural traits of one group are accepted by all groups and become a part of the new culture. A new culture is formed then by taking on parts of all the cultural traits of the various nationality groups that live in the same geographic area, in this case the state of Minnesota. Music is one example of this. Do you know which nationality group contributed polka music to our culture?

Some cultural customs and celebrations have not died out and are preserved through regular observance by various nationality groups. Let us look at some of these cultural observances in our state.

Folk Arts Fair, International Institute, St. Paul

MINNESOTA ETHNIC FESTIVALS

January	Ladies International Curling Bonspiel	Duluth
February	International Elks Curling Bonspiel	Duluth
	Vasaloppet Cross-Country Ski Race	Mora
March	St. Patrick's Celebration (Irish Club)	Janesville
	St. Urho's Day Celebration (Finnish)	Finland
April	Last Chance Curling Bonspiel	Hibbing
May	Syttende Mai (Norwegian) ·	Fergus Falls
	Jewish Festival	Edina
June	Danish Day	Minneapolis
	Mid-Summers Dag Festival (Scandinavian)	Erskine
	Centennial Celebration — Scottish Heritage Day	Mapleton

	Deutscher Tag (German)	St. Paul
	Polka Days Festival (Austria)	Mounds View
	Pow Wow	Pipestone
	Aebleskives Days (Danish)	Tyler
	Kaffe Fest	Willmar
	Fiesta Days (Uruguay)	Montevideo
	Svenskarnas Dag (Swedish)	Minneapolis
July	Pow Wow	Red Lake
	Wild Rice Festival	Kelliher
	Karl Oskar Days (Swedish)	Lindstrom
	Kesa Juhla (Finnish)	New York Mills
	Edgerton Dutch Festival	Edgerton
	Heritagefest Festival/	New Ulm
	Pageant Hermannstraum	New Ulm
	Song of Hiawatha Pageant	Pipestone
	Victorian Craft Festival	St. Paul
	Kolacky Day (Czech)	Montgomery
August	Pola-Czesky Days (Bohemian & Polish)	Silver Lake
	Folk Festival	Duluth
	Belgian-American Day	Ghent
	Berne Swissfest	West Concord
	Polska Kielbasa (Polish)	Ivanhoe
September	Minnesota Renaissance Festival	Chaska
	Mennonite Festival	Mountain Lake
October	Goose Festival & Wild West Days	Middle River
	Oktoberfest	Gibbon
November	Christmas Fair (Scandinavian)	Minneapolis
December	St. Lucia Festival (Swedish)	Minneapolis

Try to find information on these observances.
Have you ever attended any of these special events?

Words to Know — Define these words and terms. You may need to use a dictionary or encyclopedia to find some of the answers.

County seat

Culture

Ethnic group

Intensive farming

Melting pot

Platted

Squatters

Writing Activities

Write brief answers to the following questions:

1. Why did the population of Minnesota grow so much between 1849 and 1860?
2. Name some early population centers in Minnesota.
3. Name some of the ethnic groups that came to Minnesota.

CHAPTER THIRTEEN

STATEHOOD

Minnesota in the 1850's

During the period between 1849 and 1858 there was an air of optimism in the territory, and nearly everyone expected the territory to become a state at any time.

Business continued to grow in the territory, and new settlers came in increasing numbers. The lumber industry was thriving. Travelers coming into the territory left with positive impressions of the vast potential of the area. One person, John W. Bond, who had spent a few years in the area, probably succeeded in swaying the opinions of many in the East and the South to pack their bags and hasten to this new land. He wrote a book, *Minnesota and Its Resources*, published in 1856, and the following is a part of what he had to say about Minnesota:

". . . From the Iowa line to the Minnesota River — from the Mississippi reaching beyond the head-waters of the Blue Earth, lies a broad scope of territory, unsurpassed in all the necessary qualities of a richly favored agricultural country — rolling prairies, heavy timber, well watered, and quite exempt from malarious influences. So easy of access that navigable rivers wash two sides for hundreds of miles in length. Those who settle upon the Minnesota will have steamboats at their doors, while those who fill up the more central portions will not wait long for the iron road.

. . . Minnesota might proclaim to all nations, 'Come unto me all ye who are hungry and naked, and I will feed and clothe ye.' But she should add, 'Bring a good stock of industry, ambition, patience and perseverance and don't expect to find large cities, with marble palaces, but a rich open soil with plenty of wood and stone for build-

ing.' Armed with fortitude and a small capital, we say
come, and when you come, go to work, and blessings will
rapidly multiply around you."

The Slavery Question

Getting statehood was difficult in the 1850's, because the
United States government was busy with the problems of
the South and slavery. The Old South was a contradiction,
because southern politicians generally belonged to the
Democratic Party and talked about democracy, while they
still held four million blacks in chattel slavery. The term
"chattel slavery" meant that the black people had practically no legal rights or protection under the law, and could
be bought or sold like farm animals. The southern politicians were well organized and held a lot of power in national politics.

The northerners and most of the people of Minnesota
thought slavery was wrong. For years, a movement called
abolitionism had been growing. Men like Benjamin Lundy
of Ohio and William Garrison of Massachusetts had both
written and spoken out against slavery. They organized a
system called the Underground Railroad that moved
escaped slaves from the South to Canada. American
women also wrote against slavery. One of these women
was Jane Swisshelm, the editor of the newspaper at St.
Cloud, and another was Harriet Beecher Stowe of Massachusetts.

In the 1850's, the argument became hotter. There was
"Bleeding Kansas". This long fought and messy conflict
held the attention of the United States for years. In 1854,
the United States Congress had decided that the people of
Kansas and Nebraska could decide for themselves whether
they wanted to be admitted as free or slave states. The
problem with Kansas was that settlers were pouring in and
there was no clear cut rule on slavery. Northerners came

in, determined to make Kansas a free state, and southerners brought slaves into Kansas, determined to make Kansas a slave state. Both sides tried to organize a state government but neither succeeded. Southerners brought in "roughnecks" from Missouri to stuff the ballot boxes and prove that Kansas was a slave state. Open warfare developed between the two factions. The president of the United States, Franklin Pierce, ordered in federal troops but was unable to stop the trouble.

At the same time, a United States Supreme Court decision, the Dred Scott Case, made a great impression on the people of the United States and Minnesota as well. The case started in Fort Snelling, Minnesota, in the time that Minnesota was still part of the Wisconsin Territory. The surgeon at Fort Snelling, Doctor Emerson, had brought a black man, Dred Scott, from the slave state of Missouri to Illinois, and then to Fort Snelling.

At Fort Snelling, Dr. Emerson talked with other people about the legal status of Dred Scott, a slave now living in free territory. When Emerson went back to Missouri, he made a test case out of Dred Scott's status. He had Scott sue the courts for his freedom. Dr. Emerson said that the fact that Dred Scott had lived in free territory meant that he was a free man. The case bounced from court to court, and in the late 1850's, it ended up in the Supreme Court of the United States. The chief justice, a southern sympathizer from Maryland, Roger Taney, read the majority opinion in 1857. He said that Scott was a slave, and did not merit the protection of the law given white people. He also said that Scott was property, that the government could make no laws concerning property, and that slavery was legal in all states of the land.

The North was horrified. This case was one of the most shocking in America, and paved the way for the Civil War, which followed a few years later.

Minnesota Becomes a State

The idea began to spread that Minnesota ought to become a state. As long as Minnesota was a territory, its governing officers were appointed by the President. Its activity was supervised by Congress, but it was represented in that Congress only by a delegate who had no vote. If Minnesota became a state, it could elect its own government officials, and it could send senators and representatives to Washington to vote on national issues.

Becoming a state was like playing a game; there were definite rules that had to be followed. First: Congress must pass an "enabling act" — an act that "enabled", or permitted, the people of the territory to form a state. Second: the territory must hold a convention to draw up a constitution, that is, to decide the form and the rules for the new state government. Third: the people of the territory must have an election to vote on the constitution and to elect officers for the state. Fourth: Congress must approve the new constitution and government by passing an act admitting the state to the Union.

There were many problems to be solved. One of the first problems was that of the boundaries of the future state. Just what part of the big Minnesota Territory should be included in the state of Minnesota? Some of the Republicans in the southeastern counties wanted to draw an east-to-west boundary line just north of St. Paul that would make a long, narrow state of Minnesota, extending as far west as the Missouri River. They hoped to move the capital down to St. Peter and to build a railroad running westward from Winona. This plan would take the control of the government away from the Democratic traders and businessmen of the St. Paul region and give it to the Republican farmers of the Minnesota River Valley.

Naturally, the leaders in the St. Paul and St. Anthony section opposed this plan. They wanted to put the boundary line north and south along the Red River, and on the north they wanted the state to extend up to the Canadian border. They wanted to keep the capital at St. Paul, and they hoped that St. Paul and Minneapolis would be the center from which railroads would be built to the West.

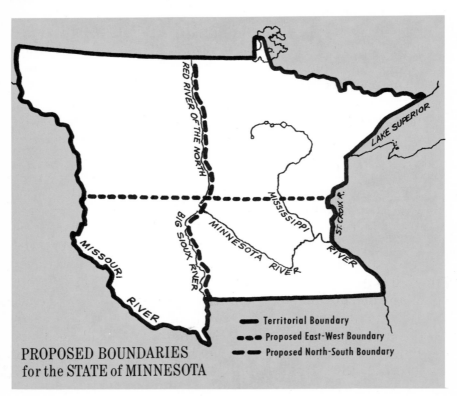

PROPOSED BOUNDARIES
for the STATE of MINNESOTA

Territorial Boundary
Proposed East-West Boundary
Proposed North-South Boundary

Which of the two plans would you have favored? If you look at a map, you will not take much time to answer that question. The east-to-west boundary would have lost for Minnesota its northern pine forests, its Iron Range, most of its lakes, and its important position at the head of the Great Lakes. Minnesota would have been just an agricultural state. But with the north-south boundary along the Red River, Minnesota has had lumbering, mining, manufacturing, the lakes and the tourist trade, as well as farming. The boundary question was very important. Much of Minnesota's future depended upon the decision that the pioneers made.

The St. Paul group had the inside position in this boundary race. Henry M. Rice, the territorial delegate to Congress, favored the north-south boundary, and he put that line into the enabling act which he drew up for Congress to pass. The southern Minnesotans saw that Rice had beaten them, but they tried one last plan to win their way. They introduced into the Minnesota territorial legislature a bill to move the capital from St. Paul to St. Peter. The bill was passed. All it needed to become a law was the signature of the governor.

Then Joe Rolette, the member from Pembina, disappeared, taking the bill with him. Hunt as they would, the legislators could not find him. Just as the clock struck midnight on March 7, 1857, Rolette walked into the hall. But it was too late; the legislature had adjourned. Rolette had been hiding in a St. Paul hotel, with the bill locked in a safe in his room. Of course, the governor had signed another copy of the bill, and the men from St. Peter thought it should be considered a law. But the courts decided that it had not been properly passed, so St. Paul remained the capital of Minnesota.

Meanwhile, Congress had passed the Enabling Act on February 26, 1857. This act fixed our boundaries and set the date for the election of representatives to the convention which would make Minnesota's constitution. It also promised important grants of public lands — including one for schools, one for a state university, one for government buildings, and one for roads and other internal improvements.

Now came the important task of making a constitution for Minnesota. Delegates had been elected in June, and on July 13, 1857, they met in St. Paul. The Republicans and the Democrats were about evenly matched in numbers, and each party wanted to control the convention. There were many disagreements. Each party started to draft its own constitution, but they soon realized it was better for them to compromise, and eventually they agreed on a constitution.

Alexander Ramsey

The next step was to present the constitution to the people of the territory and have them choose state officials. This was done in an election held on October 13, 1857. Alexander Ramsey was the Republican candidate for governor, and Henry H. Sibley was the Democratic candidate. It was a close and hard fight, and there was fraud on both sides. Votes were even reported from nonexistent people in imaginary cities, but most of them were not actually counted in the final result. The result of it all was that the constitution was adopted, and Sibley was elected as the first governor of the state of Minnesota.

Only the act of admission by Congress was necessary now in order to make Minnesota a state. Congress was very slow about taking action. The day came, in December of 1857, for the new state legislature to meet as provided in the constitution. But still Congress had not admitted Minnesota. Nevertheless the legislature met and began its work. So Minnesota had a "state legislature", but the new state officers could not take office until the state was admitted by Congress. The legislature therefore had to work with a territorial governor.

The legislature then chose Minnesota's first two United States senators. It was easy for the members to agree on Henry M. Rice as one of them, but there were a number of other men whom they might have chosen for the second senatorship. It went to General James Shields. He was an Irishman who had won a national reputation as a soldier in the Mexican War and as a senator from Illinois. He had just come to Minnesota, but everyone knew about him. Later he went to live in Missouri. He became a senator from that state too, so this one man had the honor of serving as United States senator from three different states.

Still Minnesota was not admitted to the Union. The legislators, however, went on making laws. They found that in order to do some of the things that they wanted to do, it was necessary to change the constitution. They therefore adopted two amendments to the constitution, and the people accepted these amendments in a special election — before Congress had even approved the original constitution.

Why did it take Congress so long to admit Minnesota to the Union? It was because of the struggle that was going on in Congress over the admission of Kansas. Kansas also wanted to enter the Union, but its constitution permitted slavery. Many Congressmen believed that it had not been made fairly and did not represent the wishes of the Kansas people. They were unwilling to approve it unless they could feel sure that the people of Kansas really wanted it. But the southerners would not admit Minnesota until Kansas had been accepted. So the admission of Minnesota was put off until, at last, a compromise was reached about Kansas. Then the bill admitting Minnesota was passed on May 11, 1858. Minnesota was a state, the thirty-second star on the flag, the North Star State.

As the first governor of the new state, Sibley had a lot of problems to solve. There was the problem of the continuing organization of the area as people moved in. And there was a problem in establishing new state institutions like schools and welfare groups to take care of special needs. The railroads had to be built, and there were only a few crudely marked roads. And there was always the problem of defense against the Indians. The Sioux were not adjusting to the changes, and as more settlers poured in, there was danger of an all-out fight.

Taxes were a problem too. In 1857, mostly due to world problems, there was a depression. This meant that prices for farm products fell. Immigration had slowed down too, and it was hard to get money to start a new business. Slavery was on people's minds as the newspapers with early editors like James Goodhue of St. Paul and Jane Swisshelm of St. Cloud reminded their readers about the growing division between the northern and southern states. In just four more years the problems of the new state of Minnesota would become entangled with two wars, the Civil War and the Sioux War, fought within its own borders.

There are several names for the Civil War, such as the War Between the States and the Suppression of Southern

Independence Movement. Minnesota newspaper readers got all of the background, because they lived through it. Abraham Lincoln of Illinois was selected by the Republican Party to be their candidate in 1860. The Democrats could not agree on a candidate and ended up with three presidential candidates. Lincoln was elected. South Carolina seceded from the Union in 1860. In the early part of 1861, a number of other southern states followed this lead. The seceding states formed the Confederate States of America. Southerners fired on a United States fort in a South Carolina harbor, and Lincoln called for volunteers. The Civil War had begun.

Words to Know — Define these words and terms. You may need to use a dictionary or encyclopedia to find some of the answers.

Abolitionism

Bleeding Kansas

Chattel slavery

Constitution

Dred Scott Case

Roughnecks

Underground Railroad

Names to Know — Identify these people.

Henry M. Rice

Joe Rolette

Dred Scott

General James Shields

Writing Activities

Suppose you were a newspaper correspondent sent to Minnesota by the *New York Times* in the 1850's. Write a one or two paragraph dispatch to your paper on the following topics:

Territorial Residents React to the Dred Scott Decision.

The Dispute over Where the Boundaries of the State of Minnesota Should Be.

Problems Facing Henry Sibley as He Becomes the First Governor of the State of Minnesota.

CHAPTER FOURTEEN

THE NEW STATE IN TWO WARS

Minnesota's Part in the Civil War

All of the northern states had provisions in their constitutions to form state regiments in time of need. When the Civil War began, these were formed and filled with volunteers. In time, these regiments became the Union Army. They went by state names. For example, the Minnesota regiments, about ten who saw some kind of action, were named by state and number. The federal government put them and other state regiments under the control of federal officers. The federal government also furnished uniforms, food, pay, shelter, weapons and ammunition.

There was a rush to volunteer. Minnesota, with a population of about 250,000 sent over 20,000 men into the armed forces. This meant that a great proportion of the young and able-bodied, and some of the not so young, went into the army.

We will look at the record of one regiment, the First Minnesota, in detail. Minnesota regiments in action fought in every major area of the war. Some fought west of the Mississippi in Arkansas. Others fought in the terrible battles like Shiloh, and Nashville in Tennessee. Some were with General Grant when he captured the southern fortress of Vicksburg in 1863. Others marched with Sherman through Georgia and the Carolinas toward the end of the war.

The First Minnesota Infantry built a record that ranks with the great military organizations of all time. In a time when long distance travel was not common, these people had gone a long distance. They had traveled by river boat, railroad, and a short distance by foot as well, from Minnesota to the vicinity of Washington, D.C. There they became part of the Army of the Potomac.

Civil War days at Fort Snelling

Their uniforms were the standard issue blue wool cloth. This consisted of a dark blue jacket, light blue pants, heavy leather laced shoes, and a small leather billed cap. For cold weather they were issued heavy overcoats of blue wool with a double thickness over the shoulders. They carried a heavy pack that contained a blanket, a piece of rubberized canvas that could be used as a rain cape, rations, ammunition, a bayonet and a heavy long muzzle-loading rifle.

Living conditions in the army were not good. Sanitation was often neglected, and disease raged and carried off more men than gunfire. By modern standards, the food was terrible.

One of the standard issues was hard tack. These flat loaves, looking like giant crackers, were made out of flour, salt and water. They lasted for months, until a certain fly laid eggs on them, and the larvae, called weevils, riddled the bread. Hard tack had to be soaked in coffee or broken up between two rocks so that it could be eaten. With this were rations of highly salted beef and pork. Most of the cooking was done by the soldier in his mess kit. Toward the end of the war, canned goods had appeared, but stomach and intestinal trouble followed all regiments.

The First Minnesota Regiment participated in many battles: Antietam, Fredericksburg, Chancellorsville. They also played an important part at the Battle of Gettysburg. On the afternoon of the second day of the Battle of Gettysburg, the First Minnesota Regiment made history. A northern general saw a hole in the line. He saw that the North could lose the battle and the war right there, so he ordered Colonel Colvill, commander of the Minnesota Regiment, into action. Two hundred and sixty-four men of the Minnesota Regiment charged thousands of southerners. In less than ten minutes, two hundred and sixteen Minnesotans were killed or wounded, but they bought time for those that would follow after them, and the battle was won.

Company E of the Minnesota Infantry U.S.V. taken November 1862 at Fort Snelling

During 1863, 1864 and part of 1865, the First Minnesota troops saw more action in the East. Those in the West and on the central front also saw much marching and fighting, and dying. Some of them were with Sherman when he accepted the surrender of General Joseph Johnston and the last large southern force in the field.

The terrible war ended soon after. Thousands of Americans had died, from both the North and the South. Many Minnesotans died on these battlefields, but their gallant actions had helped preserve the Union. They would not return to their homes in Minnesota, and their loss was keenly felt in the small settlements and farming communities of the state.

The Sioux War of 1862

While the Civil War was going on elsewhere, the Sioux situation in Minnesota had been simmering ever since the treaties in the early 1850's. People on the frontier in the middle of the nineteenth century were worried about the Indians. Stories from the older Indian wars in the East had been handed down.

We can see how unfair these stories were. The good deeds of so many Indians were never mentioned. The enormous Indian contribution to agriculture was hardly ever mentioned. The white people's robbing of the Indians was not told. This had been going on for many years. Land had been taken without payment in earlier times, and the payments for land in the days of the treaties were never enough. The ugly stories about how bad liquor was used in the Indian trade were regarded as funny, not bad. Knowledge of the Indian was slight; the average settler knew little about the Indians' culture, their hopes and wishes.

The summer of 1862 was tense. Newspapers carried stories of many southern victories in the Civil War. Official letters came back to many Minnesota families telling of the death of a soldier from battle or disease. But life went on. Immigrants were still coming in, and more men left to fight in the Union Army. The people left on the farms of the

Minnesota frontier planted their crops and watched the wheat, oats, corn, barley and vegetables grow in the long, hot days of summer. In the meantime, trouble was coming.

The Sioux on the reservations depended on the annuities or annual payments from the government for a living. The payments in money, food and trade goods were made at the agencies. Even in the best of times, the money was slow to arrive. Now in war time, it was even slower.

The Sioux had gone through the bleak winter of 1861 with scarcely enough food to survive. When spring came, they went to the Government Agency to get their promised amount of food and clothing, as well as money due on their agreement with the government for the sale of their lands. They found that the food and clothing were locked up in the storehouse, but their money had not yet arrived from Washington. The agent refused to distribute the food and clothing until the money arrived, and to make matters worse, the traders would not extend credit to the tribes. One brutal trader said, "Let them eat grass". This angered the Indians. They knew the white men were already at war, having noticed the young men going away. Some of the Indians had been to mission schools and could read the newspapers.

Finally, in late August, supplies came in, but money for the annuity payments still did not come. A detachment from Minnesota's Fifth Infantry took an active part in the distribution at the agency near Redwood Falls. While the distribution was going on, trouble started in another place. A band of four Sioux warriors, hungry and resentful of the actions of the white people's government toward them, lit the fuse to an explosive frontier war in August 1862.

Most accounts of this incident indicate that the four Sioux warriors stole eggs from a farm near Acton, in Meeker County. Fearful of being discovered, they challenged the settlers to a sharpshooting contest, then turned their guns on the settlers, killing three men and two women. Word of this act traveled rapidly through the tribes of the Minnesota River Valley, and a council was called to determine what to do.

The council fire burned brightly and there was excitement in the air. The young warriors wanted to go to war, while some of the elders of the tribe were against such an action. Little Crow, one of the most highly respected chiefs at the council, listened silently as the warriors demanded war. He finally spoke, cautioning against war because of the larger armies of the white people.

Many warriors, eager to get the war under way, taunted Little Crow, saying that he was a coward and had lived with the white people too long. Little Crow saw that the young warriors were determined to fight and he agreed to fight also. He put on the war paint and with real misgivings prepared to lead his people into war.

Little Crow took command of most of the Sioux forces. He was aided by such noted Indian leaders as Shakopee and Mankato. Having lived for years near agencies and trading posts, the Indians were well armed. In the looting of the settler's farms, they picked up more arms and ammunition. Raiding gave them all the food they needed.

To the Sioux, war meant fighting, killing, and what white people called "massacre". This was their cultural way of dealing with an enemy. To the white population of Minnesota, these acts were considered those of savages and they were determined that the Sioux were to be punished to the fullest extent possible.

The first attacks of the war were directed against the settlers and traders, with later attacks coming against towns and forts. Indian raids against the white settlers became general across southern Minnesota. Hundreds of

160

white settlers were killed. Farms were looted, and buildings were burned. The terrified settlers left their farms and partially harvested crops and fled. Temporary forts were thrown together where the people could find safety. Fear was widespread. Families were separated, and many settlers were prisoners of the Sioux. Not all of the Indians joined in the hostilities; John Other Day, a Sioux, organized an escape group and helped many white people to escape.

The Upper Agency near Redwood Falls was looted and agents and traders were killed. The agent who had made the remark about eating grass was later found dead, with his mouth stuffed full of grass.

Many settlers came to Fort Ridgely, and proceeded to build barricades between the buildings for defense. The Sioux attacked several times, but the rifle fire, with the additional cannon fire of Sergeant John Jones was too much for them.

Fort Ridgely in 1862

New Ulm was also the site of a Sioux attack. Settlers had come here for refuge as they had at Fort Ridgely, and they joined to defend the town under the command of Judge Charles Flandrau. The first attack of the Indians was beaten back, but part of the town was burned. Flandrau kept all of his people in a few fortified buildings of the business district. The defenders now burned all of the town except these buildings. They wanted a clear field of fire when the Sioux attack came.

The next morning over six hundred Sioux attacked over the still smoking ashes. They gave up and went away after many were killed. The concentrated fire was too much for them. Some of the defenders were killed and a number were wounded.

Battle of New Ulm, 1862

Henry Sibley, former governor of Minnesota, raised an army of 1600 men, many of them new recruits. Sibley moved fast, up the Minnesota River Valley. General Sibley sent agents ahead to contact Little Crow. A brief period of negotiation was started, but no agreement could be reached.

Sibley's scouts reported that a large village of Sioux were on the Yellow Medicine River. Sibley moved his troops toward the spot. Little Crow planned an ambush. Hundreds of his warriors were hidden in the thickly growing trees, waiting for the long column of troops. The ambush didn't work. Some soldiers, against orders, had left the column. They were hungry, and saw potatoes in an Indian garden and started to dig there. The Sioux fired on them. Sibley saw what was going on and got his men out of the woods to a ridge.

The Sioux now started an open, all-out battle against Sibley's army. This has come to be called the Battle of Wood Lake. They charged again and again uphill against the white men's position. At the height of the battle, Mankato, arrayed in all his feathers, led a wild charge and was killed. The Indians soon gave up the attack.

Sibley lost no time. Little Crow could no longer hold his warriors together. Sibley's troops covered a large area looking for both Indian and white survivors. Two hundred and sixty-nine captives of the Indians were rescued.

Over fifteen hundred Indians gave up and became prisoners. A great military court was held. Three hundred and seven captured Sioux were condemned to death for their part in the war. Henry B. Whipple, bishop of the Episcopal Church in Minnesota, intervened on the Indian's behalf and went directly to Washington, where he presented their case to President Lincoln. Lincoln decided that most of the Indians had been fighting in a war just as the white soldiers were fighting in a war. These he determined should not be punished. There were some he felt were guilty of murder or other serious crimes and these he ordered to be hanged.

On December 26, 1862, thirty-eight Sioux men were hanged at a public mass execution at Mankato, and with their passing the Sioux nation virtually disappeared from the state. The white population insisted that the Sioux be moved out of Minnesota, and public opinion was so strong that the government ended all treaties with the Sioux, stopped their annuity payments, took their Minnesota River lands from them and moved them west to the Missouri River country. The Sioux had made a desperate attempt to hold what they believed to be rightfully theirs, but failed.

In the spring of 1863, all remaining Sioux in Minnesota, except for a small number of trusted individuals, were removed from the state and placed on reservations in Nebraska and South Dakota.

In 1863, Little Crow was killed by a farmer near Hutchinson, Minnesota. It was rumored that he and his son had come down into Minnesota from Canada on a horse-stealing raid.

Little Crow will long be remembered as a leader who tried to live at peace with the white settlers, and when he became disillusioned by continued failures on the part of the government to deal fairly with his people, made a difficult decision to lead his people in a war to regain their lost lands.

Words to Know — Define these words and terms. You may need to use a dictionary or encyclopedia to find some of the answers.

Army of the Potomac

Battle of Wood Lake

Gettysburg

Hard tack

Names to Know — Identify these people.

Little Crow

Henry Sibley

Writing Activities

Write a short essay describing living conditions for the Minnesota soldiers fighting in the Civil War.

Write a short essay describing the conditions that led to the Sioux War of 1862.

UNIT FOUR: THE DEVELOPMENT OF SOCIO-ECONOMIC SYSTEMS

CHAPTER FIFTEEN
THE LUMBER ERA, 1837–1910

The story of the lumber era in Minnesota is one of both greatness and of tragedy. It provided the timber, the money and the people who helped build the state and to bring in the thousands of immigrants who were to settle and populate the area, but it also swept away the finest forests of white pine to be found anywhere in the world in just a few short years. Where nature had spent hundreds of years in producing these magnificent trees, the axe and saw of the lumber men left desolation in a few short years.

White pine

Nearly two-thirds of the state was covered by forest when the area was first discovered. Today, most of this original forest is gone, and although we still count forestry as an important industry, it is in areas other than the production of lumber from the gigantic white pine.

What became of the Minnesota lumber? Much of it went down the Mississippi in great log rafts to build cities along its course such as Dubuque, Rock Island, and St. Louis. Other cities such as Omaha, Des Moines, Kansas City and

Modern forest product mill, International Falls

Early Stillwater, lumber capital of Minnesota

Topeka used Minnesota lumber to build their stores and homes. Much of the lumber made its way to the East and to Europe, and much of it went into wooden products that brought the products of the world back to Minnesota. It went to the West Indies in the form of barrels and brought back molasses; it went to Brazil and brought back coffee; it went into the Dakota territory where it built military forts. It made millionaires of many lumber pioneers and their wealth helped build the cities of Minneapolis, St. Anthony, St. Paul, Stillwater and Duluth.

It also left its mark on the landscape. The lumber barons, in their rush to take from the land all of the timber they could cut, and as fast as they could cut it, left the slashings or waste trimmings strewn over the ground, an invitation to forest fire and disaster. These too are a part of Minnesota history.

Names such as Stanchfield, Washburn, Bovey, Morrison, Shevlin, Akeley, Hall, Walker and Weyerhauser became famous for their efforts in making Minnesota lumber available to the world, and many of them accumulated vast fortunes in the process. To them, the huge forests were a challenge. The trees were theirs for the taking. Only the Indians stood in their way, and this was no great obstacle since the government was there to help acquire the land through its process of treaty making.

Millions of acres were acquired for the price of blankets, guns, looking glasses and beads, or for a few cents an acre where cash was involved. Often the lumber barons sent their crews onto land they didn't even have cutting rights for. It didn't matter, for by the time the trees were cut down, they were ready to move on to still other areas.

Many Indian chiefs were manipulated into signing away timber that they had no right to sign away. The forests belonged to the Indian people, not just to the chiefs, but their desire to possess many of the white man's goods made them easy prey for the timber speculators. Chief Hole-In-The-Day asked Franklin Steele (first to explore the Mississippi River pine forests) for fifty cents a tree, a pony, five blankets, calico and broadcloth in exchange for the right to cut lumber near Aitkin, and said that he also had great pine woods on Leech Lake which he offered to show them. He was paid what he asked and the stately pine trees began to come down.

The white pine forests of Minnesota seemed so large to people of that era that they couldn't imagine the possibility of using up this valuable natural resource. Conservation never once entered their minds, or if it did, it was quickly covered by thoughts of quick wealth. J. W. Bond, writing about Minnesota Territory in 1853 had this to say about the lumber supply:

Pulpwood lumbering in northern Minnesota

"... *As yet, our lumbermen only go up the St. Croix and its tributaries, and the Rum River, a tributary of the Mississippi, just a few miles above St. Anthony, lying between the Mississippi and the St. Croix. From that region comes the mighty pine of the St. Croix and of the Mississippi. But far above the Rum River are other tributaries of the Mississippi, and eighty miles of solid pine timber on the shores of the Mississippi itself, and many yet unexplored tributaries, so that centuries will hardly exhaust the pineries above us."*

In the last month of 1837 the first tree was cut and the first cabin built at the town of Marine. David Hone and Lewis Judd, who came in 1838 from Marine, Illinois, took up this claim on the St. Croix River, and the next year persuaded thirteen people from their old home to join them. They went to St. Louis, where they started up the river with everything necessary for milling and farming, including oxen and cows. Mrs. Hone was the only woman in the party and was the first white woman on the western side of the St. Croix Valley. When the party arrived they found that the claim had been "jumped" by two men to whom they had to pay three hundred dollars before they could get their land back.

The mill which they built cut the first lumber in that part of the valley and did business for fifty years. It was owned later by Lewis Judd and Orange Walker, who came first as the company's clerk. The people at Marine always raised enough food for their own use and were very prosperous until the mill burned down in 1863. It was entirely destroyed, as were almost half of the early sawmills in Minnesota, for fire was their worst enemy. More of our woods have been burned than have been cut and much of the money which was gained by such hard work in the early days had to be used to rebuild mills which were burned.

171

In 1853, the St. Croix Valley was probably the lumbering capital of the world. Sawmills were being built up and down the river, and people were pouring into the valley either to work in the lumbering operations or to engage in businesses that provided goods and services for that growing industry. Here is the way Mr. Bond described the valley of the St Croix at that time:

". . . the St. Croix, with population on both sides of the river, from Point Douglas to the farthest point of the lumbering operations, will send to market this year nearly sixty million feet of sawed lumber and logs. Circumstances have greatly favored the lumber men of the St. Croix this year. The high spring water has enabled them to send all of their logs down river. The boom was filled very early and many millions have already reached the markets below. From Stillwater to the boom, sixty miles below Taylors Falls, you can see nothing but rafts and strings of logs."

The boom was a unique part of the lumber era. It made it possible for the lumber men to send millions of logs down river in a short time, to a sort of "corral" or holding point, at which they could be sorted out, credited to their proper owner, whose brand was stamped on the log and then sawed into lumber for the waiting markets of the world. Here is how Mr. Bond described the St. Croix boom:

". . . Piers of immense size were sunk at intervals from the Minnesota shore to an island in midstream and from the island on to the Wisconsin shore. Boom timbers were hung from pier to pier and when finished not a single log could get past. This boom is undoubtly the most complete and expensive work of its kind in the Northwest. It is a curiosity to see the huge size of some of the log rafts from this boom. Two noted St. Croix river *pilots passed Stillwater with a fleet of three million feet of logs under their command. We believe this is the largest body of logs that ever went out of the St. Croix at one time."*

Sawmills were being built all along the St. Croix. The first, downriver from Taylors Falls was at Osceola on the Wisconsin side of the river. There was the Marine Mills on the St. Croix and the Arcola Mill six miles above Stillwater. At the upper end of Stillwater there was an expensive steam mill, and just beyond was the McKusick Mill, noted for its excellent finished product. Below Stillwater several other mills were either finished or in various stages of construction. Names such as Perrin, Mears, Bowron, and Stevens were connected with many of the early saw mills. In 1853 there were eleven active saw mills in the valley capable of cutting up to 250,000 feet of lumber every twenty-four hours, which when sent on to the St. Louis market brought up to fourteen dollars per thousand feet.

The Lumberjacks

Probably no story of the lumber era would be complete without telling about the men who cut the big pines and made them ready for their float trip down river. These were the lumberjacks. They were a tough, hardy mixture of rough and ready souls from the forests of Maine, the French-Canadians and the Scandinavians. Most had worked in the forest before and they brought their skills to the infant Minnesota timber country. Their strength, courage and endurance were trademarks of the profession.

A logging crew included a foreman or boss; a cook (who was usually the most popular man in camp); his assistant called the "bull cook"; the teamsters who drove the camp teams; the choppers who were the most skillful with the ax; the swampers, who cleared the roads and slashed branches from the fallen trees; the barkers who ripped the bark from

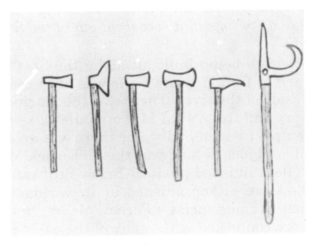

Tools used by the lumberjacks

Dining hall in early lumber camp

the fallen trees so they would slide easily; the sled tenders; the blacksmiths; and a camp utility man or boy whose job it was to do all the odd jobs about the camp. The camp store was called the wanagan box and its keeper was the wanaganeer.

Their work was dangerous and the hours long. Rising before dawn, they would eat a gigantic breakfast, then go into the woods and work all day in what was often freezing temperatures. In the log drives down stream they would often ride logs and became quite skillful in spinning the floating logs while keeping their balance.

When they arrived in the lumber towns after a log drive, they received their pay, and the celebrating that followed would put the cowboys of the Old West to shame. Most of their money was spent in celebrating, and many a bar top was left with the imprints of the jack's spiked shoes after he had danced on it. Some who declined to celebrate and saved their money might take their wages and look for a farm in the new country. Those who spent their wages in a few nights of merriment went back into the forest for more work, more money, always looking forward to the next pay day and its accompanying celebration.

Everything about the lumber era was big. The pines were big, the forests were big, so big that no one knew where they ended at that time. The men were big and they thought big. The lumber kings amassed giant fortunes in a hurry, and the lumberjacks performed work of great strength and feats of bravery. No wonder then, that this era produced the stories of Paul Bunyan and his blue ox, Babe.

The End of the Lumber Era

The peak year for lumber production in the St. Croix Valley was 1895, when over 373 million feet of lumber were cut. In 1905 Minnesota reached its highest statewide total, nearly two billion feet, and it was nearly all white pine.

The lumber men did not replant the land from which they took the trees. As the lumber regions of the Rum River, St. Croix Valley and other areas gave out, the lumber men looked to new regions further west, and as they left Minnesota they also left behind thousands and thousands of acres of wasteland with its stumps, slashings and rubble.

Rounding up the logs

The lumber era was nearly over by the early 1900's as the white pine was used up, but the problems remained. Replanting and conservation measures were to come in later years, but what could people do to replace the majestic white pines which had taken nature hundreds of years to grow to maturity?

It was the end of an era. It was good and it was bad, but it was a part of our history and of our growth period. It took something away from our heritage but it gave us something too. How would you evaluate this era in our state history?

Words to Know — Define these words and terms. You may need to use a dictionary or encyclopedia to find some of the answers.

Conservation

Lumber boom

Lumberjacks

Timber

Wanagan box

Wanaganeer

Writing Activities

Suppose you are a newspaper reporter sent to interview a lumberjack to find out about Minnesota's lumber industry. Write out a series of questions you would like to ask, and from what you have learned about the lumber industry, supply the answers to your questions.

CHAPTER SIXTEEN

AGRICULTURE IN MINNESOTA

Indian Farming

The first agricultural efforts in Minnesota were undertaken by the Indians. As a matter of record, many farm practices have been credited to the American Indians north of Mexico, and it is likely that some of these were practiced by those tribes that inhabited what is now Minnesota.

The Indian's supply of food from cultivated plants was limited and varied in quantity from year to year. Samuel W. Pond, one of the early missionaries in the state, said in commenting on the Sioux in Minnesota as they were in 1834:

> *"At most of the (Indian) villages a very little corn was raised by some of the families, but only enough to supply them with food for a few days. Before 1834, no land had been plowed by or for them except a little at Lake Calhoun. Mr. Renville's relatives raised a little corn at Lac qui Parle, but only a little. More corn was raised at that time at Lake Traverse than anywhere else among the Sioux."*

Early Pioneer Farmers

The white people began farming in Minnesota around trading posts, military posts and missions. Early accounts of traders in this area mention food products which were produced in their gardens and small fields nearby.

The person who is sometimes given credit for being the territory's first pioneer farmer was Joseph R. Brown, for whom one of Minnesota's counties was named. Primarily a trader and early lumberman, he is said to have broken a piece of prairie near Minnehaha Falls and in 1829 to have raised a crop there.

In 1821 a group of Swiss merchants and tradesmen came to the Selkirk settlement at Pembina. Five of the Swiss families decided not to stay and migrated south to the "States," and were permitted to squat near Fort Snelling. In 1823, thirteen other Swiss families left the colony in Canada and some of these came to Fort Snelling. Again, in 1826, over two hundred people, mostly Swiss, left Pembina and came to Fort Snelling. Some stayed, others went on down the river.

In 1840, all squatters were removed from the Fort Snelling reservation. Some of them moved to what is now St. Paul, and one, Gervais by name, founded an agricultural colony about nine miles north of St. Paul in what is now known as Little Canada.

Most agricultural historians are agreed that the first real agricultural locality to be settled was in southern Washington County. The first farmers were Joseph Haskell and James S. Norris who settled near Afton about 1839. Later, in 1841, Norris moved to a new claim in Cottage Grove. The first field of forty acres of broken sod was planted to wheat. This is said to be the first farm north of Prairie du Chien.

The census of 1850 reported 6,077 persons. The number of people reported as farmers was 340, including 77 in St. Paul; it probably also included others elsewhere who were not actually farming. Total land in farms was 28,881 acres, improved land 5,035 acres, and the number of separate farms 157. Some of these farms, however, were only garden plots. By way of comparison, agricultural statistics compiled by the Minnesota Crop and Livestock Reporting Service in 1979 showed that there were 104,000 farms in Minnesota. What a remarkable change in the short space of 130 years.

The census of 1850 tells us that of Minnesota's crops, oats made up 37%, potatoes 26%, corn 20%, peas and beans

12%, and other crops 5%. Ten years later wheat had entered the picture: corn 29%, potatoes 25%, wheat about 22%, oats 21%, and other crops 3%. By 1875, wheat alone made up nearly 66%.

The largest farms were in three counties: Ramsey, Benton and Washington. The honor of having the largest farms went to Washington County, with one of 339 acres.

While the number of farms has grown steadily, there has been a slowing up of the movement of land into farm use since 1900. In the early years, prairie homesteads could be had for the taking, but by 1900 most of the prairie land was occupied. We saw that in 1850 there were 5,035 acres of improved land in the state. In 1900 there were 26,248,498 acres of improved land for farms. Today there are approximately 30,300,000 acres of improved farm land.

The Sod House Frontier in Minnesota

The Civil War was over by the spring of 1865, but a century would pass before the descendants of the slaves would have their full human rights. The U.S. Congress passed important laws during the war years. One of these laws was the Homestead Act of 1862; and under this law, a man or a woman could get 160 acres of land free. In order to get the land, the settlers had to choose their surveyed 160 acres, and then go to the nearest land office and sign a paper, promising that they would live on the land, plow part of the land, and build a house.

In western Minnesota, many thousands of people took homesteads. Unfortunately, there was cheating; people signed up for land and did not do what they had promised. The homesteaders had five years to finish rights to land on their claim, but they could sell their rights to other settlers who wanted land. They would sign their rights to the land away in a document called a relinquishment. The new settlers would buy their right to the land for a few dollars per acre.

The lives of people settling homesteads were grim. Western Minnesota was open prairie country. Trees for fuel and building grew only near the few lakes and streams. Most settlers, short of money, built their houses and barns from sod. Sod is the upper layer of earth bound together by grass roots. The settler would come in with a team of oxen or horses, a wagon, plow, and household goods.

Early spring was the best time to get started. That way a crop could be grown. Getting started was never easy. Think about a settler family. They would come to an open, brown, grassy area. As far as they could see, there were no trees. Here and there on slopes, green grass might be starting to work through last year's drouth. The March wind rippled the grass as the people looked at it.

Early immigrant sod house

They had to locate a place for a homesite. This included a house and a barn, also a chicken coop and garden. Next, they started on the sod house. The man yoked or hitched his oxen to the single blade plow and set it in the ground. The heavy oxen leaned forward as the pioneer held the wooden handles of the plow. Roots popped and grass rustled as the plow turned the sod, leaving a long black strip behind. After a half dozen or so strips were made, the sod house was built. The man took a sharp, square spade and cut the tough, six-inch-thick sod into chunks several feet long. These were laid up in walls like bricks. A roof of poles and more sod, or maybe of tar paper was put on. A door and several windows were put in. A metal stove pipe was put through the roof and the family was ready to move in.

There are a few good things to say about these houses. The sod walls stopped the wind and kept out the cold fairly well. In the hot summer months the sod houses were fairly cool. However, the earth floor picked up all the smells of the household. Often it got so strong that the pioneers dug it out and replaced it with fresh earth. In dry weather, dust came down from the sod walls. Insects of all kinds liked to share the house with the settlers.

Money was scarce and wood for fuel was often far away. People burned dry cow manure, or cow chips, as it was called. Some settlers took long slough or swamp grass, twisted it into ropes, and burned these. Even when twisted, grass burned fast. It was a lot of work to keep a fire going, and in the winter, fire was life itself.

In spite of drouth, insects, and all of the problems, the pioneers came and worked their farms.

During the 1850's, new kinds of farm machinery came into the state. These included steel plows, mechanical threshers and well drilling machines. The scarcity of labor during the Civil War accelerated the use of machinery.

Watching John Deere's steel plow at work

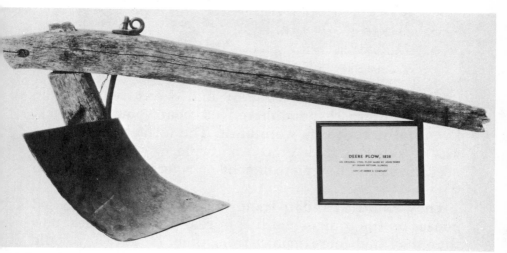

The first Deere plow

There were many improvements in farm machines in the 1860's. One of these was the self-raking reaper. Steam threshers came in about 1867. Various types of grain drills were offered for sale. Other implements in use were horse hay rakes, small grain reapers, potato diggers, harrows, straw cutters, iron corn shellers, and fanning mills. Mowing machines and hay stackers meant more and better feed for cattle and horses. Better plows, manure spreaders and cultivators helped bring in a better crop.

Automatic self-rake reaper, invented in 1858

Good tame hay like timothy and clover replaced the coarse wild grasses, and more feed meant more livestock. Eventually, railroads were built. The farmers now had a way to ship out their crops and bring in goods that they needed without having to depend on rivers and long wagon trips.

They could abandon their hated, uncomfortable sod houses on the prairie and live in real wooden houses, now that they had more money from their crops. They could burn coal, brought in by train, instead of cow manure and grass. Coal produced a longer-lasting fire. They planted trees around their land to break up the force of the winter winds which whipped across the flat or rolling prairies.

In the last twenty-five years of the nineteenth century, a new fence material called barbed wire came into use. After that, someone invented woven wire, which was even stronger than barbed wire. Now, instead of depending only on wheat, the farmer could also raise hogs and keep them safely penned up.

Early Wheat Farming

The most practical — and profitable — form of frontier farming was vegetable gardening, for the farm homes and for such local markets as could be reached. Experiments in grain growing were made early in Minnesota. In 1841, James Norris harvested forty acres of spring wheat in Washington County, and the next year ninety acres. He gave a definite answer to one of the questions of the time:

An early farm in Minnesota

wheat did well in Minnesota. It seemed to be easy to raise, and there was promise of an expanding market for it. So as the settlers swept in, and as more soil came under cultivation, many turned to wheat raising. The earlier subsistence farming gave way to a one-crop system.

It was not easy to transport wheat to market. The railroad did not reach Minnesota until the 1860's, and the farmers had to depend on horses or oxen to get the crops to river towns for transportation to St. Louis and other centers. If steamboats were few, wheat supplies might pile up in the shipping ports. A visitor in 1859 to Hastings, a bustling Minnesota town on the Mississippi, described the scene he saw:

> *"Wheat everywhere; wheat on the levee; wagon loads of wheat pouring down to the levee; wheat in the streets; wheat on the sidewalks."*

McCormick's reaper

Many factors influenced the rise of wheat farming: the swarming of people onto the western lands in the 1860's, the coming of the McCormick reaper and other farm machinery, the Civil War with its demand for increased production, and the gradual westward extension of railroads. More and more the open land was wheat land, and by the mid-seventies wheat made up two-thirds of all the agricultural production of Minnesota. Much of this wheat was the new dark, hard northern wheat that made excellent flour.

Some people even created fabulous "bonanza farms", making a gigantic business from the combination of land, machines, and wheat. This was farming on a very large scale, and demonstrated for a time, at least, the possibility of mass production of wheat at a profit in the Red River Valley region. Oliver Dalyrymple, in 1875, broke 1,280 acres which in 1876 produced a crop of 32,000 bushels of wheat. In 1877 he had 4,500 acres which produced twenty-five bushels of wheat to the acre. It is said that a typical threshing crew on a "bonanza farm" (and there were many such on the larger farms), included twenty-three people, a foreman, and ten teams of horses. They could thresh fifty acres a day. Labor, of course, was one of the problems of such farms.

As wheat became more and more important, Minneapolis grew into the Mill City of the world as pioneer millers like the Washburns and Pillsburys turned the mountains of wheat into flour.

Problems and Politics

Eventually Minnesota farmers depending on wheat growing were beset with problems. For one thing, farming moved westward to the rich prairies of the Dakotas; for another, there were wheat producers in other parts of the world — Argentina, Australia, Russia — who added to the world market. As production increased, not only in the West but throughout the world, prices dropped. Yields began to decline as the soil gave up its nutrients. Smaller yields, lower prices, worldwide competition, and the profits of middlemen and railroads created problems for the farmer. These problems led to a political crusade and to a mechanical revolution that modernized farming.

It was not easy to fight competition from far-off countries, but the railroads and elevator men and millers were close at hand, and in the 1860's and the years that followed the farmers organized and fought their battles through such institutions as the Grange and the Farmers' Alliance and through radical third parties, with gifted leaders like Oliver H. Kelley and Ignatius Donnelly. The farmers used politics in an attempt to restore what they regarded as the economic democracy of the earlier frontier.

Ignatius Donnelly

A Minnesota pioneer farmer, Oliver H. Kelley, was chiefly responsible for founding the Grange. He was early interested in agricultural organization, was one of the founders in 1852 of the first county agricultural society in Minnesota, and took part in the founding of the Minnesota Territorial Agricultural Society two years later. A tour of the South in 1866 convinced Kelley of the need for cooperative action among farmers, and the next year, with six associates, he founded the National Grange, or the Patrons of Husbandry, a secret order of farmers. Its object was the advancement of agriculture by educational processes. The plan was to enrich the social and intellectual life of the farmers; and the local granges, open to both men and women, were to function as clubs, with specially prepared programs for their meetings. It is of interest to know that as early as 1865 a "Farmers' Association", primarily a mutual insurance project, was started in Minnesota, and that two years later this "Farmers' Union" as it was then called, launched a campaign for the organization of farmers' social clubs. In 1868 Kelley set out for St. Paul, and there, on September 2, with Colonel Daniel A. Robertson, founder of the Minnesota Horticultural Society, he established the North Star Grange. A practical tone was given to the project by including among its goals the protection of members against corporations and the establishment of depots for cooperative buying and selling. The Farmers' Union approved heartily of the new plan of agricultural organization. Early in 1869 eleven local granges united to form the Minnesota State Grange, the first state federation of its kind. By the close of that year Minnesota had forty out of forty-nine local granges in the United States. The movement spread, and by 1874 Minnesota alone had 538 granges.

Though the Grange itself was non-political, its members throughout the Middle West agitated for reasonable railroad rates, against discrimination, and for regulation through state laws; and legislatures took action. The Granger legislation established the principle that railroads and other corporations were properly subject to public regulation, a principle set forth by the Supreme Court in 1876.

The Change from Wheat Farming

In the early days of Minnesota farming, there were some pioneers of the new agriculture. One was Wendelin Grimm, a German immigrant who settled in Carver County in 1857. He brought with him a bag of alfalfa seed. He planted this seed in the fall, and some of it survived the severe Minnesota winter. Each year he kept on planting seed from the alfalfa that grew, until, out of his patience and persistence, came Grimm alfalfa, the hardiest variety known. That was a great contribution to agriculture.

Another pioneer was Peter Gideon, who came to Minnesota from Ohio in 1853 and settled on the south shore of Lake Minnetonka. He was especially interested in apples and one that he grew was the Wealthy, a hardy northern variety well suited for the climate of Minnesota.

Earlier it was mentioned that wheat and small grains became important in the economy of Minnesota. The period of specialized wheat farming for the state roughly covered the years 1860–1885. Actually, the high point in this period came in 1878. Grasshopper plagues and a plant disease called stem rust seriously damaged wheat harvests in the 1870's, and by 1880 wheat farming was giving way to diversified farming. Other crops such as potatoes, flax, some of the other small grains, and hay began to assume more importance. Attention began to be focused on the importance of livestock.

Corn and hogs grew to replace wheat as the crops on the rich land of southern and central Minnesota. There was a demand for more good beef from the people who lived in cities of Minnesota and the eastern United States. The farmers fattened cattle on corn and oats they raised themselves, and then shipped them to market, chiefly by railroad. Packing houses developed in places like South St. Paul, Austin and Albert Lea, to process beef and pork for customers in Minnesota and all over the United States.

Education and Agriculture

Early in the history of the state, farmers began thinking about specialized education for the farm youth and the need for research in agriculture. Colonel John H. Stevens, along with others, brought to the West the New England idea of public institutions. Upon election to the legislature in 1857, he began to work for legislation that would provide for agricultural education.

Legislation establishing an experimental farm and agricultural college at Glencoe was passed in 1858, but unfortunately no funds were provided for the new institution. Stevens donated some of his own land, and a public subscription of $10,000 provided some funds.

The Civil War came on and the college at Glencoe never got underway. In 1865 a grant of land became available to the college under the Morrill Act of 1862. In 1868 the University of Minnesota was reorganized. The land grant of 1862, for the encouragement of agricultural education, which had been made to the Agricultural College at Glencoe in 1865, was given to the University on the condition that it provide for a college of agriculture, a college of mechanical arts, and an experimental farm.

Gradually, there developed what is today known as the College of Agriculture, Forestry and Home Economics. In 1947 the legislature established a School of Veterinary Medicine. This was a part of the College of Agriculture, Forestry, Home Economics and Veterinary Medicine until July 1, 1957 when it became a separate college.

In 1882 the Glencoe land was sold by the Board of Regents of the University and under legislative authority the proceeds from the sale were to be used for the purchase of a new farm at St. Anthony Park, St. Paul.

In 1884 Experiment Station buildings were erected on the new farm, which for many years was known as the

University Farm and which now, by the Board of Regents' action, is known as the St. Paul Campus of the University of Minnesota.

The School of Agriculture (non-degree) opened at St. Paul in October of 1888. Later Schools of Agriculture were opened at Crookston (1906), Morris (1910), Grand Rapids (1926) and Waseca (1952).

The teaching of agriculture was established in the public high schools of the state in the early years of the 1900's. The Smith-Hughes Act, passed by Congress in 1917, stimulated this development until today there are almost three hundred high schools in the state offering courses in vocational agriculture.

Today there are County Agricultural Agents in every one of the eighty-seven counties, Home Demonstration Agents in most of them, and temporary or full time 4-H Club Agents in a majority of the counties.

Agriculture and Politics in the 1920's

The 1920's was a time of real discouragement for the business of agriculture. Due to several reasons, including possible over-expansion in World War I, prices were low. Our once great agricultural export business had been hurt by the unrealistic Treaty of Versailles that ended the war.

Prices for farm products were low. There had been a severe financial recession in agriculture in the early twenties. Prices recovered to some extent after that, but were still troubled. During this entire period, farmers never received enough money for their products. They had to pay high prices for what they were required to buy. They received low prices for what they had to sell.

This was not a new problem. The farmers had been faced with this in the nineteenth century. At that time, a great man of Minnesota, Ignatius Donnelly, helped organize the Northwest Farmers' Alliance. This, in time, had merged into the Populist or People's Party. The movement had apparently failed, but its social ideas had not. The Populist ideas resurfaced in the 20th century in the Progressive Party. This party represented laboring people who worked in industry.

In the meantime, the Farmer-Labor Party had developed in the 1920's. This party represented all the working people, farmers and laborers alike. It opposed the extremely conservative group in the state that was led by Governor Theodore Christianson. In spite of the Farmer-Labor Party's strenuous campaigns for a good economic plan for the working people, they seemed to make little progress. Finally in the late 1920's, the Farmer-Labor Party won and Floyd B. Olson became governor of Minnesota.

New Farm Power

Up until World War I most of the power used on farms was horse power. Then came the introduction of gasoline tractors. The first of these machines was mounted on steel wheels, and was heavy and clumsy. They were patterned somewhat after the steam tractors which were used a great deal prior to World War I for the operation of threshing machines, and to some extent on larger farms for plowing.

Gradually, however, the machinery manufacturers built lighter and more competent tractors. Rubber tires for tractors and other farm machines were introduced in the early 1930's, and from that time on the use of tractors increased by leaps and bounds, and the faithful old horse gradually faded out of the picture.

The real push in the use of mechanized implements came during and after World War II.

The Dairy Industry in Minnesota

Dairy farming in Minnesota has a history of its own. During the days of the sod house frontier and the older forest frontier, the dairy industry got its start. People in the middle of the nineteenth century were hungry. They wanted fat, especially butter, which is an energy food. The market was there. Butter always sold well. Modern feeds were far in the future, but cows could be kept which ate the short northern grass. Farmers arranged their cattle year by year so that cows would have calves in early May. Many of the calves were fed on skim milk and butchered for veal, which meant that the rich whole milk could be used to provide cream and butter. The dairying operation worked mainly through the summer season.

Cows were milked from April until November. People who kept cows would put the milk in shallow pans, which would be set in the cool water of the spring house, or well house. When the cream rose to the top, it was skimmed off. Milk was poured into wooden pails. Some housewives scalded the pails after washing, but many merely rinsed them in cold water, and germs of every kind were present.

A cow would come in from the pasture loaded with mud on her udder. The milker merely brushed this off, and often dirt would drop into the milk pail. Some housewives strained the milk and some did not. After the cream turned sour, it was churned, generally in an old-fashioned wooden dasher churn.

Dairy farmers in the 19th century used wooden barrel churns like this one.

It is hard to make good butter. After the butter is churned from the cream, it separates from the buttermilk, and the buttermilk must be drained off. After this the butter is washed in clear water to remove all traces of buttermilk, and then salted. The farm wife did all of this. She made mistakes. If the baby cried just when the washing was going on, she often changed the diapers, and forgot to wash her hands before she went to finish the butter. Sometimes her hair came loose, and strands fell into the butter.

Finally the butter was packed into small tubs, and covers were put on the tubs. They were stored in the cellar or the outside root cellar. The tubs piled up until November, and when winter was just around the corner, the butter buyer came. He would look over the pile of tubs and open some of them. These he would probe with a tube, and examine the core he had removed. If the butter buyer was not by nature a distrustful man, he soon got that way. Now and then, his probe would hit a big stone the housewife was trying to sell as butter. He would hold the core to the light. Sometimes he would find cattle hair, human hair, dead flies and other things. Once in a while, he would open a tub and turn green! Butter that has been neglected too long in a warm place develops a terrible smelling substance called butyric acid.

After checking, the buyer would make an offer, generally less than fifteen cents a pound. Though this sounds like a very low price, it helped the farmer's income. If the farmer had twelve cows milking, and each produced only two hundred pounds of butter in a season, that would mean that the yield at the end of the season would be twenty-four hundred pounds of butter.

Changes came to the dairy industry in Minnesota. Danish people came to Minnesota. They had knowledge of better, cleaner dairying. They and other people started both creameries and cheese factories, where the milk was collected, and handled under sanitary conditions. The introduction of the cooperative creamery also stimulated dairying. What is generally recognized as the first cooperative creamery was established at Clark's Grove in Freeborn County by a group of Danish farmers in May, 1890. From this humble beginning has sprung the great cooperative dairy product marketing organizations in the state today.

From Wisconsin came a brilliant German-American, Professor T. L. Haecker. He taught at the school of dairy husbandry at the University of Minnesota. And he traveled all over the state, telling the farmers to clean up their dairies. In Sweden, Gustav P. DeLavel invented a machine to take cream away from milk. It was called a separator, and made butter dairying much easier and cleaner. Professor Babcock of Wisconsin invented a butter-fat tester in 1890 that was accurate, and it was accepted. From western Europe the idea of fermented green feed, called silage, came to Illinois and Wisconsin, and then to Minnesota. Warm barns were built, and dairying became a year-round program.

In the latter part of the nineteenth century, and in this century many more advances were made. Improved breeds of European and British cattle came in. A true American genius, studying all that had been written about stock nutrition, wrote a fine work called *Feeds and Feeding*. Milking machines came into use. The U.S. government, in the early part of this century put through sweeping laws controlling foods and drugs. Minnesota passed many sanitary laws of its own, and such milk-borne diseases as brucellosis and bovine tuberculosis were finally eliminated.

The true value of milk as a food was realized, and new sanitation laws cleaned up milk distribution as well as butter and cheese production. America, including Minnesota, has had something of a sweet tooth for a long time, and it witnessed the development of ice cream, which became another product of the Minnesota dairy story.

Today dried skim milk is produced in great quantities, and found on grocery shelves. It also goes into candy, baking, and livestock feed, as well as cat and dog food. All this makes Minnesota big in the dairying business. Only the future can tell us whether it will continue to be as successful.

Dairying is important in Minnesota.

Factors of Change

There are many forces which have helped to change the course of agriculture since Minnesota became a state.

Some of these have already been mentioned, such as the mechanization of most farm operations, the founding of educational institutions, and the spread of railroads throughout the state.

Others would include such things as the introduction of electricity to most farms in the state, the development of new knowledge and techniques for the farmer by the Agricultural Experiment Stations, the cooperative movement in agriculture and the organization of Soil Conservation districts.

Farm youth of the state have been influenced by the 4-H Club Movement and its counterpart in the public high schools, the Future Farmers of America. In fact, many youths of high school age are members of both organizations.

The modern farm is a far cry from the early farm. The farmer has as much money invested in the machinery on one typical farm as the cost of all implements in the entire territory in 1840. The cash cost of operation has increased tremendously. The modern farmers can make money faster, but they also run the chance of going bankrupt faster than their predecessors. The farmers of today must be good managers or expensive machinery can mean their downfall.

Minnesota—a leading agricultural state

The products of Minnesota farms now help to feed the United States and the world. In the early years of statehood, with few exceptions, most of the farm products produced were consumed within the state, and in many instances, it was necessary to import food into the state. Now Minnesota farmers sell more than a billion and a quarter dollars worth of agricultural products each year. Truly, this is a far cry from the days of 1858 when the territory became a state.

What is the future for the Minnesota farmer? Farms are becoming larger, more machinery and equipment is required for effective operation, operating expenses are higher. There will, no doubt, continue to be ups and downs in prosperity as there has been in the past. Farm life will always hold a certain attraction for some people. Those who operate efficiently will probably continue to make a satisfactory living. The next hundred years will see developments unheard of today. Farm life today is much improved over that of the first farmers. The modern generation has much to be thankful for, and not a little is owed to those who have gone before. The challenge of tomorrow is to live to pay in part that debt to the past, so that those who come after may look at what people of today are doing and be satisfied with what has been done.

Today the fertile soil of Minnesota is producing crops of corn, beans and grain that would bring smiles of disbelief to the faces of Joseph Haskell and James Norris, should they return to their first farm sites in Afton and Cottage Grove. Where Norris worked nearly all of the year in breaking his forty acres of prairie and planting it to wheat, today the modern farmer rides in air-conditioned comfort atop the multi-horsepower machines that dig up over one hundred acres of field in a twenty-four hour period, or harvest as many acres of golden grain in the same period of time. Even Joseph R. Brown, the opportunist and forward thinker of his time, would find it hard to believe the progress that agriculture has made in Minnesota since his lifetime.

Words to Know — Define these words and terms. You may need to use a dictionary or encyclopedia to find some of the answers.

Alfalfa	One-crop system
Bonanza farm	Reapers
Cooperative	Silage
Drouth	Sod
Farmer-Labor Party	Sod house
Homestead Act of 1862	Subsistence farming
National Grange	Threshers
Northwest Farmers' Alliance	Yield
Nutrients	

Names to Know — Identify these people.

Ignatius Donnelly
Oliver H. Kelley

Writing Activities

Write brief answers to the following questions:

1. What are some factors that assisted the growth of farming in the second half of the 1800's?
2. What factors led to the rise in wheat farming in the 1860's?
3. What caused the change from wheat farming to more diversified farming?
4. The change to diversified farming led to the growth of what industry?
5. What important legal principle was established as a result of the Granger legislation?

CHAPTER SEVENTEEN

INDUSTRY IN MINNESOTA

Mineral Resources

Minnesota, in the earlier 19th century, was not known as a mining state. The state of Wisconsin got part of its start from lead mining, and Iowa did the same, but valuable mineral deposits were not found in our state until late in the 19th century.

Valuable deposits of granite were found in the St. Cloud area and both St. Cloud and Cold Spring became quarrying centers. Granite was also found in the Minnesota River Valley at Morton, Minnesota. Valuable limestone deposits were found near Mankato and Winona. The Kasota stone of the Mankato area and the limestone of Winona are still worked today.

Clay for bricks was once a major part of Minnesota's economic resource. Construction in the growing state of Minnesota boomed. Because of the need for bricks, wherever clay could be found to make bricks, brickyards sprang up. Many of these are now abandoned but Springfield and New Ulm are still producing bricks. Fine clay was found at Red Wing, Minnesota, fine enough to make delicate pottery. For many years, Red Wing jars, platters and other dishes were widely exported.

The biggest Minnesota mineral resource was found in the northern part of our state. Not far from Ely, Minnesota, iron ore was discovered. Charlemagne Tower and his Minnesota Iron Company played an important part in the development of iron ore mining in Minnesota. At Ely and other towns like Tower and Soudan, workers dug shafts hundreds of feet into the earth to reach the iron ore. A railroad between Two Harbors on Lake Superior and the mines enabled Minnesota iron ore to be shipped by lake

Ore locks, Lake Superior

schooners and steamers to Pennsylvania, Illinois and Ohio.

By the 1890's, rich iron ore was found almost on the surface near Virginia, Minnesota. Not long after that, an even larger deposit was found near the surface at a logging camp that in time became the city of Hibbing. The Merritt brothers, sometimes known as the "seven iron men", started work in this field. Under their leadership, great open iron ore pits were operated and a railroad was built to Duluth to carry the ore. The Merritts drove hard, but the United States was in a financial recession in the 1890's, and they lost their great holdings to larger, more developed companies.

From the beginning of our country's economic history, Minnesota iron ore has played a very important role. With the growth of heavy industry, there seemed no limit to the demand for iron ore. Great machinery, at first steam shovels, and later great electric cable drag lines, bit into the red earth. A constant flow of ore cars streamed down to Duluth and emptied into the holds of the huge lake steamers. From April to November, when the season was open, the people were working.

A fantastic amount of iron ore was mined out of Minnesota. Much went to build great American industries. Much of it went to build weapons and other materials for two world wars. Some people thought there was no end to the rich iron ore, but by the 1950's, the Vermilion, Mesabi, and later the Cuyuna ranges were running low on rich ore.

Mining on Minnesota's Iron Range

There was an immense amount of low grade ore, called taconite, left. This low grade ore was not wanted by the steel companies because of all the wastes mixed with it. Great plants were built on the Iron Range however, right in Minnesota, to wash out the impurities. The end result was a pure iron product. Today, Minnesota still ships out much of this enriched taconite.

Taconite tailings (waste) were once dumped into Lake Superior.

The development has not been easy, however. One company threw the wastes, or tailings, into Lake Superior, creating severe health problems. Finally, after a court battle, the company has been required to dump its tailings on land several miles from Lake Superior.

The Grain Milling Industry in Minnesota

The industrial period that followed was a time of great economic explosion and expansion for some, and of economic discouragement for others. Large manufacturing companies like the Twin City Tractor Company, that in time became Minneapolis Moline, expanded. The Ford Motor Company of Detroit, Michigan, built a large assembly plant on the east bank of the Mississippi River in St. Paul.

A number of smaller, but important manufacturing plants were built in the state. Other small plants expanded. The great milling industry remained active during this time.

For many years, Minnesota was the leading flour-producing state. White flour, made from wheat, was the core of this industry. Minnesota has also milled rye, barley, oats and other grains; but it all began with wheat. Wheat has been the number-one source of bread for thousands of years. When people first domesticated wheat in Asia and Africa, they became true farmers and were on the road to civilization. The making of bread from wheat flour is a great story in itself. References are made to bread in the Bible and in most of western literature. Equally important is the subject of mills that make flour.

In Minnesota, the first flour to be made was manufactured at Fort Snelling. Soldier-farmers raised wheat at the fort in the 1820's. Other soldiers built a water-driven flour mill at the Falls of St. Anthony. When the first real agricultural settlers came to Minnesota, mills were started. A man with a French name, Benjamin Gervais, ran a mill at Little Canada, before 1850. When settlers poured into the valleys of the St. Croix, the Minnesota, and the Mississippi, they built mills to make flour. Flour and wheat were shipped down the river to St. Louis. It always had a ready market. Wheat was the first cash crop of early Minnesota farmers.

Actually, it was wasteful to ship wheat out. Transportation costs money. Why ship out the grain with the bran and the waste parts of the wheat, when flour could be shipped more cheaply?

In southeastern Minnesota, there are many fast running streams. This part of Minnesota is rough hill country, with streams which run down to the mighty Mississippi. Settlers built flour mills on the Zumbro, the Cannon, the Root and Whitewater Rivers, and also on many creeks. Settlers farming the nearby valleys and slopes brought wheat to be ground at these water-powered mills. Much of this flour was packed in barrels, at two hundred pounds to the barrel, and shipped down the Mississippi. The sale of flour was the first real money product for this part of the state.

Millstones from an old mill

Improved Milling Methods

In order to make flour, wheat was ground. When it came out from between the great millstones, it was very hot. It was hoisted to the top of a high building and stirred until cool. Then it was dropped to the lower floor, where the basic meal was sifted through fine screens and filters to remove the bran or pericarp of the wheat, and most of the germ. What was left was unbleached white flour. This was used to make bread. Bread was in great demand.

By the time the Minnesota mills started, an American genius, Oliver Evans, had improved the milling industry.

Evans had developed automatic machinery for mills. They were driven by the same source of power that drove the mill. Now machines cooled the meal and filtered it into flour.

But even with machines, the life of the millers was hard. They had to watch the water, because if there was too much, it could wash away the mill, and if there was too little water, the mills could not run. Then, at times, the miller had to heave the heavy stones apart, and with a punch and chisel, cut new grinding grooves in the stones.

In Hungary, Germany, Switzerland and France a new milling system had been developed, called the rolling mill system. Instead of being slowly torn apart by rough stones, wheat was finely crushed between a series of rollers. These rollers were made of materials other than stone, such as steel. Edmund LaCroix set up the first roller mill in Minnesota before 1870. In the lonely valley of Stockton Creek, an immigrant from England, A. C. Mowbray, owned a traditional mill. Mowbray had the new milling machinery installed in his mill. The development of this type of milling at Stockton helped make Minnesota a milling leader.

There were also changes in the wheat itself. To make bread, the flour is mixed with other materials to make dough. The dough is filled with gas from working yeast. If the dough will hold this gas for a while, all is well. The expanding gas will make the dough rise.

High risen dough means high, nourishing bread. This is because the elastic, high-protein element in wheat, called gluten, holds the gas in. The traditional fall and spring wheat that the settler brought to Minnesota was a soft wheat. This soft wheat had a low protein, weak gluten quality, but it was the only kind of wheat at the time. Not until a new wheat from Russia came to Canada and from there to Minnesota, was there a hard, dark, quick maturing, high-protein wheat.

The new wheat made the best bread flour in the world, but with the old fashioned stone mill, it was hard to handle. The roller mills, however, gave better results. By the 1880's Minnesota had both the new, wonderful wheat and the new mill. Minnesota was ready to move ahead in milling and it did. The flour markets quickly saw that much would come from Minnesota. The demand for flour was there, and more and more high quality spring wheat flour was required. Minnesota farmers responded to this demand.

Home-baked bread

The clattering water wheel mills kept going. Many of them lasted into the 20th century. But the big move was for concentration. Minneapolis became the number-one flour producing city in the world. Railroads led from Minneapolis to the hard spring wheat areas of the Dakotas and northwestern Minnesota. In the hot days of late summer, long lines of wagons came to the railroads, where the wheat was quickly unloaded by machine and loaded onto freight cars. It was shipped to Minneapolis.

In addition to the mills, Minneapolis had gigantic, hundred-foot wooden towers, called elevators, to store grain. The Falls of St. Anthony furnished water power. Grain and flour dust rose in a fine cloud in the milling district and the flour moved out. People like Pillsbury and Washburn, who had been in the lumber industry, turned to milling. More and more new machinery was developed and used, but troubles arose. Fires were a great danger in the big elevators, and rats loved the old fashioned wooden elevators where there was a lot of food. Pigeons loved them too, and splattered droppings from one end of the mill to the other.

Problems and Change in the Milling Industry

The millers and grain traders developed financial power. They put pressure on the railroads to give them favored rates for shipping their product. That meant they would haul at a low rate. The railroads made up for this by charging the farmers high prices for hauling the basic wheat. The farmers were not organized, and for years took a financial beating. This was one of the causes for much of the financial trouble on the plains.

The milling of flour led to other financial problems. Some of the smaller mills went out of business because they could not compete with the larger mills. Southern Minnesota turned to crops other than wheat. The national scene changed too.

Great areas of land for the growing of wheat were opened in the state of Washington. It was not good milling wheat, but there was a lot of it. Kansas, Oklahoma, Nebraska and Texas started to grow winter wheat on a large scale. It was not as good for milling as Minnesota's, but it made bread.

There were a number of changes in the home. People started to buy more bakery bread, and bread factories developed across the land. The factories were interested in using cheap flour, and selling bread for as high a price as they could. They found out that they could mix the high protein and the inferior wheat flour, and still make bread that would sell.

By the middle of the 1920's, two cities passed Minneapolis in flour production. Kansas City, Missouri was close to the southwest winter wheat area and moved into flour production. Buffalo, New York was also close to the railroad and lake shipping systems, and became a great milling center. As the years passed, less and less home baked bread was made and people cared less about quality.

Today Minneapolis, Hastings, Winona, Lake City, Duluth and some other Minnesota towns still make flour, mostly from blended wheat. In 1980, Minnesota startled the business world by once more leading in flour production. Really good bread flour is still made. The Enright Company makes high quality flour in Lakefield, Minnesota. In the fall of 1980 two brilliant young millers reopened the old Stockton mill. These men, Farren and Moore, take South Dakota dark hard northern wheat and make high quality bread flour.

The Stockton mill

The Breakfast Cereal Era

When the great period of flour production was over, Minnesota turned to other types of milling. During the Depression, General Mills was formed in Minneapolis. They developed "Bisquick", which was one of the first packaged mixes on the market. It consisted of flour, salt, baking powder and shortening that would not go rancid easily. During World War II the packaged cake mix was produced by General Mills. After the war they led in producing the pre-mixed cake. Today great amounts of money are spent on advertising, and though professional cooks still say the packaged cakes are inferior, they seem to be here to stay.

Minnesota started one of the national "firsts" in breakfast food with the production of "Cream of Wheat." Small bits of the white interior of wheat kernels that could be boiled were packaged. "Wheaties" was produced as breakfast food. The Washburn, Crosby company hired a quartet in the 1920's to sing on radio about "Wheaties", and developed the first singing commercial. They also advertised the radio program about Jack Armstrong, the all American boy. This caused Wheaties sales to boom. Then corn syrup from Iowa was added to make a pre-sweetened cereal — no more reaching for the sugar bowl.

Minnesota milling has come a long way. Pancake flour is made in great quantities, and northwestern Minnesota and North Dakota also raise durum wheat for the best macaroni and spaghetti. Large Minnesota mills make semolina, a meal made from the inside of durum wheat. Most of this is made into macaroni in our home state. Noodles are made from local wheat too. Minnesota also raises large quantities of barley, some of which goes to malting plants for the basic raw material in beer.

Livestock feed is still another part of the milling industry. Pink-nosed little pigs love Minnesota-produced feed, as do calves, lambs, big hogs and cattle. Large numbers of turkeys are fattened on it, as well as chickens. These same materials are also used in dog and cat food, produced by the Minnesota milling industry.

Now let's summarize: the milling industry began with the clashing of stones of the mill at St. Anthony Falls, spread out over the state and now makes everything from pancake mixes to cake mixes to cat food. The milling industry has been very important in Minnesota history, and remains a major industry even today.

Words to Know — Define these words and terms. You may need to use a dictionary or encyclopedia to find some of the answers.

Gluten

Iron ore

Taconite

Tailings

Rolling mill

Names to Know — Identify these people.

the Merritt brothers

Charlemagne Tower

Oliver Evans

Pillsbury

Writing Activities

Write a short essay discussing the iron ore and taconite industries and their importance in Minnesota history.

Write a short essay discussing the grain milling industry and its importance in Minnesota history.

CHAPTER EIGHTEEN

THE GROWTH OF TRANSPORTATION

Early Transportation

The earliest routes of transportation in Minnesota were those traveled by the Sioux and Chippewa. Entire villages would move from place to place in their search for food. Often these routes went overland, as a short cut from one place to another. These shortcuts were used a great deal, and became trails that could be easily followed. Later, when the fur traders came into the territory, they too used the Indian trails to get from place to place.

The waterways of Minnesota were favorite travel routes of the Indians, and their light birch canoes could go almost anywhere. Sometimes portages had to be made, but these often provided a convenient place to camp before resuming the journey.

The birch bark canoes were most important to the Chippewa in the harvesting of wild rice which grew in lakes and rivers. It took skill to make a birch bark canoe, as well as skill to paddle one. The canoes were usually made for two. The first step was to build a tough frame made from spruce. This was covered with cedar planking; then with birch bark sewn together and sealed with spruce gum.

These water routes were also used by the fur traders in establishing their early trade routes. These highways froze over in the winter months, however, and early travelers had to devise new means of transportation. They used "dog travois" and "pony travois". The travois pulled by dogs was a crude sledge with two poles fastened to it. These poles were fastened over the dog's shoulders with hide thongs. The other ends dragged on the ground and on these the load or pack was tied.

Pony travois were much the same, only larger, but were not used in severe winter weather since ponies could not stand the extreme cold as well as dogs. For traveling great distances in winter, the trappers and traders used toboggans pulled by teams of dogs. They could travel distances of thirty to forty miles in a day, pulling great loads of furs and provisions.

Dog sled and team in St. Paul—1859

This was early transportation in Minnesota, and these early people — the Sioux, the Chippewa and the fur traders — were our first highway engineers.

The Steamboat and the Development of Early Minnesota

In the beginning, Indians and traders in Minnesota used canoes to travel the various rivers. Zebulon Pike and some of the fur traders used the keelboat. The keelboat was a boat up to sixty feet long, that was rowed, pushed with poles, or towed by men on shore, who pulled it along with a rope. Pulling it was the most difficult way, because sometimes there was no solid land on shore. Then the men had to wade along the river's edge, pulling with all of their might, while deer flies, black flies and mosquitoes bit their faces and hands.

Poling a keelboat upstream

But a new day was coming. In Scotland, a brilliant man, James Watt, had invented a low pressure steam engine. And in England, Richard Trevithick developed a high pressure boiler steam engine, which was very powerful. There is still a dispute over who really invented the steamboat, but Symington of Scotland, Trevithick of England and Fitch of America, plus others, all built successful boats powered by steam before 1809.

Robert Fulton introduced the steamboat in the United States, but his steamboats weren't much good on the wild western rivers. They would often run aground on sandbars and rocks, and their low pressure boilers simply lacked the power to drive the boat upstream against the powerful Mississippi current.

Then Henry Miller Shreve built a better type of steamboat. Shreve designed a boat that was long, wide and shallow in the water, unlike Fulton's which was often too deep. Shreve used the Evans-Trevithick type of high pressure boiler. His boats were able to travel up the mighty Mississippi and its branches or tributaries.

The first steamboat ever to come up the Mississippi River to Minnesota was named the *Virginia*, and it came upriver from St. Louis to Fort Snelling in 1823. As it chugged and smoked and whistled up the river, it must have been very frightening to the Indians, for they had never seen such a thing. They called it "Pata Wata", which meant "fire canoe".

These shallow draft steamers carried out the produce of the Red River Colony. When Minnesota had ideas of becoming an organized United States territory, steam was ready to do its part. Small steamers moved further on. Many were built in Minneapolis, above the Falls of St. Anthony. They ran all the way up to St. Cloud. The immigrants they transported there and the produce they brought back helped to build St. Cloud into a major city in Minnesota.

An early steamboat, the Anson Northrup

The first steamer to navigate the St. Croix River was the *Palmyra* in about 1838. It came from St. Louis loaded with sawmill equipment and docked at St. Croix Falls.

Other steamboats soon followed the trail blazed by the *Palmyra* up the rugged St. Croix. The *Fayette*, loaded with the first livestock and necessary supplies to build a mill and establish a settlement, arrived May 13, 1839 at Marine Mills.

From that time, more and more steamers traveled the rivers, transporting people, food, clothing, machinery, and just about everything that was needed by the settlers. The steamboat was intended mainly to carry freight and supplies, but it did a great amount of passenger business, too. Many steamers were like floating palaces, trimmed in gold, velvet, leather and glass. Some were nearly 250 feet long and could carry from three hundred to four hundred passengers in first-class luxury.

While travel was luxurious for a person with a lot of money, the poor immigrants were huddled together in large dormitories on the lower deck of the boat. They had barely enough food to stay alive, but they survived in spite of the way they were treated.

Imagine yourself living in one of the early towns or settlements on the Mississippi River — no trains, no cars, no airplanes or buses, and very few roads or trails leading to any other towns. Food supplies might be low, medicine in short supply and the only newspapers published miles down the river. Letters and packages could be delivered only when a steamer brought them upriver. Steamboats could not travel in winter, so it might be several months before the first steamer of the spring came upriver.

You have waited all winter, and now spring has arrived and with it the ice is disappearing little by little each day. The air is chilly yet, and the wild geese are seen flying northward. Suddenly you hear the shrill whistle of the steamer and see a tail of white smoke coming around a bend in the distance. Others see it too, and there is excitement in the air. The cry goes up, "Steamboat 'round the bend!"

Every man, woman and child runs down to the landing to await the big boat. Even the dogs sense the excitement. There will be cause for a big celebration tonight. Winter is over and the first steamboat has arrived. Letters from loved ones are delivered. Medicine and food are unpacked. Catalog clothing, ordered last fall, has finally arrived. Perhaps a friend or relative has arrived on the steamer. There are newspapers, and news from the outside world. Can you feel the excitement? Will you join in the singing and dancing tonight?

The steamboats are gone now, for several reasons. As the forests were cut along the rivers, this affected the water run-off and some rivers became too shallow for these big boats. The coming of the railroads was also a factor in the decline of the steamers. There are only a few steamers left today, and these are mainly excursion boats that travel only in limited areas. The *Delta Queen* and the *Mississippi Queen* are perhaps the only ones of their kind in existence today.

The *Delta Queen,* proud reminder of the days when many steamboats traveled on the Mississippi

In the 1930's, the federal government established a series of dams on the Mississippi to supply a minimum

Whitman Dam on the Mississippi River

nine-foot depth from St. Louis to St. Paul. As a consequence, river traffic again began to flow. The boats were far
different from the bulging stern-wheelers of an earlier day.
Now they were barges being pushed along by a relatively
small tug. The St. Croix and the Mississippi Rivers are
used quite extensively by river barges today. The freight
they move is again considerable in quantity, several million tons a year. The up-bound traffic is made up mostly of
petroleum and coal. The down-bound traffic is usually
grain. Savage is now an important port, as the lower
reaches of the Minnesota River have been dredged. A
tremendous amount of grain is loaded into barges at Savage.

Today towboats travel the Mississippi River, pushing barges up
and down.

Perhaps Minnesota's most important waterway is Lake Superior and the Duluth Harbor. This was one of the routes used to bring the first white people into the territory. Fur traders and explorers used this waterway as their entry into the wilderness of their day. Ships from all over the world come into the Duluth-Superior Harbor at the western end of the St. Lawrence Seaway today. They bring products from other countries and they take back the products of Minnesota industry and agriculture to markets all around the world.

Duluth—inland seaport to the world

Waterways have always been important to transportation in Minnesota, and they still are important today, but for different reasons.

The Red River Oxcarts

In 1843, when trade was growing between Pembina and St. Paul, there was no road, and a strange new transportation vehicle was brought into use. It was a two-wheeled cart made of wood and buffalo hide. Everything was fastened

Red River oxcarts in 1857—St. Paul

together with wooden pegs. The spokes of the wheels, sometimes five feet across, were straight, and the rims were from three to five inches wide. The cart was attached by shafts to one ox.

These carts were ideal for the rough, swampy country because they could ride right over nearly anything. They followed any trail, but soon their huge wheels had established their own rut-scarred roads. They bumped along the trail at the rate of twenty miles a day, their ungreased wooden wheels screeching so loud they could be heard for miles. Within the next fifteen years about five hundred of these carts were in constant use, making regular scheduled trips, often in long trains of fifty to one hundred carts.

These oxcarts carried up to a thousand pounds of buffalo hides, pemmican and pelts to St. Paul, and then after much celebrating, the drivers loaded their carts with tea, tobacco, hardware and anything else that was needed at the other

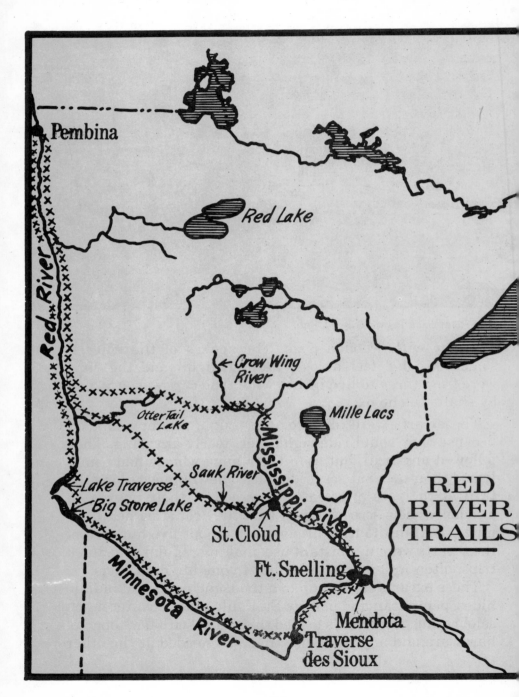

Pembina

Red River

Red Lake

Crow Wing River

Mille Lacs

Otter Tail Lake

Mississippi River

Sauk River

Lake Traverse

Big Stone Lake

St. Cloud

Ft. Snelling

Minnesota River

Mendota
Traverse
des Sioux

RED
RIVER
TRAILS

end of the line. These early oxcart trains followed the west bank of the Red River as far south as the ridge called Brown's Valley, between Lake Traverse and Big Stone Lake, and then across the prairie to the Minnesota River near where St. Peter is located today. This place became known as "Traverse des Sioux".

From here the big carts followed the Minnesota River Valley into St. Paul. Other routes were followed later, as shortcuts were charted, but the early route along the bank of the Red River gave these strange-looking vehicles their name.

The First Military Roads

With the creation of Minnesota Territory in 1849, better roads were necessary for settlement and trade, as well as for protection against possible Indian attacks. Without funds to build the roads that would attract settlers, the territorial legislature, following the precedent set by every other territory and several states, turned to the United States Congress. Henry H. Sibley, Minnesota's first territorial delegate to Congress, asked for money to build military roads in a bill introduced in the House of Representatives on February 4, 1850.

After debating this request for several months, Congress passed the bill on July 8, 1850, and it became effective on July 18. Forty thousand dollars was appropriated to carry out the provisions of the bill, and the money was to be immediately available for constructing four roads and for surveying a fifth.

There already existed a haphazard network of rough ungraded roads in Minnesota. Earliest of these were the Indian trails that connected major waterways and that were adopted by fur traders in conducting their widespread business. As the fur trade grew, so did the number of more or less defined routes — all established to serve isolated trading posts and transport valuable pelts to collecting stations. Other pre-territorial roads, most of them little more than logging trails, had been cut by lumbermen in the St. Croix Valley.

In laying out the military roads, the engineers made use of these rough trails whenever it was convenient. Actual construction was limited to building bridges, clearing timber, removing undergrowth, and making swamps passable. Sections of road over open prairie needed little or no roadwork at all.

The road right-of-way was to be opened a hundred feet wide, with a center strip for wheeled vehicles to be thoroughly cleared to a width of fifty feet. To make swampy areas passable, building log causeways covered with earth and digging drainage ditches was suggested.

The military roads played a vital role in the growth of Minnesota Territory. Built by the federal government primarily to promote military strength along the frontier, these roads served the causes of commerce and population expansion just as efficiently. As the number of people in the territory multiplied, so did the demand for roads, especially in the later 1850's. And many of the roads needed to take the thousands of newcomers to isolated settlements were designated as branches of the military roads. These roads laid the framework upon which was built a statewide network of communication and trade.

The Corduroy Road

Early settlements were usually connected by waterways, but it was often necessary to have a land route as well. The first road of this kind was the "corduroy road" connecting Grand Portage and Fort William, thirty-six miles away. It had to be built with logs because so much of the area was swampland, making a regular road impossible.

Thousands of logs were laid side by side, creating a sort of floating road surface over the soft, swampy areas. This road was probably very rough, but it served its purpose. Do you know why it was called a "corduroy road"?

The early "corduroy" road

Stage Coach Travel

As travel in the territory increased, the means of transportation were improved and people took to "wheels" in order to get from place to place with their cargoes. This new form of travel led to the development of suitable "trails" over which people and their wheels could travel across Minnesota.

Stillwater's stage coach line to St. Paul was started in 1849, one of the first in the territory. One was operated for a short time between St. Paul and St. Anthony. Then the Galena stage was started by way of Stillwater, Hudson and

Menomonie, Wisconsin to Galena, Illinois, to take care of business between steamboat seasons. Roads were poor and inns few, breakdowns frequent and passengers had to be prepared to camp in the snow whenever disaster overtook them.

Early Minnesota stagecoach

So fast was the country opening up and so great was the need of conveyance in a country without a railroad, that in 1859 the Minnesota Stage Company was formed to manage the various lines. By 1862 there were eight lines going out of St. Paul, and at the end of the Civil War there were 1300 miles of stage lines, 300 miles of Pony Express mail routes, with 700 horses and 200 people employed in carrying out the schedules.

Railroads

Minnesota, by the 1850's, had developed "railroad fever" and within the next thirty years developed a system of railroads that established the Twin Cities as the market center for the entire Upper Midwest. The new system of

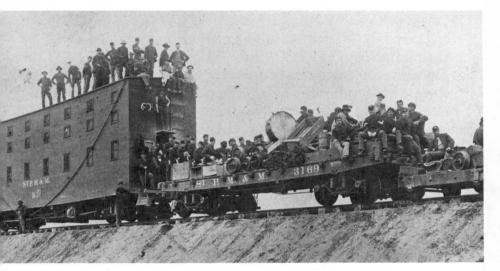

The early railroad builders

rails connected the East to the Midwest and the Upper Midwest, bringing both people and progress to the areas along the way.

In 1862, the Minnesota and Pacific Railroad connected St. Paul and St. Anthony by rail, and on July 2, the first train puffed into St. Anthony, pulled by a wood-burning engine called the *William Crooks*. This historic locomotive, the first in Minnesota, was brought up the Mississippi by steamboat from LaCrosse, Wisconsin.

An early, wood-burning locomotive

The early Minnesota and Pacific line extended as far as Breckenridge by 1871, and to Winona by 1872. This pioneer effort was made possible by the work of Edmund Rice, a man who has been called the father of railroading in Minnesota. He went to England and secured money with which to build the railroad.

Among the early roads to be built was the Minneapolis and Cedar Valley. Its first track opened in 1865 between Mendota and Northfield, and later it ran from Minneapolis to Faribault. Another important railroad was the Winona and St. Peter, which eventually ran to the eastern part of the Dakota territory.

The Minnesota Valley road began its first line to Shakopee in 1865, and in 1880 joined the Omaha, later to become the Northwestern system. This road followed the Minnesota River Valley, linking cities along the way. The first railroad to go north was the Lake Superior and Mississippi Valley, connecting the Twin Cities and Duluth. It later became part of the Northern Pacific System. In 1889, the Great Northern Railroad began running all the way to the Pacific Ocean. This road was a combination of many smaller companies and was masterminded by the greatest railroad man in our history, James J. Hill.

Hill came to Minnesota from eastern Canada in 1856. He did not intend to stay here but he missed the last oxcart caravan to what is now Winnipeg and being the kind of young fellow he was, it was not long before he was immersed in river traffic. That led to an interest in the extension of traffic north and west beyond the river terminus of St. Paul. It became an obsession with him. There had to be a railroad! Eventually it must reach to the Pacific. He, Jim Hill, was going to build that railroad. And he did.

The road he built went through various names; he was often threatened with complete failure; he borrowed and

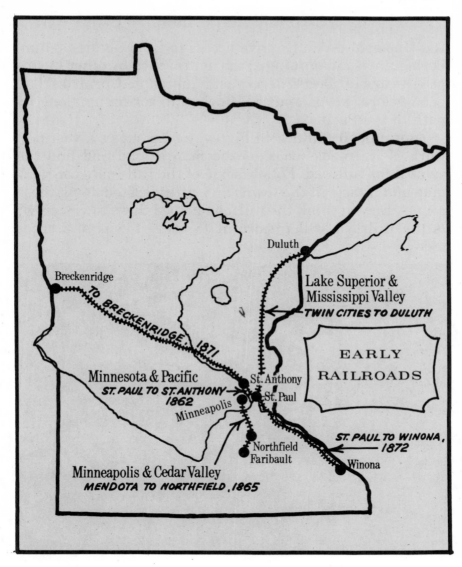

Breckenridge

TO BRECKENRIDGE, 1871

Duluth

Lake Superior &
Mississippi Valley
TWIN CITIES TO DULUTH

EARLY
RAILROADS

Minnesota & Pacific
*ST. PAUL TO ST. ANTHONY
1862*

St. Anthony

St. Paul

Minneapolis

Northfield
Faribault

*ST. PAUL TO WINONA,
1872*

Winona

Minneapolis & Cedar Valley
MENDOTA TO NORTHFIELD, 1865

invested with apparent reckless energy, but he built his
railroad — the Great Northern. And in building it, he did
more than make a fortune for himself and his associates.
He made and earned the title of Empire Builder.

This road opened a new era in westward expansion and
probably did more than anything else to bring settlers into

the Upper Midwest. It gave access to farming areas, lumbering areas and mining areas not reached by other means of transportation. Where vast, unoccupied prairies had been before, towns and cities began to spring up along its path to the Pacific.

Your official Minnesota highway map shows a vast network of railroads. Look at the map legend and find the symbol for railroad. Follow some of the rail routes on your map and notice all the towns and cities located along these routes. Do you think the railroad helped these towns grow? Is the railroad still important to these towns and cities today?

Modern diesel-powered locomotive

Railroad Monopoly

In the first part of the 20th century, Minnesota had a governor named Samuel Van Sant. This strong Dutchman was born in Illinois, and fought against the South in the Civil War. He moved from Illinois to Iowa, and finally to Winona, Minnesota, where he worked on the river and became one of the most important log raftsmen of all time. Then he went into politics.

When he was governor of Minnesota, Governor Van Sant saw something alarming. James J. Hill of St. Paul, president of the Great Northern Railways, had made an alliance with the Northern Pacific head, Harriman. Harriman and Hill had combined forces with the Morgan banking firm of New York and formed a company known as the Northern Securities Corporation. The purpose of consolidating was to put all western railroads of the United States together and form a monopoly.

Van Sant knew a monopoly like this was against United States law. His administration started a legal fight against the corporation. In time, the Supreme Court saw the struggle Van Sant was in, and ordered the corporation dissolved. Van Sant had won a great fight for honesty in government. A really tough man of great courage, he is ranked as one of Minnesota's greatest governors.

Street Cars or Trolley Cars

In the early 1900's a new means of rapid transportation developed in and around the metropolitan Twin Cities area. Miles of iron tracks wound in and around the lakes, hills and streets of the area. This system was known as the Twin City Rapid Transit Company, and for the price of a nickel one could ride a street car or trolley to a variety of destinations. Here is how one writer describes this early means of transportation:

"Every known device for the comfort and the safety of passengers is employed to make its service pre-eminent. Its tracks are unusually smooth and heavy. The large, 45-foot cars, built by the company in its own shops, are of the most modern and expensive construction and are the

wonder of strangers. They are roomy, easy-riding, comfortable, and handsomely furnished. They are mounted on heavy double trucks and equipped with powerful motors, air brakes, whistles, and electric signal bells. Easy, spring-cane seats accommodate fifty-two persons. The windows, with their peculiar disappearing sash, are unusually large and deep, insuring the freest circulation of air, and admitting the cooling breezes of summer delightfully. It is a real treat to make a trip in one of these big, smooth-rolling, yellow cars.

"All Twin City trolley trips are over the lines of the Twin City Rapid Transit Company, whose well-equipped lines reach every resort and point of interest in and around the Twin Cities, as well as their desirable residence sections. The company operates over three hundred miles of standard-gauge track in Minneapolis, St. Paul and Stillwater, serving a populous and well-settled area of over six hundred square miles, and enjoys the well-earned reputation of being one of the most progressive electric transportation companies in the United States."

Today there are some people who remember these street cars, and as they hear of the traffic and fuel problems of the 1980's they may well ask, "Why did they disappear?" One might also ask, "When will they return?" Do you think they will?

The Automobile Age

Charles Babcock is a name as significant in Minnesota in association with automobiles as Jim Hill is in association with locomotives. Babcock was a small town general store operator at Elk River. His home and store were on the edge of the highway carrying traffic north and west of the Twin Cities. He watched the traffic move over the rutty road and conceived the idea, quite revolutionary at the time, of having the owners of cars using the highways pay for their improvements.

He conceived of a great state highway system of hard surfaced roads, which auto licenses and gasoline taxes would finance. First, he sold the idea to Governor Christianson, who made him highway commissioner, and then he sold it to the people of the state. Babcock was not an engineer, but he gave Minnesota leadership in highway construction because he possessed imagination and public leadership.

Educational Affairs Dept., Ford Motor Co.

MODEL A
FIRST FORD MOTOR COMPANY CAR
1903

MODEL B TOURING CAR
FIRST FOUR-CYLINDER FORD
1905

MODEL K TOURING CAR
FIRST SIX-CYLINDER CAR
1906

MODEL T TOURING CAR
FIRST FORD MODEL T
1909

Early Ford motor cars

Putting wheels on a gasoline-driven motor has changed Minnesota life in many ways. The most pronounced of its effects may be that of making us more alike. Travel now being easy, the ordinary Minnesotan sees much of the world and becomes very familiar with those parts of it which are not many miles away.

The business associated with automobiles has as completely overshadowed that previously associated with horses as the bus station overshadows the former livery stable. At least one out of ten has a job directly connected with the automobile.

The automobile in its various applications has made a mighty mark on the picture of Minnesota life. Its benefits in bringing color, variety and a feeling of freedom are impossible to measure. Like every good gift, it carries a price tag. Sometimes when noting the accident reports, it seems quite high.

The First Bus System

Did you know that the bus transportation industry had its start right here in Minnesota? It all started in Hibbing, Minnesota, back in 1914 when an enterprising man by the name of Eric Wickman put an idea into action. He started a short bus service between Hibbing and the nearby mine. He began with one old touring car, then added a second, but his idea was so popular that he couldn't handle all the business. He went to the blacksmith shop and supervised the construction of a twelve-passenger bus. Business boomed, and he soon expanded his service to Nashwauk, fifteen miles away.

In 1916, he acquired financial backing and organized the Mesaba Transportation Company. By 1918, he had a fleet of eighteen buses operating in northern Minnesota. He moved his headquarters to Duluth, and in 1922 bought up several small bus companies, extending routes to the Twin

The first Greyhound bus—a 1914 Hupmobile

The Greyhound of today

Cities and other points. Expansion followed each move he made, and eventually his idea grew into the Greyhound System that we know today.

Looking at the Minnesota Highway Map

Highways: Classes and Symbols

Look at your official highway map of Minnesota. It is so full of lines it almost resembles a spider's web, doesn't it?

Do you know what all of these lines represent? If you said roads, you are correct, but what kinds of roads? Look at the map legend and find the symbols that represent various kinds of roads. The more heavily traveled highways are of four types. These are called interstate highways, multilane divided highways, multilane undivided highways, and high type highways. All are either concrete or blacktop (asphalt) surfaced. Find some examples of each on your map.

Intermediate highways are those that carry a lower rate of traffic but are still hard-surfaced (concrete or asphalt). Can you find some examples of this type on your map? Secondary roads are those that carry the least amount of traffic and are mostly gravel-surfaced, although some secondary roads may be asphalt-surfaced. Can you find examples of both kinds of secondary roads on your map?

Some people refer to our highways as "trunk highways" and "arterial" or "feeder" highways. What do you think these names mean?

Let's take an imaginary trip from St. Paul to Moorhead. Look at your map and determine the best route to take. What kinds of highways will we travel on?

Can you find a town or city in Minnesota that does not have a highway of any kind connecting it to the rest of the state?

Mileage Charts and Scale

There is a mileage chart on the back of your official Minnesota highway map that lists over forty of the major cities of the state. This chart tells you the mileage or distance between any two of these cities. When would this chart be helpful to a motorist? Study the chart and find out how it works. How far is it from Albert Lea to Worthington? From Fergus Falls to Red Wing?

Solve this problem: How long would it take you to drive from Detroit Lakes to Northfield if you maintain a speed of fifty-five miles per hour?

There is more mileage information contained on your map. Notice the tiny red numbers that appear next to highways. These are always placed between two towns or cities, and show the distance between them. How far is it from Gaylord to Winthrop? From Gaylord to Morton?

There is still another method of measuring distance on your map. Look at the map legend for the "scale of miles." In this case, your map will tell you that one inch on the map is equal to sixteen miles. Using your ruler, can you find approximately how far it is from Duluth to Grand Marais? From Lake Benton to New Ulm?

How many ways are there to find mileage distances on your map?

Air Travel

Transportation has taken many forms in our state's history and probably the most amazing of all is the airplane. If early residents of our state were surprised and frightened by their first look at the steamboat, what do you think their feeling would be if they could see one of today's large airplanes glide in for a landing, and then watch as two hundred people walk out of the plane?

The airplane came into existence in the early 1900's, and by 1920, experimental flights had started in Minnesota, carrying mail between the Twin Cities and Chicago. Northwest Airways originated at about this time and has grown over the years into what is known today as Northwest Orient Airlines.

The first air passenger service, the Jefferson Transportation Company, began in 1926, and operated between the Twin Cities and Rochester. Universal Airlines started service between Minnesota and Chicago that same year.

Soon all of these pioneer airlines merged with Northwest Airways and enlarged the operation with routes going to Seattle on the Pacific Coast.

Today there are two major airline companies located in Minnesota, Northwest Orient Airlines and Republic Airlines. These companies, along with several out-of-state companies, now use the Minneapolis-St. Paul International Airport as a major base of operation, offering both passenger and freight service to all parts of the world. Today you can travel from New York to Minnesota in four hours or less. How long do you suppose it took the early settlers to travel from New York to Minnesota?

Northwest Airlines in 1929. Pilot was "Speed" Holman, pioneer aviator

The Boeing 747, Northwest Airlines today

Look again at your official Minnesota highway map. It contains information on air travel and uses symbols to locate all airports in the state. Can you find several commercial airport locations on your map? Can you find several smaller noncommercial airports? Where can you find seaplane ports in Minnesota?

Words to Know — Define these words and terms. You may need to use a dictionary or encyclopedia to find some of the answers.

Barge

Corduroy road

Keelboat

Portage

Red River oxcarts

Steamboat

Travois

Trunk or arterial highway

Names to Know — Identify these people.

Charles Babcock

James J. Hill

Edmund Rice

Henry Miller Shreve

Writing Activities

Write brief answers to the following questions:

1. What improvements did Henry Miller Shreve make in steamboat design?
2. How was the Red River oxcart especially suited to use by the people of the Red River Valley?
3. How did the railroads help in the settlement of the country?
4. What are some of the effects the automobile has had on our lives?

CHAPTER NINETEEN

COMMUNICATION THROUGH THE YEARS

Primitive Communication

Tens of thousands of years ago, primitive people learned to communicate, first by signs, then by grunts, and then, as their brain powers gradually developed, by spoken words. With the discovery of fire, far back in the history of human development, it was learned that the glow of light from a fire, or a column of smoke could be seen for long distances, and the practice of communication by lights and smoke signals came into being.

In America the Indians learned early that messages could be sent in a sort of pre-arranged code by alternately blocking off and releasing bursts from the heavy smoke of a campfire through the use of skins or blankets. Such signals were very useful in rough country. Soldiers on the frontiers during the Indian wars were kept on the alert for puffs of smoke signals sent up around them by unseen but watchful Indian scouts.

Pioneer Communication

By the early 1820's, mail communication of a sort was maintained with the outside world by the use of keelboats of the traders and the supply boats of the military via Prairie du Chien, the nearest point of settlement some two hundred miles to the south. Such service, however, was irregular and uncertain. The journals kept by Major Lawrence Taliaferro, the Indian agent near Fort Snelling, are full of complaints over his failure to receive his mail and official instructions from Washington.

Such boat service could only be carried on during the months from April to November when the Mississippi was free from ice. During the winter months, attempts were made to maintain a monthly mail service with Prairie du Chien by dispatching soldier carriers or half-breeds under contract up and down the river on the ice. A post office was established at Fort Snelling as early as 1827, but carrier service with down river points left much to be desired.

Point Douglas was the early depot from which supplies were purchased and transported to interior settlements in the 1840's. In July of 1840, the first post office in the state, outside of the military installation at Fort Snelling, was established at Point Douglas, located just above present day Hastings, Minnesota, where the St. Croix River joins the Mississippi.

St. Paul's first post office

In 1846, offices were opened at St. Paul and Stillwater. Postage rates were high, the costs usually being paid by the sender, and depending upon the distance the letter had to travel. Twenty-five cents for a one-page letter going four hundred miles was normal.

When St. Paul was established as a post office in 1846, with Henry Jackson, a store keeper, as its first postmaster, a rude box with twelve cubbyholes was nailed together for service, and that original postbox is still preserved in the museum of the Minnesota Historical Society. As regular steamboat lines came into existence, the river boats contracted for the carrying of the mail during the months of navigation, and "mail packets", operating on regular schedules were favored by travelers. Stagecoaches carried the mails during the winter months. Fogs, low water, wrecks, fires and accidents hindered the steamboat service, and the mail stages encountered flooded streams, storms, and endless mud.

Newspapers

Try to imagine yourself living in early St. Paul. The only news you could get would be from reports of people who came up the Mississippi by boat, by newspapers brought with them, or reports of happenings from traders or soldiers coming overland by foot or horseback. Your news would be pretty old and probably pretty limited. If something important happened in the nation's capital, it might be weeks or months before that news reached you. Letters from friends and relatives in distant places might take many weeks to reach you. Can you think of some problems this might cause? Even local news in early St. Paul might be missed if there was no way to report it to you. You could check the trees and fronts of buildings in the young settlement. Often notices and news articles were tacked up in these places for everyone to see.

This was the situation in 1849 when James Goodhue decided to leave his newspaper business in Lancaster, Wisconsin, and come to St. Paul to start another paper. He was a newspaper pioneer and he saw the need for a paper in the young city. He set up his operation in a drafty, one-room

James Goodhue

building and published the first copy of *The Minnesota Pioneer* on April 28, 1849.

The people of St. Paul eagerly snatched up all the papers he could produce. He delivered the papers himself and also acted as his own news reporter. His press was capable of printing only 225 pages in an hour and his supply of metal type had to come all the way from Chicago.

Mr. Goodhue saw his small weekly paper gain steadily in importance, and his editorials and comments on local and national politics won him fame that was noted all across the country. He died only three years later, but his pioneering efforts had set the stage for other papers and publishers that would follow.

Interior restoration of Goodhue's first newspaper office

Early papers like *The Minnesota Pioneer* gave lengthy accounts of the proceedings of the territorial legislatures and the courts, the messages and reports of the governors, officials, and public and semi-public groups, published the laws, and spread presidential messages and congressional debates over many columns.

Local politics were handled with great vigor, and editorial rivalries used language that today would give cause for criminal and civil libel suits. In many towns barely able to support one paper, preceding a political campaign there would be both a Republican and a Democratic paper. Each appealed for support from dutiful party members, and frequently the defeat of a party candidate meant the end of the corresponding party paper, amid the rapturous outbursts of the successful rival editor. The cultural side was not neglected, for practically every issue contained literary efforts good or bad, original or clipped, and bits of poetry.

These pioneer editors encountered endless difficulties in getting their supplies of paper, and their columns contained frequent references to this problem. As a consequence, there were occasional failures to print for a week or two, and often there were but single sheets of varying sizes. The paper used was made from rags, and as a result, the issues preserved in the collections of the Minnesota Historical Society, dating back over a hundred years, are in surprisingly good condition as compared with those printed on the wood pulp paper of the period from 1880 onward.

St. Anthony was the location of another early newspaper, *The St. Anthony Express*, first published in 1851. The decade of the 1850's saw some ninety newspapers come into existence, many of which lasted only a short time. Twelve pioneer papers survived the early period of hardship and continued to make their contribution to the growing area of Minnesota. These papers were: *St. Paul Pioneer Press*,

1849; *The Minnehaha*, 1855; *The Winona Republican Herald*, 1855; *The Chatfield News*, 1856; *The Stillwater Post-Messenger*, 1856; *The Mantorville Express*, 1857; *The Monticello Times*, 1857; *The Red Wing Republican*, 1857; *The St. Cloud Daily Times* and *Daily Journal Express*, 1857; and *The Wabasha County Herald Standard* in 1857.

The roll call of Minnesota's newspaper editors is virtually unending. It begins with James M. Goodhue and his *Minnesota Pioneer* of 1849. Ignatius Donnelly, gifted radical leader of Minnesota politics who edited the *Emigrant Aid Journal* of Nininger, and Jane Swisshelm, fiery abolitionist who founded the *St. Cloud Visitor*, joined the list in the 1850's. John A. Johnson, first three-time governor of Minnesota and Democratic party leader of the turn of the century, was an early president of the Minnesota Editorial Association while editor of the *St. Peter Herald*. Scores of other editors have served in state offices and the legislature, in Congress, and in other public service.

The newspaper has an interesting history in the development of our state. Perhaps one of the reasons Minnesota is such a progressive state is the fact that the people have been so well informed through the newspapers of their times.

The Telegraph

In the 1850's as the flood of settlers continued to pour into the region, Minnesota Territory became less remote from the outside world. That marvel of rapid communication, the electric or "magnetic" telegraph, patented by Samuel F. B. Morse in 1837, came into general use after long years of struggle, and its lines of iron wire were reaching to the Mississippi. News dispatches were being carried over the wires to the river towns, and then the newspapers of these communities were rushed onto the steamboats for delivery upstream. Word of the admission of Minnesota as a state on May 11, 1858, came by telegraph to Prairie du Chien. The citizens of the newly admitted state learned the glad news on May 13, upon the arrival of the first upbound steamboat.

Telegraph companies had sprung up almost by magic throughout the states east of the Mississippi amid legal complications, bitter competition, and lack of coordination. Local groups set up stock companies to run telegraph lines in various areas, and then solicited the towns along the proposed routes for subscriptions to insure their being serviced by the wires.

Newspapers now carried dispatches brought by the telegraph, but there were constant complaints about the service, due to breaks in the line, storms and other mechanical difficulties, to say nothing of operator "coffee breaks" and deliberate holdups in transmission. In the middle of dispatches concerning exciting events such as major battles of the Civil War, the line would go dead and Minnesotans would realize how out of touch they were with the outside world.

The Telephone

In 1876, Alexander Graham Bell succeeded in transmitting the human voice over distance by wire. The telephone entered the age of communication, and soon spread across the country. Minneapolis and St. Paul were among the leaders in setting up a telephone system. Private experimental lines were run in both cities in 1877, and the following year found the Northwestern Telephone Company in operation in Minneapolis, with about a dozen subscribers.

Numerous independent companies sprang up, some of them using the constantly improving Bell equipment, and some adopting independently developed devices utilizing early types of dial phones. As late as the first decade of the twentieth century there were two major telephone systems operating in the Twin Cities, and it was necessary for business and professional people to have phones of both companies to transact their business. Eventually the two were consolidated into the Northwestern Bell Telephone Company, a subsidiary of the American Telephone and Telegraph Company.

An early telephone

Today you can pick up a telephone and in a matter of seconds talk directly with a specific person on the Atlantic or Pacific seaboard, or with people in other countries, via the wonders of electronics.

Radio and Television

The next step in communication didn't come until the beginning of the 1900's. Voice broadcasting came into being in 1906. It didn't really come into use (as radio) until 1919.

The University of Minnesota began utilizing radio broadcasts in 1912, and by 1921 was offering musical broadcasts. This station, originally called WLB, is the country's oldest station of its type to be in continuous operation since its beginning. WCAL, operated by St. Olaf College in Northfield, received its broadcast license in 1921, and WLB in 1922. WLB was renamed KUOM in 1931. Do you know what those call letters stand for?

Commercial broadcasting began nationally in 1922, and pioneer stations in Minnesota were WLAG (later to become WCCO), WAMD (later to become KSTP), WDGY, and WRHM (later to become WTCN).

An early radio

Most early broadcasting stations featured Swedish or German band music, and the market reports, which the farmers and stock growers appreciated. Since 1930, many radio stations have come into existence all across the state. How many do you know of? Do you have a favorite?

Television entered the experimental stage in 1939 through the efforts of KSTP, and became a reality through Channel 5 in 1948. WTCN-TV began operation on Channel 4 in 1949, and WMIN-TV opened Channel 11 in 1952. KEYD-TV began on Channel 9 in 1955. KTCA-TV, the state's first educational station, began on Channel 2 in 1957.

Several changes in ownership shifted some of these early stations to different channels and network affiliations. Today you probably know the call letters and channel of most of them quite well. How many can you name?

Communication has progressed over the years to the point where you can now turn on your radio or television set and listen to or watch an event as it is happening any place in the world (or even in space). What do you think early pioneers of Minnesota would think if they could see the communications systems we have today?

Words to Know — Define these words and terms. You may need to use a dictionary or encyclopedia to find some of the answers.

Communication

Minnesota Pioneer

Telegraph

Names to Know — Identify these people.

James M. Goodhue

Samuel F. B. Morse

Jane Swisshelm

Writing Activities

Imagine that you are a newspaper publisher in early Minnesota. Write a letter to a friend, describing your newspaper.

CHAPTER TWENTY
EDUCATION IN MINNESOTA

The First Schools

Many years before there were any settlers' children in Minnesota, plans for their education were made in our nation's capitol. The Ordinance of 1787 provided that all children who were to live in the Northwest Territory should be entitled to an education.

When the government surveyed this new land it divided it into sections of one square mile each. Thirty-six sections made up a larger unit, called a township. The western states asked the federal government to give them one section out of every township to be used for education. Usually a school house was built on this section, and it served as a school, a community meeting place and a voting center for all elections. Section number 16 was usually chosen as the school section. Can you think of a reason for choosing this particular section?

6	5	4	3	2	1
7	8	9	10	11	12
18	17	16	15	14	13
19	20	21	22	23	24
30	29	28	27	26	25
31	32	33	34	35	36

Section

Township and section plot

When Minnesota Territory came into being, it asked the federal government to give it two sections out of each township for schools. This request was granted and sections 16 and 36 were set aside as school areas. Over the years this request has proved to be very valuable to school children in Minnesota. Timber was sold from many of these sections, providing money for education. Iron ore was later discovered and mined from other school sections and a special tax was placed on all ore mined. This tax money provided millions of dollars for education in Minnesota.

The first school in Minnesota was at Fort Snelling and was set up to educate the children of people stationed there. Their education consisted mainly of reading, writing, and arithmetic, with special instruction in politeness and manners. French was taught to these children by a French officer stationed at the fort. How does this early education compare to your education today?

The first school outside of Fort Snelling was organized by the Pond brothers in 1835, and was a log building on the west bank of what is now Lake Harriet in Minneapolis. This missionary school was started mainly to teach the Sioux how to follow the white people's customs in farming, cooking and Christianity.

Another early school was in existence in 1832, before the Pond brothers' school. This school was organized by a Mr. Aitkin, and was located within the trading post at Sandy Lake.

In 1839, the first Catholic school was established among the Chippewa at Grand Portage. Later, in 1847, the first school of historic importance was started in St. Paul. It had a very modest beginning, as it was located in a building that had been used as a blacksmith shop. The first teacher in this school was Miss Harriet Bishop, who came all the way to St. Paul from the East.

Other schools followed, many established by Catholic and Protestant groups. There were only three public schools in the state by 1849, one in Stillwater, one in St. Anthony and the one taught by Miss Bishop in St. Paul.

Early Day Education

The early rural schools were on a low budget. Before the people could pay adequate taxes for good schools, their land had to be developed to produce a good income. At the start, with only a few acres under cultivation, there could be only small taxes.

Under the system that developed, time was laid out in "Terms". There would be two and sometimes three terms a year of several months each. Pay for teachers was low. In early Minnesota, twelve to fifteen dollars a month for women, and eighteen to twenty-five dollars for men was common. The qualifications were also low. The only qualification for teaching was to be able to read and write and have the ability to do basic arithmetic.

An early one-room school in Minnesota

An early day school

Since there was little tax money, but plenty of timber, rough log school houses were built. Try to picture a log building about twenty feet long and twelve feet wide, with a split shingle or shake roof, and possibly three or four small windows. Inside there would be an iron stove, a rough split log floor, and rows of benches with no backs, also made of split logs. On one end was a raised platform, and a table and chair for the teacher. On a cold winter morning, the teacher might face up to thirty shivering students.

There were no grades. The teacher grouped the students by reading ability. Reading, writing and arithmetic were often the only subjects taught. Now and then, some teacher would offer a little science, history or geography. Until well into the 1870's there were no free school books. There was always a shortage of books and often no uniformity. This meant that in a class of fifth form reading, there might be six students and six different texts. Cheap paper was not yet available, so the students generally wrote their lessons on heavy slates.

The teacher was expected to maintain discipline. Many of the students were in their upper teens, going to school for only the winter term, when their farm chores were at a minimum. They fought with each other, they bullied the smaller children, and made the teacher's life miserable. There are a number of instances where the students drove the teacher out of the school. Teachers commonly used a plentiful supply of hickory, ash, or ironwood rods to whip the students who would not behave. Such was the early public school in Minnesota.

In time, improvements came. In the 1860's, a county superintendent system was started. The county superintendents of schools did what they could to improve education. A state superintendent of schools tried to provide more information to all schools. Using the land law already mentioned, a fund was developed to provide state aid for many school districts where the tax base was small. In this early period, State Superintendent of Schools Edward Neill provided outstanding leadership.

Edward Neill

As the economic picture of the state improved, more taxes were levied. With more money, the log school houses disappeared. Even today, one can see many of the small white buildings that replaced them.

During the second half of the nineteenth century, education changed significantly. Free text books were provided. Many county superintendents organized special short classes, called institutes, to help teachers learn new methods of education. In the twentieth century, a compulsory school law was passed, and a system of grades established. The primary school was divided into eight grades.

These rural schools lasted for over a century in Minnesota, but finally came to an end. With better roads and improved education, consolidated systems emerged. This provided for the smaller school districts to be consolidated into larger school districts. The consolidation law also provided buses for transportation of students to the larger schools. It is believed that with the larger schools, better education results.

Horse-drawn buses

High schools in Minnesota had a slow start. Secondary education, or classes beyond grade school, had been handled by private academies for a long time. Gradually, however, tax supported high schools gained in number. Several things are responsible for this. Our gradually industrializing civilization demanded people who had more education than just basic reading and writing. Before the end of the Civil War, there were a few public high schools in Minnesota at places like Mankato, the Twin Cities and Winona. High schools grew in number in the late nineteenth century, and in the twentieth century, their number increased even more.

Early 20th century high school building in Minnesota

Before general consolidation it was often not easy for a rural student to attend high school. Tuition was paid by the country school district but there were no school buses. Either their parents took them, they drove to school themselves, or they stayed in town to go to school. The same consolidated system that helped the grade schools also gave the high schools a big boost. This brought about many changes. Many small towns that at one time had high schools saw their schools close as they became part of a larger school system. More classes could be offered, and provisions were made for children with learning difficulties. Teachers with special training were hired to teach these classes.

Private education has been part of Minnesota for well over a century. Many immigrants from the European countries wanted their children to have a full religious education. Many schools, Catholic and Protestant, were built, and there are still a number operating in Minnesota today. There are fewer, however, than there were at one time in our state. Education is an expensive process. Many people believe that they simply can not afford the money it takes to keep these schools going.

Our Schools Today

The schools in Minnesota today are much different than the early blacksmith shop where Harriet Bishop taught in early St. Paul. The wood-burning stoves have been replaced by modern gas and oil furnaces and steam boilers. The early benches have been replaced with modern desks and study tables. Libraries that consisted of perhaps half a dozen books in the early days have changed into large rooms containing hundreds or thousands of books. How many books does your school library have?

Today school buses transport many children from their homes to their schools. In the early days, children often walked several miles each day to attend school. Some rode horses to school and kept them in small barns on the school grounds until the end of the school day. Can you imagine a lunch period where you would have to feed both yourself and your horse?

Years ago, many children dropped out of school after the eighth year because they were needed to work in the fields or to help support the family. Is this expected of you today?

Our high schools of today offer a wide variety of training for the future. Students may choose subjects that will pre-

A modern school building

pare them for many kinds of work. Some of these special subject areas are: business, home economics, agriculture, science, and vocational or skilled trades training. If students want to become doctors, lawyers, teachers, or any other professional worker, they may choose subjects in high school that will prepare them to enter a college for special training in that field. If students want to become secretaries, carpenters, mechanics, or skilled in other fields, high schools offer special subjects to provide training in those areas.

Many school districts now have vocational-technical schools that offer special training in skilled occupations. Does your school district have a vocational-technical school? Do you think it should?

The schools of today are indeed a great deal different from the little one-room school house of years ago. Your grandparents may have gone to one of these one-room schools. Ask them to tell you about their school experiences.

Colleges

With the start of the public educational system in Minnesota, a real need arose: the need for trained teachers. The low standards for teachers of the old country schools were no longer accepted. The first teacher training institution in Minnesota was authorized by the legislature in 1858. This was a "Normal School", which opened in Winona in 1860. More were added in various large towns in the state. All of them trained and certified teachers, at first requiring only that their students had graduated from elementary school.

As more high schools came into being, the more basic elements of the normal schools were dropped. In time, the normal schools became the teacher's colleges that trained teachers for both the primary and secondary schools. After World War II, they gradually dropped the name "teacher's college", and offered other degrees not connected with the teaching profession. They were then called "state colleges". In time, they added graduate schools for people who wished to take courses above the minimum level. At the present time there are full degree state universities at Moorhead, St. Cloud, Bemidji, Mankato, Marshall and Winona.

Private colleges (those that are not supported by taxes) were founded early in Minnesota's history. The oldest college in Minnesota was founded at Red Wing in 1854 by the Methodists and was named Hamline University. It closed in 1857, due to lack of money, but started up again eleven years later, and was relocated in St. Paul. Gustavus Adolphus College was also founded at Red Wing, in 1862, and in 1876 was moved to St. Peter.

Even before the University of Minnesota or Winona Normal School were started, both Protestant and Catholic churches had established colleges. St. John's Seminary, a Catholic school, in time became a university. Today these colleges and universities are located across the state and some of them are known on a national scale.

Hamline University at Red Wing

Some famous people have taught or studied at these private colleges. A famous writer, Ole Rolvaag, taught for many years at St. Olaf College in Northfield. His *Giants in the Earth* is regarded as a great frontier novel. Thorstein Veblen, who was an economist and social thinker, studied at Carleton College in Northfield.

Shortly before the First World War, a municipal, or city-supported, two-year junior college was established at Rochester. People believed that it would be good to have a college of this type to provide a place for local students to start their college training. Many graduates of high school, who could not enter colleges or universities for financial

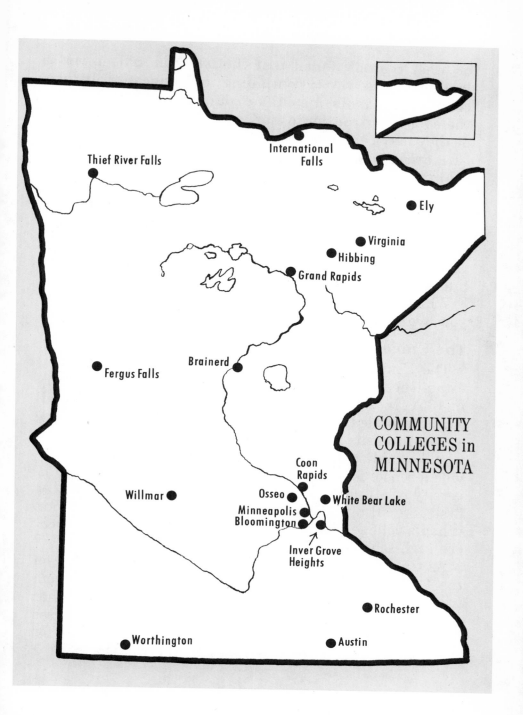

Thief River Falls

International
Falls

Ely

Virginia

Hibbing

Grand Rapids

Fergus Falls

Brainerd

COMMUNITY
COLLEGES in
MINNESOTA

Coon
Rapids

Osseo

Willmar

White Bear Lake

Minneapolis
Bloomington

Inver Grove
Heights

Rochester

Worthington

Austin

or other reasons, found that the two-year college was a less expensive way of continuing their education. In these colleges, students may take courses that will prepare them for later transfer to four-year colleges or universities, or they may choose courses that will train them in special skill areas in only two years.

Many other junior colleges, now called community colleges, have been built in our state. After World War II, the state of Minnesota took over the administration of the community colleges. There were only nine state-supported community colleges in Minnesota by 1958. Since then, more have been established, and today there are eighteen public-supported community colleges in Minnesota.

Which of the state community colleges is closest to where you live?

The University of Minnesota

The University of Minnesota at Minneapolis was first established by the legislature of the Minnesota Territory in 1851. In 1862, a government act known as the Morrill Act passed the United States Congress. This act gave every state university system a grant of government land if it would establish an agricultural school, and if it would provide a school for future reserve military officers. The University of Minnesota opened right after the Civil War. At first, like all upper educational institutions of Minnesota, it had a college preparatory department, similar to a modern high school.

As time passed, it developed into a university based on the German model, offering professional schools which train doctors, veterinarians, scientists, nurses and other professional people. Today it has a wide range of courses leading to the bachelor's degree, including training for teachers. A graduate school was also established. At a

Modern University of Minnesota—aerial view

graduate school, people can take advanced degrees. Some world famous people have taught at the University of Minnesota. Today it has over forty thousand students in campuses in Minneapolis, St. Paul, Duluth and Morris.

The State Historical Society

Do you know that the State Historical Society is older than the state it serves? It's true. The territorial legislature, in 1849, established the State Historical Society in a farsighted action that has become a rich heritage for all Minnesotans.

These early leaders realized that someday vast changes would occur in the territory. They wanted to record and save materials from the early days, and they knew that generations yet to come would appreciate having a record of what their state had been like in years past.

Today the vast collection is divided into five groupings: books, newspapers, pictures, manuscripts, and museum objects. The society publishes a variety of materials that enable people to learn of their state's history. Each year thousands of people visit the society and see history come alive through the materials on display. The entire collection in all departments serves as a research and resource center for anyone who wishes to find out about anything connected to Minnesota history.

Minnesota Historical Society building

Words to Know — Define these words and terms. You may need to use a dictionary or encyclopedia to find some of the answers.

Community college
Consolidation (of schools)
Morrill Act
Normal school
Ordinance of 1787
Secondary schools
Township
Tuition
Vocational-technical school

Names to Know — Identify these people.

Harriet Bishop

Edward Neill

Ole Rolvaag

Writing Activities

Imagine that you are attending school in Minnesota in the middle of the 1800's. Write a letter to a friend describing what your school is like.

CHAPTER TWENTY-ONE

GOVERNMENT

Tribal Government

Whenever human beings group together to form a society, there must be some kind of government. If this were not so, you can imagine the confusion and problems that would arise. This government may be made up of either written or unwritten laws (code of behavior). There must be a recognized source of power or authority and there must be a means of enforcing laws.

The earliest forms of government in Minnesota that we know of were those of the Sioux and the Chippewa. The white people came into contact with Sioux and Chippewa governmental systems as early as the periods of exploration and fur trade. In these contacts the white people's government was always considered to be better (at least by the white people). Their government was stronger due to the power of their armies and weapons of warfare.

Often the representatives of the white government did not understand how the Indians' government functioned and this created many situations in which the Sioux and the Chippewa were forced to accept unfair decisions. These decisions were not open to compromise or discussion by the Indian tribes, for they knew very little of the way in which the white people's government worked. This often created situations in which the following results came about:

1. Territory was given up to the white government.
2. One tribal chief might be induced to sign or agree to something that affected other tribes who had nothing to say in the matter.
3. Conflict and war.

The following diagrams and descriptions may give you some idea of how the Sioux or Dakota government operated. This information is also true to some degree for other Indian systems. To obtain more information on the Chippewa system of tribal government consult resource and reference books or community resource people who are knowledgeable on the subject.

■ Government of the Dakota Nation

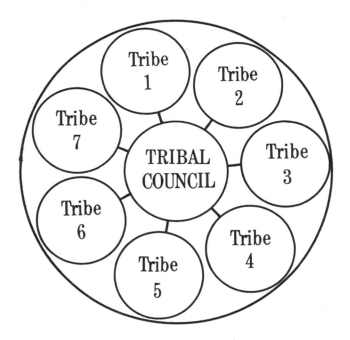

The outer circle suggests that everything within it is called a nation (seven Dakota tribes). This nation is made up of the seven tribes, each with its own form of government. All tribes are united by this larger unit of government to which each tribe has equal representation. Is this similar to our own present day county and state government structure?

A Tribal Government

This diagram represents one tribe and its main units of government. The chief was usually a highly respected warrior. His main duties were to judge those accused of doing wrong and to select encampment sites for his traveling village. His council of advisors was made up of the older, experienced men of the tribe. They helped him make decisions. Special police guards were authorized to enforce their decisions. Sometimes the death penalty was given if the crime was considered serious enough. More often lesser penalties were given, and it was not uncommon for a guilty party to be banished from the tribe. In some cases, the guilty person was required to give up his personal possessions, such as horses, robes and food, to the victim's family as payment for his crime.

The Plains Indian (Dakota) ■ Tribal System of Government

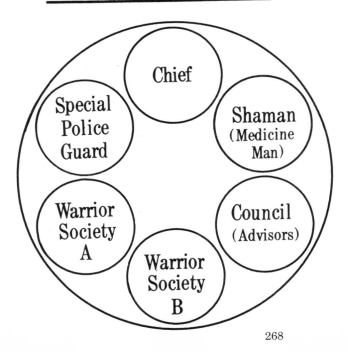

Each tribe usually had from two to four warrior societies, each of which had a great deal of authority in the tribe. One warrior society might have complete control of the buffalo hunts, another might have most of the authority in conducting warfare. These societies each might have highly respected leaders, often called chiefs, but their roles were not the same as that of the tribal chief.

The warrior societies usually had charge of the training of young boys in such matters as archery, horsemanship, hunting and other required warrior traits. Tribal traditions, stories, and other sacred matters were usually taught to the young by the older members of the tribe, often the council members.

The various bands or tribes of the nation would usually gather for a tribal council each June (or more often if the need arose). Tepees of each tribe would be set up in circles around the encampment area. A large council lodge or tepee would be located at the center of this circle. Chiefs, advisors, medicine men and respected warrior society chiefs would meet in this council and discuss problems of the nation. Their decision was usually accepted as law by all tribes. This council session has some similarities to our own present day state legislature.

In addition to solving problems and making decisions, this council would also receive delegates from other nations or tribes, and in such sessions they often met with representatives from the white people's government. Other duties of the council included that of interpreting the dreams of their young. This council was the one and only court of law, and its decision was final. Do you see any resemblance between this council and our own state or national supreme court?

State Government

Our Minnesota state government system is patterned after the Federal system, having three main branches. These are the Legislative, Executive and Judicial.

The **Legislative Branch** is composed of two parts or houses, the "Senate" and the "House of Representatives." The men and women elected to these "houses" are called senators and representatives. They are elected by the voters of their district to represent them at the state level of government.

Both houses together are called the "legislature." The legislature meets every year, beginning in January. The length of the meeting session is limited to 120 days for every two-year period. During this time, the legislature makes the laws it believes are necessary for the state and its people. Sometimes the work cannot be completed in this amount of time, so special sessions must be called by the governor.

The **Judicial Branch** is made up of all the court systems. These include the state supreme court, court of appeals, district courts, and county courts. The function of the courts is mainly to interpret the meaning of laws and to determine if any of the laws have been broken.

The Supreme Court is the highest court in the state. It is composed of nine judges or "justices." One is called the "chief justice" and the others are "associate justices." This court decides on cases which cannot be decided in lower courts, and their decision is the final word in all cases concerning state government. Although decisions of the state courts may be appealed to the federal courts and the Supreme Court of the United States, most legal problems are settled in the state court system.

How the Three Branches of State Government are Selected

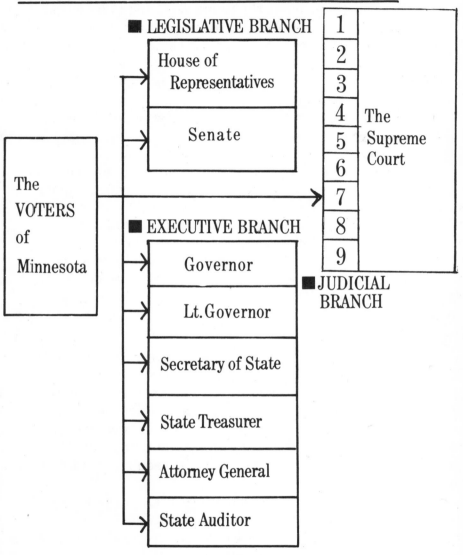

■ LEGISLATIVE BRANCH

House of Representatives

Senate

The VOTERS of Minnesota

■ EXECUTIVE BRANCH

Governor

Lt. Governor

Secretary of State

State Treasurer

Attorney General

State Auditor

1	The Supreme Court
2	
3	
4	
5	
6	
7	
8	
9	

■ JUDICIAL BRANCH

Minnesota is in the process of establishing a "Court of Appeals." This court will assist the Supreme Court in its work.

At the next level, we find the state divided into ten districts. Each district has a district court and is composed of three or more judges. Most cases that come before the district courts are decided there, but some cases may be sent on to the Supreme Court if the need arises.

Beneath the district courts are the county courts. Judges in these courts are elected for six-year terms.

The **Executive Branch** of state government is headed by the governor. The governor is assisted by a lieutenant governor, a secretary of state, a state treasurer, an attorney general, and a state auditor. Each of these officials is elected to a four-year term by all the voters of the state. The main duty of this branch of government is to administer or carry out the laws passed by the legislature, and to see that the business of the state is handled efficiently and correctly. This branch of our state government cannot make laws, but it can make recommendations to the legislature for new laws.

County Government

Minnesota has eighty-seven counties. Each has its own government. These county governments make and enforce the laws and regulations of the county. Each county has a "county seat town," where the county government offices and courthouse are located. Usually one building, the county courthouse, contains all the county offices, but sometimes space requirements or condition of the courthouse requires additional buildings.

The following diagram will show the basic framework of county government in Minnesota. This will differ slightly from county to county, but it is still the basic organization of our county government.

◼ COUNTY GOVERNMENT

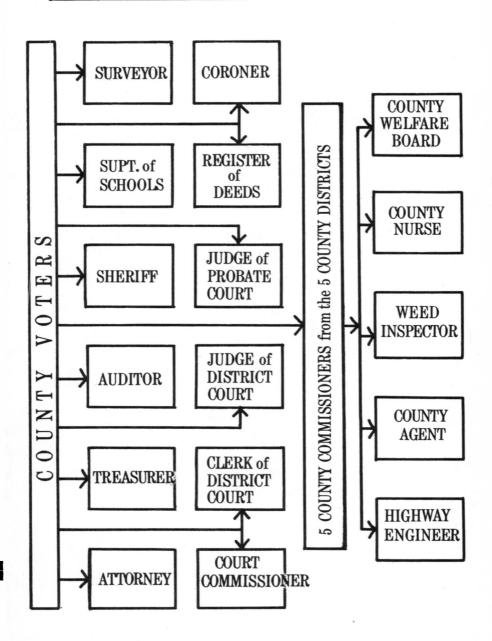

Municipal Governments

Municipal governments are the governing bodies of cities. They are divided into four groups:

- Cities of the first class.
- Cities of the second class.
- Cities of the third class.
- Cities of the fourth class.

Large cities such as Minneapolis, St. Paul, and Duluth are cities of the first class and other cities fall into the other classes depending upon their population size. All municipal governments are similar in that they have a mayor and a council elected by the voters of the city. Sometimes a city will have a city manager to handle the city's business. This person is not elected, but appointed by the mayor and council.

Township Government

Township government is the structure set up by people living in rural areas. This is a more simplified governing system than other forms, for in this system all the residents of the township meet once a year. This annual meeting is called a "town meeting," and it is a time to discuss problems and to elect officials for the coming year. The following diagram will show the common structure of township government:

■ MUNICIPAL GOVERNMENT STRUCTURE

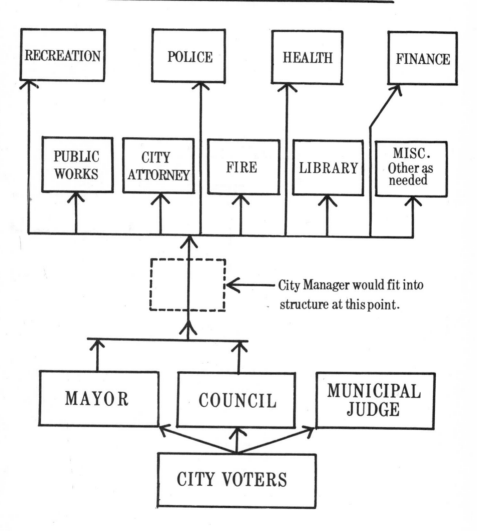

City Manager would fit into structure at this point.

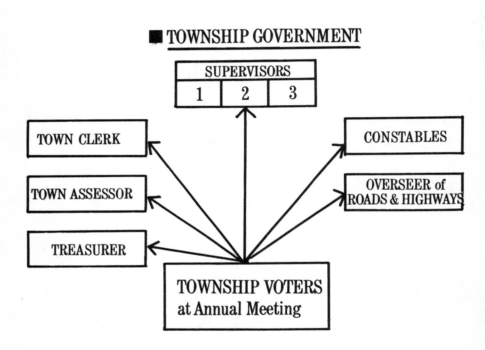

■ TOWNSHIP GOVERNMENT

SUPERVISORS

| 1 | 2 | 3 |

TOWN CLERK

CONSTABLES

TOWN ASSESSOR

OVERSEER of ROADS & HIGHWAYS

TREASURER

TOWNSHIP VOTERS
at Annual Meeting

School District Government

School District Government in Minnesota consists of five types. These are: Common School Districts, Independent Districts, Special Districts, Districts of Unorganized Territory, and Associated School Districts. The Independent School District is perhaps the best known and most numerous of these types. The Independent District is usually set up as the following diagram shows.

■ INDEPENDENT SCHOOL DISTRICT

TEACHERS	BUSINESS MANAGER	OFFICE WORKERS	FOOD SERVICE	TRANS-PORTATION

SUPT. of SCHOOLS

BOARD of EDUCATION					
1	2	3	4	5	6

VOTERS of the School District

Relationship Between State and Federal Governments

What powers does the federal government have and what powers do the state governments have? Where does one stop and the other begin? It does seem confusing, and it was confusing until our forefathers met in Philadelphia back in 1787 to end the confusion. They wrote a document that was to become perhaps the most famous the world has ever seen. This document was called the Constitution of the United States of America, and it defined clearly the function and power of the federal government and the function and power to be assumed by each state.

■ Distribution of Constitutional Power

STATES MAY	STATES MAY NOT
Control elections, local governments, public health, safety and morals, within their boundaries (includes such things as marriage, divorce, education and general voting qualifications).	Interfere with functions of the federal government, such as making war, writing treaties with foreign countries, maintaining armies or navies, printing their own money.
FEDERAL GOVERMENT MAY	FEDERAL GOV'T MAY NOT
Regulate commerce over state lines and with foreign nations. Ratify treaties and carry on foreign relations. Maintain postal systems, grant copyrights, coin money, declare war, and raise, support and make rules for the regulation of an army and navy.	Favor one state at expense of another. Grant titles of nobility, or restrict an individual from knowing the statement of charges against him or prevent him from the right of a speedy trial, except in cases of rebellion or invasion.
BOTH MAY	BOTH MAY NOT
Levy taxes. Build roads. Borrow money. Spend money for the general welfare.	Deprive persons of life or property without due process of law, or pass laws incriminating persons for acts that were not illegal when committed.

This document has enabled our nation to prosper and grow for nearly two hundred years. This constitution is the framework under which a free people could take an active part in making their government work for them. Each state has modeled its own state constitution after the federal model and made the model work at the state level just as efficiently as it does at the national level.

The chart on the previous page shows those powers given to the federal government and those reserved for the states. It will show what each government can do and what it cannot do.

Citizens' Responsibilities to Their Governments

No democratic form of government can survive unless its citizens carry out their responsibilities to it. Each person has been given a role to play in this process. If citizens take their role seriously, they will continue to enjoy the benefits of a government that is responsive to their needs and wishes. Individual citizens have many responsibilities to their various governments, some of which are:

1. To obey the laws their government (local, state, and national) has established.
2. To vote for officials who will speak for them and carry out their feelings in matters of legislation.
3. To keep informed of problems and issues of the day, on local, state, and national levels, in order to vote intelligently.
4. To share in the cost of operating government by paying their fair share of taxes at all levels of government.

Can you think of other responsibilities that a citizen in our democratic society might have?

Many years ago, near the end of the Civil War in America, President Lincoln gave a speech near the Gettysburg, Pennsylvania, battlefield. In this speech he referred to our government as . . . "of the people, by the people and for the people . . ." What do you think this quotation means?

The following diagram may help you understand the several roles citizens play in the various types of government under which they live. Note that the citizen is placed at the center of the diagram, enclosed by circles representing the increasing size of the units of government to which the citizen belongs.

The citizen's role in government

Words to Know — Define these words and terms. You may need to use a dictionary or encyclopedia to find some of the answers.

Chief

County seat

Executive branch

Government

Judicial branch

Legislative branch

Township government

Warrior societies

Writing Activities

Find out the names of the state officials who presently hold the following offices:

Governor

Lieutenant Governor

Secretary of State

State Auditor

State Treasurer

Attorney General

U.S. Senators from our state

U.S. Representative from your district

State Senator from your area

State Representative from your area

Find out the names and offices of your county officials

If you live in a town or city, find out the names and offices of your town or city officials.

CHAPTER TWENTY-TWO

RECREATION
AND HISTORIC SITES

There's a lot to see and do in Minnesota if you like to spend your time outdoors: hiking, boating, canoeing, fishing, and hunting, to name just a few activities. Winter doesn't stop the outdoor activities. There are downhill and cross-country ski areas and snowmobile trails throughout the state. There are also many historic sites to visit, such as Fort Snelling in the Twin Cities and the Tower-Soudan mine on the Iron Range.

Winter activities in Minnesota

Two departments in the state government deal with our natural and historic sites. The Tourism Division of the Department of Economic Development provides information on parks, camping, historical sites, tours, festivals, snowmobile trails, ski areas, and bicycle routes. The Department of Natural Resources (DNR) is in charge of state

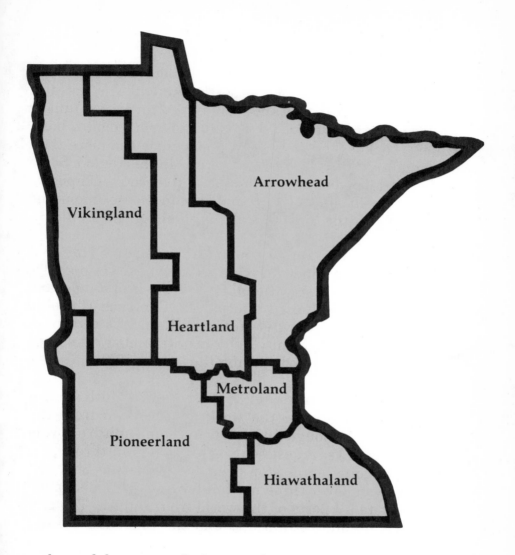

parks and forests, and also regulates hunting and fishing.

The Department of Economic Development — Tourism Division can tell you about all the different things there are to do and see in our state. They divide the state into six tourism regions. We will take a closer look at these regions.

Arrowhead

The Arrowhead region is a place where the visitor can enjoy the naturalness of the north country. The lakes in the Boundary Waters Canoe Area are famous for lunker walleye, northern pike, lake trout and small-mouth bass. Hikers, backpackers and snowshoers enjoy the more than one hundred miles of state forest trails in this region. Some of these trails were once followed by the Sioux, Chippewa and French explorers. Rock climbers can choose among the many cliffs in the Taylors Falls area along the scenic St. Croix River.

The Arrowhead region includes Voyageurs National Park, along with nineteen state parks which are open for campers. South of the National Park is the Iron Range, and nearby is the Iron Range Interpretive Center at Chisolm. The Forest History Center in Grand Rapids is a turn-of-the-century logging camp. It shows how lumberjacks lived and worked in the woods during the height of Minnesota's lumbering era.

Arrowhead's urban center is the port of Duluth. Ocean freighters from around the world can be seen from the aerial bridge. Although far from the ocean, Duluth's port is one of the world's largest sea ports. More than three hundred ocean-going ships stop every year, via the St. Lawrence Seaway. Over three million tons of cargo is shipped every year to all ports of the world from Duluth. The city highlights unique restaurants and the St. Louis County Heritage and Arts Center. The Lake Superior agate, Minnesota's state stone, can be found all the way up Superior's shore.

In 1804, traders landed on the banks of the Snake River and set up a wintering post. Today an authentically reconstructed fur post near Pine City is stocked with the goods of those early times and guides dressed as voyageurs are en-

Split Rock Lighthouse—historic North Shore marker

gaged in activities typical of the post in the 1880's. Other historic sites include the Grand Mound Interpretive Center where the largest prehistoric Indian burial mound in Minnesota is located. The mound is one of the largest in the entire Upper Midwest. At the center, the culture of the mound people is explained.

Heartland

Lakes and rivers are everywhere in the Heartland region. Heartland's waters provide excellent hunting and fishing, and are also good for swimming and water skiing.

The tale of Paul Bunyan and Babe, his blue ox companion are preserved throughout the Heartland. It is said that Babe helped create Heartland by wandering the country-

Paul Bunyan and Babe

side for days. When he did, his thundering tracks formed the basins for what are now Heartland's lakes. In Brainerd at the Paul Bunyan Amusement Center, tourists can talk to the animated fifty-foot statue of Paul, who is accompanied by a fifteen-foot replica of Babe. More statues of Paul and Babe guard the shores of Lake Bemidji at the southern entrance to the city.

While Heartland preserves it memories of folk heroes, it also has its real heroes. In Little Falls, Charles Lindbergh, the man who made the first flight across the Atlantic Ocean, is commemorated with a state park and interpretive center. His house, near the center, was built in 1906 by Lindbergh's father. In Sauk Centre, the "Sinclair Lewis Boyhood Home" has also been restored and designated a national and historic site.

Other attractions in the Heartland are Lumbertown USA, a full-size replica of an 1870's lumbertown located at Gull Lake, and an international raceway for top notch auto racing near Brainerd. The Mille Lacs Indian Museum is on the southwest shore of Mille Lacs Lake. The area around the museum was settled by the Chippewa whose descendants still live there. The museum features displays portraying Chippewa life in each of the four seasons.

Heartland's Northwest Angle, jutting into Lake of the Woods is the northernmost point of Minnesota. Not long ago it was accessible only by air or water, but now there is an all weather road through Canada to accommodate travelers. Fort St. Charles, founded in 1732, is located on a Lake of the Woods island. The Northwest Angle State Forest is a true wilderness.

Marker at Sinclair Lewis historic site

Hiawathaland

Hiawathaland in the southeastern corner of the state is characterized by rolling hills and deep valleys. One of the most stunning scenic drives in the United States is the route from Red Wing to Winona. The drive is flanked by the Mississippi River on one side and steep bluffs on the other. This route was once a segment of the historical Great River Road.

Many river towns line this drive. Red Wing, famous for its shoes and pottery is a city full of river legend and history. Downriver is Old Frontenac which dates back to 1723 when it was the site of a French fort. Frontenac State Park surrounds the historic site. Further down the drive is Lake City where the Mississippi River has widened to form Lake Pepin. Waterskiing originated here in 1922 and is still enjoyed today.

Another interesting town is Wabasha, which sits on a terrace in the Hiawatha Valley, with tree-lined bluffs on each side. Minnesota's oldest operating hotel is in Wabasha and it is filled with antiques. Hiawathaland boasts of having more antique shops per person than anywhere in the United States.

The four southernmost counties of this region possess natural wonders unique to Minnesota. Because it was part of the "Driftless" region, it was unaltered by glaciers. Rock formations carved beneath the surface in caverns can be found and some of the most impressive limestone formations and hardwood forests are in the four state parks that encompass more than three thousand acres.

Other attractions of Hiawathaland are the Steamboat Museum in Winona's Levee Park where "Steamboat Days" are celebrated annually, and Mantorville, a historic site which was once a stage depot. Mantorville has been restored to its original 1880's appearance. The only Civil War

The Hiawatha Valley

Lake Pepin—near Lake City

recruiting station left in Minnesota is located in Wasioja. Meighen Store is another historic site, located in Forestville State Park. Under the management of Robert Foster and Felix Meighen, this country store provided the village of Forestville with dry goods, hardware and foodstuffs from 1857 to 1910.

Metroland

Metroland includes the eight counties surrounding St. Paul and Minneapolis, and it prides itself on its lakes and rivers, parks, camping sites, restaurants and nightclubs, theatres, major league sports and extensive winter sports facilities.

Festivals, fairs and parades are part of the year round entertainment in Metroland. The Minneapolis Aquatennial highlights the summer festivities, and the St. Paul Winter Carnival tops the winter fun. The country's largest Swedish festival, Svenskarnas Dag, is held in Minneapolis every June. The Minnesota Renaissance Festival celebrated annually recreates the sights and sounds of that age. But the greatest event of the year is the Minnesota State Fair held at the end of summer in Metroland, attracting more than one million people annually.

The Minnesota Valley Restoration is another exciting attraction, featuring a turn-of-the-century theme park near Shakopee. Nearby a mid-1800's Minnesota river community has been recreated with period buildings. South of the Twin Cities, exotic animals and vegetation can be viewed at the Minnesota Zoological Garden.

A part of Metroland's history has been preserved at Fort Snelling. The fort was built between 1820 and 1824 by United States soldiers under Josiah Snelling. Today the fort is a living museum with costumed soldiers actively involved in the traditional military life of the 1820's.

No visit to the Twin Cities would be complete without viewing the Minnesota State Capitol. The marble-domed statehouse is the largest in the world and was designed by Cass Gilbert, architect of the United States Supreme Court building and the George Washington Bridge.

The Minnesota State Capitol building

In St. Paul, the Science Museum of Minnesota's Omnitheatre features an audio visual system that can take you on fantastic voyages through space and time. The IDS Center, Minneapolis' fifty-seven story monolith, overlooks it all, the entire two thousand square miles of Metroland.

The arts are represented in Metroland too, with large collections of masterpieces in its many museums and institutes. The Minneapolis Institute of Art and the Walker Art Center are open year round to visitors. Adjoining the Walker Art Center is the nationally acclaimed Tyrone Guthrie

Repertory Theatre which is recognized for its significant contribution to the theatre arts.

Tyrone Guthrie Theatre in Minneapolis

Pioneerland

Fifty percent of Minnesota's historic sites can be found in Pioneerland, the southwest corner of Minnesota. A replica of an early chapel and a sod house can be seen at the start of the Hiawatha-Pioneer trail near Jackson.

In Cottonwood County ancient rock carvings called the Jeffers Petroglyphs show the work of native Americans from as long ago as 3000 B.C. The carvings are comprised of nearly two thousand reproductions of human figures, weapons and animals, indicating life in the Little Cottonwood River Valley. The Pipestone National Monument contains the famous soft red stone that American Indians used to make ceremonial pipes.

Fort Ridgely's ruins can be viewed in the Fort Ridgely State Park. A restored stone commissary now stands ex-

Early writing—what does it say?

plaining Fort Ridgely's two crucial battles that turned the tide of the 1862 Sioux war. Other historic attractions can be found near New Ulm. This German town is dotted with architectural masterpieces and highlighted by the Gothic Post Office built in 1910. A brick mural just off the main street authentically depicts pioneer life in the Minnesota River Valley during the 1850's.

The Upper and Lower Sioux Agencies are also open to the public. The Upper Sioux Agency was established in 1854 as a center for teaching farming methods to the Sioux. The Lower Sioux Agency was the scene of the first organized Indian attack in the war of 1862. An interpretive center at the site tells of the Indian struggles during this period.

Along the Minnesota River is the college town of St. Peter and the Traverse des Sioux State Park where the 1851 treaty was signed with over five thousand Santee Sioux present. This park is one of the seventeen state parks in Pioneerland.

New Ulm post office

Pioneerland has some of the most prosperous farmland in the state, and much of the rich soil that has made the state so agriculturally successful. The region boasts of the world's largest constructed tiller, corn and pea processing plants, turkey processing plant, and rye mill.

Vikingland

Vikingland is also a region rich in history. The Kensington Runestone was found in Vikingland, creating the still unsettled controversy over who really discovered America. Other fourteenth century artifacts of Scandinavian design are on display in Vikingland's Alexandria.

Vikingland's history is preserved in many of the seventeen counties. The Solomon Comstock house in Moorhead offers a glimpse into the lives of a community leader and his family in the 1880's.

Vikingland has ten state parks and more wildlife areas than any other Minnesota region. Vikingland has two of the state's four national wildlife management refuges where deer, moose and bear abound. There are thousands of acres of prime unposted marsh and timberland for the hunter. Hundreds of acres of wild rice paddies bring in the waterfowl. Hungarian partridge and sharptails also provide game for the sportsman.

Near Bagley is Itasca State Park with 32,000 acres. The park has two hundred campsites and is situated where the Mississippi River begins its 2,552 mile journey to the Gulf of Mexico. The Agassiz National Wildlife Refuge is in Marshall County and lies on the bay of the prehistoric Lake Agassiz. The refuge was once featured on television's "Wild Kingdom" because of the wildlife resources. It is a favorite spot for photographers and birdwatchers.

Glacial Lakes State Park, an oak forested area, is a scenic area for rock hounds. The park was formed by the last glacier. The glacier cut a deep valley nearly eleven thousand years ago which remains today.

The region has several thousand lakes which can be used by campers, scuba divers, swimmers, water skiers and fishermen. Detroit Lakes hosts a Northwest Water Carnival annually in July which brings people into the four hundred lakes which surround the area. Vikingland's Red Lake County is a canoeist's dreamland with seven rivers and seven streams.

Summer activities in Minnesota

Words to Know — Define these words and terms. You may need to use a dictionary or encyclopedia to find some of the answers.

Department of Economic Development —
  Tourism Division
Department of Natural Resources
Interpretive Center
Petroglyphs

Writing Activities

If a friend from another state were to visit you for a week, what would you like to show him or her? With the aid of a map, plan a week-long tour that would allow your visitor to see the most interesting and important sights in Minnesota. Explain why you would include these points of interest on your tour.

Is there a prominent landmark, an unusual physical structure, or any other important natural formation in your community? If there is, write a brief report about it and if possible, take pictures to illustrate your report.

CHAPTER TWENTY-THREE

WHO'S WHO IN
MINNESOTA HISTORY

What Makes a Person Famous?

Have you ever thought why we put the label "famous" on some people in our society? Is it because they manage to get their names in the newspapers a lot? Is it because they are wealthy? Is it because they are great speakers or writers or leaders? Perhaps these are reasons in some cases, but there is a more important reason. Let's see if we can find out what it might be.

There are many qualities that tend to make people famous in their society. Often people are not recognized for their achievements in their own lifetime, but many years later these achievements take on added meaning. A new generation, looking back through time, can judge the contributions of individuals or groups.

Famous is a word that must be measured in degrees. Some people are considered famous for one contribution or achievement, while others may be famous for many. Some people may be considered famous for a seemingly unimportant accomplishment and others for accomplishments of far greater importance. Perhaps the best criteria for judging a person's fame is to ask the question: "Did this person do anything in his or her lifetime that benefitted the society to which he or she belonged?" (Did he or she help people?)

The social group or society that we are concerned with here is that composed of Minnesota residents, past, present and future. The following list contains names of those who have contributed something toward making Minnesota a better place in which to live. There are many, many more names that could be added to this list, but space will permit only a few.

The people selected for this list come from all walks of life and represent contributions in nearly every field of endeavor. These people were (are) a part of Minnesota history and it is hoped that you will try to learn about as many of them as possible.

Antell, Will
Andrews, Christopher C.
Anderson, Mrs. Eugenie
Beltrami, Giacomo
Bishop, Harriet
Bonza, Pierre and George
Brown, Dr. Robert S.
Brown, Joseph R.
Buffington, Le Roy
Butler, Pierce
Babcock, Charles M.
Carver, Jonathan
Cass, Lewis
Catlin, George
Christiansen, F. Melius
Cooke, Jay
Colvill, William
Cretin, Joseph
Crosby, John
Davis, Edward W.
Davis, Cushman
Du Luth (Duluth), Daniel
Dowling, Michael
Donnelly, Ignatius
Densmore, Frances
Eastman, Dr. Charles A.
Faribault, Alexander
Faribault, Jean Baptiste
Featherstonehaugh, George
Flandrau, Charles
Fitzgerald, F. Scott
Folwell, William
Fjelde, Jacob

Ford, John D.
Francis, William T.
Galtier, Father Lucien
Gilbert, Cass
Goodhue, James
Goodrich, Aaron
Goodrich, Earle
Gideon, Peter
Gorman, Willis A.
Gould, Dr. Lawrence
Grimm, Wendelin
Hart, Hastings
Haecker, T. L.
Hauge, Lars
Heaton, Herbert
Hench, Dr. Phillip
Hennepin, Father
Hill, James J.
Horn, Esther B.
Humphrey, Hubert H.
Ireland, John
Jones, Frederick M.
Kelley, Oliver
Kendall, Dr. Edward
Kellogg, Frank B.
Kenny, Sister Elizabeth
Kittson, Norman
La Verendrye
Le Duc, William G.
La Croix, Edmund
Lea, Albert
Lewis, Sinclair
Lindbergh, Charles A.

Lillehei, Dr. C. Walton
Little Crow
Manfred, Frederick
Mayo, Will
Mayo, W. W.
Mayo, Charles
Mattson, Hans
Mayer, Frank B.
Martin, Homer D.
Manship, Paul
McKusick, John
McGhee, Frederick L.
Merritt, Leonidas
Mondale, Walter
Moran, George
Mower, Martin
Nelson, Knute
Nettleton, William
Neill, Edward
Nicollet, Joseph
Norelius, Erik
Northrup, Cyrus
Norstad, Gen. Lauris
Oberhoffer, Emil
Oliver, Henry W.
Olson, Floyd B.
Ormandy, Eugene
Other Day, John
Parrant, Pierre
Perrot
Pierz, Francis
Pike, Zebulon
Pond, Samuel and Gideon
Powers, Le Grand
Powderly, Terrance

Radisson
Ramsey, Alexander
Renville, Joseph
Rolette, Joseph
Rolvaag, O. E.
Rowan, Carl
Sanford, Maria
Sanborn, John
Schoolcraft, Henry
Schiller, Friedrich
Shields, Gen. James
Steele, Franklin
Stevens, Col. John
Stem, A. H.
Stassen, Harold
Stub, Dr. Hans
Swisshelm, Jane
Tyler, Alice
Van Cleve, Horatio
Van Sant, Samuel
Veblen, Thorstein
Verbruggen, Henry
Walker, T. B.
Wangensteen, Owen
Washburn, C. C.
Weyerhaeuser, Frederick
Whipple, Henry
Whitefield, Edwin
Wickman, Eric
Williams, William F.
Williamson, Thomas
Wheelock, Joseph
Windom, William
Zon, Dr. Raphael

The "One-a-Day" Research Plan

Try the "one-a-day" research plan for finding out about the people on this list. Make an effort to look up information on one of these people each day until you have gone completely through the list. Jot down a few brief notes that will tell you what each person is noted for.

Writing Activities

Divide a paper into three columns. In the first column list at least ten people from the list given in this chapter. Arrange the names in order in terms of the time or period in which they lived (or are living). In column two write the field or profession in which each person made his or her contribution (Government, Science, Education, Art, Music, etc.). In column three briefly tell what each person's contribution was.

NAME	FIELD OR PROFESSION	CONTRIBUTION

UNIT FIVE: MINNESOTA SINCE 1920

CHAPTER TWENTY-FOUR

THE 1920'S AND THE 1930'S

The 20th Century

The twentieth century saw many advances. Electric light replaced gas lights and kerosene lamps in Minnesota. Electric street cars ran in the Twin Cities, Winona, Duluth, St. Cloud and some other population centers. Medicine made great advances and gradually some of the worst diseases like diphtheria and tuberculosis were conquered. The German development of the internal combustion gasoline engine brought automobiles to our state. Slowly good roads were built.

The United States watched a tragic holocaust in Europe, World War I. In 1917, the United States of America was involved in the war, and Minnesota sent soldiers to fight for the allied side against Germany, Austria, Turkey and Bulgaria. Many Minnesotans were killed on the battlefields. At the same time, Spanish influenza struck the world and killed more people than the war. The disease spread to Minnesota and many people, young and old, died.

When young Minnesotans came home from the war, they had trouble adjusting to civilian life again. Some were still hurt or sick, so Minnesota built a veteran's hospital. It is near the edge of Fort Snelling today.

Several national changes came right after the war. One of these was a new national amendment that gave women the right to vote. Under the law of our land, from the very start of settlement, women had been treated as second class citizens, but Minnesota had done a little more than most states concerning the rights of women. Under our state law, women had been able to vote in school elections since the 1870's. This did not mean that they had equal rights, however. In industry, business, and education, they were paid less for doing the same work as men. The 19th amendment gave women the unlimited right to vote, but their long fight against other troubles had just started.

The Roaring Twenties

The Roaring Twenties was a turbulent period of American history. It was a period when major crimes, some of them in Minnesota, were in the national headlines. Part of the violence resulted from prohibition, which was enacted with the 18th amendment to the United States Constitution. Prohibition was the abolition of the manufacture and sale of brewed and distilled alcoholic beverages. The law prohibited alcohol except for medical and industrial purposes.

Some people in the 19th century thought alcohol was a great evil. They formed prohibition groups. They were determined to eliminate it from society. In the 20th century, they stepped up their campaign. In World War I, grain was in short supply, and was needed to make alcohol for the war effort. The eighteenth amendment outlawed alcoholic beverages in the entire United States. A representative from Minnesota, Andrew Volstead of Granite Falls, wrote the act that defined an intoxicating beverage.

By 1920, the breweries were closed, and there were no legal saloons to sell distilled beverages. People who were used to alcohol broke the law on a large scale. Much beer was brewed at home, and illegal stills could be found in many places. Outlaw gangsters saw a chance to make money out of illegal alcohol, and started importing it into the state and mass-producing it. It was often sold in "speakeasies" or "blind pigs", two names for illegal bars.

Chicago became a center for this illegal business. One often hears of Al Capone, the worst of the Prohibition-era gang leaders. Minnesota also produced a national Prohibition-era gangster, George Moran, who became one of the leading Chicago gangsters. Moran was finally caught, convicted for his crimes, and was sentenced to spend the rest of his life in a federal penitentiary in Kansas.

Cultural Changes in the 20's

Other changes came to Minnesota in the 1920's. The radio became a common appliance. Telephones, which were rare early in the century, became a common item in the home. Styles also changed. With the improved status of women, dress styles changed. Women for centuries had dressed in long, voluminous skirts. In the 1920's, much briefer clothes became popular.

Literature was advancing too. Sinclair Lewis, of Sauk Centre, had published a number of widely-read novels. F. Scott Fitzgerald became a national literary figure with such books as *Tender is the Night* and *The Great Gatsby*. Fitzgerald really caught the spirit of the 20's.

In the same period, Minnesota made a great advance in music. In the late 19th and early 20th century, Emil Oberhoffer, a German immigrant, started the Minneapolis Symphony Orchestra. A Dutchman, Henry Verbruggen, followed him, and the orchestra became one of the best in the nation, with a worldwide reputation.

Agriculture in the 20's

In Minnesota, as in other states, there was a period of prosperity on the surface. Jobs were plentiful in industry. There were more new cars around than ever before. In towns, where electricity was common, people had new appliances such as electric toasters, washing machines, refrigerators and radios. Many new homes and movie theaters were built. People were investing in stock market securities.

The farmers, however, did not enjoy this prosperity. Prices for farm products after World War I remained low.

Farmers saw the town prosper, but all too often did not share in it due to the low prices. The farmers had been working hard. They had advanced their methods of farming. They looked at the national and international picture and wondered why they were not getting help.

In Minnesota, as well as in other states in the Upper Midwest, a new movement was building. The farmers thought that the government should help them. In both Minnesota and North Dakota an organization was formed, called the Non-Partisan League. This was an organization that worked through the existing political parties. The political parties were supposed to help the farmers. The idea seemed good, but the power groups in the political parties gave the farmers little help. In Minnesota, the people formed a new party called the Farmer-Labor Party.

The new party was organized along socialist ideals. The party believed that the national government should control the railroads and help the farm prices, as well as protect the wages and rights of the working people. In spite of the fact that many people were afraid of this radical new political organization, it gained in popularity. The Farmer-Labor Party had an outstanding leader, Floyd B. Olson, a Twin Cities lawyer who understood both politics and economics. Olson was one of the early organizers of this new and strong party in Minnesota.

Floyd B. Olson

In the fall of 1929, the stock markets of New York crashed. This affected business all over the country, including Minnesota. Farm prices fell, then fell more. They fell until the cost of producing either grain or livestock was more than the products would bring in the market. Many small businesses went bankrupt, and some large companies as well. In the country millions of people were out of work. Unemployment was very high in Minnesota.

The 1930's

The economic problems of the country continued into the 1930's. These discouraging times saw Floyd B. Olson elected governor with strong Farmer-Labor backing in the legislature. On the national scene, Franklin Delano Roosevelt of the Democratic Party was elected president. Roosevelt, with Democratic backing in the Senate and the House of Representatives, took action at once. He straightened out the precarious banking situation. He and the Democrats put through a number of new programs to help the country.

Here in Minnesota, the unemployed found work on government relief programs. These relief workers built many roads and public buildings. A new program was started for the young unemployed. This was called the C.C.C., or Civilian Conservation Corps. Young men lived in camps, building roads, working on soil conservation projects, and working on forest and state park improvements. At that time one could see these camps all over the state, with most of them in the north forest areas. The government also had a program for college and university students called the N.Y.A., or National Youth Administration. Minnesota was helped by all of these programs.

Olson proved himself a very strong leader. When the farmers dragged their feet on paying back debts and devised ways of getting around them, Olson encouraged them to wait until the federal government began a program to re-finance farmers.

In 1934, Governor Olson had to face a real crisis. Hard times had eased up a little bit and the truckers of the Twin Cities area, who were paid only a little above a starvation wage by private employers, went on a strike for more money and better working conditions. In the past, laboring people had often been treated very badly, and their rights not recognized. The employers organized and fought with the laboring people. With riots increasing, Governor Olson called out the National Guard. He did not, however, use the Guard to break the strike; instead he used them to keep order and conducted marathon negotiations between employers and strikers. This method worked and the strike was settled.

Governor Olson helped the state in other ways. He led the legislature in helping public education, and in putting through a state income tax. Under the conservative Republicans of the 1920's, little had been done to improve highway conditions. Governor Olson promoted laws that built many new roads and established a Minnesota Highway Patrol.

By the time he died at a young age, of cancer, Governor Olson was a nationally known figure because of his outstanding leadership and work. Seldom has a political figure been missed so much. Governor Floyd B. Olson certainly ranks as one of Minnesota's great political leaders.

The Farmer-Labor Party held power for a few years and then the Republicans under the leadership of Harold Stassen regained control. Stassen was elected governor in 1939.

The farms, after terrible times in the early 1930's made a comeback. The government programs helped farmers hold on to their land and start farming again. Farm prices made a very slow comeback with government support. In addition to these problems, farmers had to face both drouth and grasshoppers in the early part of the thirties. No farmer would forget 1934, the worst year of drouth that the Upper Midwest had ever seen. Industry made a slow comeback, helped along by orders from Europe for war materials.

A special note might be taken of the Mississippi River. In the 1930's, the river was dredged and dammed from southern Illinois to the Twin Cities. Engineers created a system that included a nine-foot deep channel between the two points. Instead of individual steamboats, rivermen now used barges. A tow tug, or sometimes a steamer, would push six or even eight heavy steel barges.

River barge traffic below St. Paul

These barges brought many things to Minnesota. Coal was the major cargo. As they moved down river they were loaded chiefly with grain. Red Wing and Winona became important river ports.

The engineers dredged out the lower Minnesota River so that barges could get to Savage, Minnesota. Savage became an important grain shipping port. The dredging and dams on the rivers helped industry and agriculture alike.

Words to Know — Define these words and terms. You may need to use a dictionary or encyclopedia to find some of the answers.

C.C.C.

Channel

Dredged

Farmer-Labor Party

Prohibition

Prosperity

Names to Know — Identify these people.

F. Scott Fitzgerald

Sinclair Lewis

George Moran

Floyd B. Olson

Andrew Volstead

Writing Activities

Write brief answers to the following questions:

1. What led to the formation of the Farmer-Labor Party?
2. Which amendment to the United States Constitution gave women the right to vote?
3. What helped the development of a new Mississippi River transportation system in the 1930's?
4. What programs advocated by Governor Floyd B. Olson helped the state?

CHAPTER TWENTY-FIVE

THE 1940'S

The state of Minnesota had not entirely recovered from the Great Depression by 1940. There were still some Civilian Conservation Corps camps in the state, and there were still some older people working on government relief projects.

In spite of that, there were many signs of economic recovery. Many of the one-time unemployed had gone back to work in industry. Companies like Minneapolis Moline were making farm machinery. The Ford assembly plant in St. Paul was putting together many automobiles. Smaller factories scattered through the state were beginning to grow. Due to the needs created by the war in Europe, the iron mines were increasing production.

Thanks to the overhaul of agriculture by the Roosevelt administration, Minnesota farmers were more secure than they had been for a long time. Minnesota grain milling was doing well. Tremendous amounts of grain were moved through both Minneapolis and Duluth. Flour, breakfast food and stock food were manufactured in quantity.

In the 40's a popular activity was to go on an excursion trip down the river. Fancy steamboats would pull into a port, like St. Paul, Red Wing or Winona, and advertise their excursion. The trip would last for several hours. A deck of the boat would be converted into a dance floor, and an orchestra was provided so passengers could dance by the moonlight.

Life was better in Minnesota during the 40's than it had been in the Depression. But people were worried about the war in Europe. Adolph Hitler had become dictator of Germany. He had fooled Great Britain and France for years, but when he invaded Poland in the fall of 1939, they went to war with Germany. The people of Minnesota listened to the news when Germany conquered most of France and western Europe in 1940. President Roosevelt declared an unlimited emergency in the United States in the fall of 1940. A draft of young men for the military was implemented. Minnesotans of military age were required to register for the draft.

This action brought about a change for the state. Fort Snelling, in the Twin Cities, was greatly enlarged to be used as a reception center for new army men, and in the winter of 1940–41 some men were trained for the infantry there. Government contracts were secured by Minnesota industries for the production of war materials. This helped our economy and increased employment. The military planning and preparation increased as thousands of men were inducted into the army at Fort Snelling and sent to various training camps. Meanwhile the war had become more horrible. Germany tried to defeat Great Britain by air strikes. They pushed into southeastern Europe. Minnesotans followed the war by newspapers and radios.

A new problem arose when Japan (a power in the Pacific) and the United States began arguing over oil supplies. Negotiations were under way when Japan, without warning, bombed Pearl Harbor and destroyed a large part of the American Pacific fleet. Most Minnesotans who lived during this time will not forget that day, December 7, 1941.

The reaction by the United States was swift: we were at war with Japan. Germany then declared war on the United States. Minnesotans went to all parts of Europe. The war with Germany lasted until the spring of 1945, when Germany was defeated. The war in the Pacific came to an end in the late summer of 1945, after the dropping of two atomic bombs on Japan.

Much had happened in Minnesota during the war. More war material was made than ever before. A shipyard was built at Savage, Minnesota. Small flat-bottomed ships for landing soldiers on beaches were built there. They were then navigated down the Minnesota and Mississippi Rivers to the ocean and sent to the fighting fronts. The army built a camp and organized a Japanese intelligence school at Savage. American-born Japanese were trained as interpreters there. With the pressure of the war, more men were drafted than any time before, and many thousands were inducted at Fort Snelling and shipped to training camps around the nation.

When the war ended, the people of Minnesota were relieved. It had been a busy time and a sad time for many. Many Minnesotans who had gone into the army never came back. Some were killed in the Pacific, in Africa, in Europe. Many others were permanently wounded or disabled because of the war. Others were sick in spirit from the terrible things they had seen and lived through.

The United States government started a program called the G.I. Bill of Rights during the 1940's. The bill provided funds for veterans who wanted to go to college or vocational school. The University of Minnesota, the state colleges, and the private colleges of Minnesota filled their student bodies with former soldiers, sailors and marines.

Agriculture made great strides after the war. New machinery was made available to farmers. Profits increased with the removal of wartime restrictions. Modern scientific farming brought greater yields than ever before.

Industry improved, too. There had been a limited amount of civilian goods produced during the war. Now they were made in abundance. Automobile dealers had long waiting lists of customers who wanted to buy the first available new cars. With the tremendous demand for iron to keep the eastern steel mills busy, the laborers on the Iron Range worked long hours.

In politics, Minnesota was active during this period. Harold Stassen was re-elected to a second term as governor. He did not finish his second term, however, because he resigned to serve as an officer in the United States Navy. He was succeeded by Edward Thye. Hubert Humphrey was mayor of Minneapolis during this time. He managed to bring the Democrats and the Farmer-Laborites together to form a new party known as the Democratic Farmer-Labor Party, or D.F.L. Humphrey was then elected senator for Minnesota.

In the late 1940's, governor Luther Youngdahl was probably the outstanding leader. Under his leadership a very active social program was formed, called the Youth Conservation Commission, and many needed reforms were made in the social welfare field. The reforms in the state hospitals were much appreciated by Minnesota people.

Words to Know — Define these words and terms. You may need to use a dictionary or encyclopedia to find some of the answers.

Democratic Farmer-Labor Party

G.I. Bill of Rights

Military draft

Names to Know — Identify these people.

Hubert Humphrey

Luther Youngdahl

Writing Activities

Write brief answers to the following questions:

1. What helped the economy of Minnesota in the 1940's?
2. What ways were Minnesotans involved in World War Two?

CHAPTER TWENTY-SIX

THE 1950'S

In the 1950's Minnesota continued its post-war prosperity boom. Incomes were higher than they had ever been in history. Unemployment was very low.

Agriculture probably made the fastest march forward. Scientific agriculture was now more than a name, with the tremendous research conducted by the United States Department of Agriculture, and the local research by the University of Minnesota School of Agriculture. The School of Agriculture started a new school, the School of Veterinary Medicine. Now men and women who wanted to become veterinarians need not get their education elsewhere, but could study in St. Paul.

Scientists studied animal nutrition in detail. The findings of the scientists were used by the feed manufacturers and new feeds of many types were soon on the market. Now people learned how to get hogs, cattle and sheep up to slaughter age in record time, and how to produce animals with better cuts of meat than ever before.

Progress was not confined to feeding. The breeders used scientific selection to produce animals that would grow faster and make better use of the feed. New breeds were imported from Europe and established here.

It was not only the production of meat animals that was emphasized, for dairy animals were studied and improved upon also. Old-fashioned milking techniques were replaced with sanitary milking parlors. Cows were put on platforms and milked with machines. The milk was piped into stainless steel cooling tanks and hauled away regularly in sanitary trucks. Bigger and better creameries were built, and Minnesota produced more butter than any state in the Union. Cheese manufacturing increased and it too became an important export of our state.

New varieties of corn and wheat were grown in Minnesota in the 1950's.

Scientists at the University of Minnesota had learned the techniques of producing hybrid corn. Minnesota became a major producer of seed corn, and the corn from hybrid varieties far out-yielded the older varieties of the past. New varieties of wheat were grown, and the yield was far better. Wheat from the Red River Valley and other parts of western Minnesota poured down to the shipping points. New varieties of barley were raised. These varieties were better for malting, the first step in making barley into beer. Hog production and sheep production expanded at this time.

Life in Minnesota experienced other changes. New roads and highways were built. More automobiles were on the road than ever before, and bus use increased. Newer, more comfortable buses cut deeply into the passenger traffic which was once carried by the local railroads. Big trucks, especially diesel semi-trailers, started to compete with railroad freight traffic. These trucks and buses added to the traffic on the road.

In homes, people readily accepted the television set. Television had been developed in various places before the Second World War, but did not come into production until after the war. The 1950's saw the establishment of large television stations. People of Minnesota were fascinated with a machine that brought both a moving and talking picture into their homes. These sets were expensive and led rapidly to a big business. Service and repair were required, which added new jobs.

At the end of the Second World War there had been a tremendous market for home appliances. In the 1950's this market expanded. Electricity was now available to remote rural areas, and appliances like refrigerators, toasters and vacuum sweepers were in demand. One appliance had a tremendous sale in rural areas. The refrigerator manufacturers made a large refrigerator called a deep freeze. This machine froze meat, fruit and vegetables, and kept them frozen indefinitely. Farmers now did not have to preserve so much of their meat by salting, smoking and canning. Now they could freeze cuts of meat and have fresh meat the year around.

The year 1959 saw the opening of the St. Lawrence Seaway. The seaway was a channel between the Great Lakes and the upper reaches of the St. Lawrence River to Montreal. Proposals for this had been made years before but had been blocked by eastern interests. Now ocean-going ships could come to Duluth. Many did, and the harbor of Duluth-Superior became one of the greatest grain shipping ports in the world.

Duluth Harbor—gateway to the world

In politics, Senator Hubert Humphrey made national headlines with his continuing campaign for human rights for blacks. After the Civil War, laws had been passed to free the blacks from slavery, and give them the right to vote. The conservative whites in the South had blocked these laws for almost a hundred years. The courageous president of the United States in the late 1940's, Harry Truman, had started a movement to allow the blacks more than just token human rights. Humphrey had followed this idea, and with dynamic leadership in the Senate, had started a series of acts that in time would make the blacks full citizens. Humphrey was criticized by conservative southerners and northerners alike, but he continued his push for civil rights legislation.

A new congressman, formerly a college professor, Eugene McCarthy, was elected to Congress and followed the liberal line of action. From Minnesota's Iron Range, Congressman Blatnik was also known as a liberal. No one in Congress understood the laboring class better than he did. Blatnik could be counted on at all times to help the poor and the people who had been overlooked by the government. Early in the 1950's a Minneapolis attorney, Orville Freeman, lost in the governor's race to C. Elmer Anderson, but he was later elected governor in 1954.

Words to Know — Define these words and terms. You may need to use a dictionary or encyclopedia to find some of the answers.
Hybrid corn
St. Lawrence Seaway
Veterinary medicine

Names to Know — Identify these people.
Congressman Blatnik
Hubert Humphrey

Writing Activities
   Write brief answers to the following questions:
1. What were some of the advances in agriculture in the 1950's?
2. What made Duluth an important port city in the late 50's?

CHAPTER TWENTY-SEVEN

THE 1960'S

Minnesota agriculture advanced again in the 1960's. Farm machinery became more sophisticated and diesel tractors were starting to become common on farms. The steel-wheeled tractor became a museum piece. Modern tractors rolled on rubber tires with liquid in them to give greater weight for traction. The old-fashioned threshing machine was seen only now and then. New combines, some of them built in Minnesota, cut the small-grain crops. In the Red River Valley, where the wheat fields were really large, huge self-propelled machines worked long hours in harvest time to cut the grain.

Farmers were better organized than they had been in the past. Back in the 1920's, a bill called the Capper-Volstead Act had given farmers the right to form cooperatives. A liberal farm organization, the Farmers Union, had been active among the farmers. The farmers who belonged to this organization held regular meetings in which farm problems were discussed, but more important, they formed farm union cooperatives, both for buying and selling. In this way they had an advantage in buying everything from tractor fuel to farm machinery.

The selling program of the cooperative started modestly, but by the 1960's had grown into one of the biggest farm selling organizations in Minnesota. The organization, which covered the entire Northwest, was called the Grain Terminal Association or G.T.A. This amounted to a series of grain elevators in the small towns, with a large terminal in the Twin Cities. Under the able leadership of M. W. Thatcher, the G.T.A. became very strong, and has proved of great help to the farmers.

Other farm cooperatives, under the leadership of the Midland Cooperatives, formed units around the state. A

Rubber-tired tractor

Steel-tired tractor

very conservative farm organization, called the Farm Bureau, had begun in these same years. The impact of these farm organizations in politics was important. Hubert Humphrey, as senator, did all that he could for farmers and listened to the liberal farm organizations. In general, this period of time in Minnesota was relatively prosperous with fair to high farm prices and much employment.

Early day threshing machines were replaced by huge combines.

More appliances were bought than ever before. There was a continuing housing boom. This was especially true in the large urban areas. The more prosperous middle classes tended to leave the older sections of the cities and move to the suburbs. One could travel in these suburbs and see new houses with double-car garages, well-kept lawns and shrubbery, and gardens. It became popular for a family to have two or more cars; a car to drive to work, a station wagon or a van to do the shopping with, and sometimes a four-wheel drive recreational vehicle.

It might be said that the standards of health in the state reached a height far beyond anything reached before. There were more hospitals and more clinics. People experienced improved dental health; and children who would have otherwise had crooked teeth were sent to a specialist called an orthodontist, who put teeth-straightening braces in the children's mouths.

More immunizations were given in schools than ever before, and childhood diseases were greatly reduced. For example, in the early part of the century polio or infantile paralysis had caused great trouble among the children of the state. Many who survived polio were left crippled. Now immunization made such diseases a thing of the past.

At the start of the 60's, the president of the United States, John Kennedy, ordered a blockade around Cuba when the Soviet Union moved nuclear missiles onto the island. The Soviets backed down and removed the missiles. Another foreign involvement caused much bitterness during this period, when the United States became involved in the Viet Nam War. The United States again drafted young men of military age. Many of them served in Viet Nam and came home wounded. Many never came home. Students at the University of Minnesota reflected the bitterness of the entire country in regard to the United States participation in the war, by staging demonstrations against the war.

President Kennedy was assassinated, and Lyndon Johnson became president. He served out Kennedy's term and was elected again. President Johnson strongly supported the civil rights legislation that Senator Humphrey had been involved with, and for the first time in the United States, blacks were allowed the rights of full-fledged citizens.

On the state level in the early 60's, the political competition between the Democratic Farmer-Labor Party and the Republicans was close. Karl Rolvaag won a disputed election over C. Elmer Anderson, but neither party had a large majority of the state's voters. Republican Harold Levander became the governor in the mid 1960's. Hubert Humphrey was now vice-president of the United States. He had been elected as a running mate for Lyndon Johnson. An able speaker, Humphrey had become one of the best-known Minnesotans in history and was in great demand as a speaker around the nation. Humphrey was being recognized as one of our nation's true leaders.

Biographies were written about Hubert Humphrey. His life story is interesting. He was born in the tiny village of Wallace, South Dakota, the son of a druggist. He grew up in Doland, South Dakota, where his father had a pharmacy. During the Depression he went to the Denver College of Pharmacy and became a licensed pharmacist. For several years he worked as a pharmacist in the family store, then in the larger South Dakota town of Huron. He went on to get his master's degree in political science in the south. He came back north, settled in Minneapolis, and taught college in the area. He was elected mayor of Minneapolis, and from there went on to the political career mentioned earlier.

Words to Know — Define these words and terms. You may need to use a dictionary or encyclopedia to find some of the answers.

Combine

Cooperative

Grain Terminal Association

Immunization

Suburbs

Urban

Names to Know — Identify these people.

Lyndon Johnson

John Kennedy

Writing Activities

Write brief answers to the following questions:

1. What changes occurred in agriculture during this period?
2. What reduced the occurrence of many childhood diseases?

CHAPTER TWENTY-EIGHT

THE 1970'S

As it had for the two previous decades, agriculture in Minnesota continued its growth in the 1970's. The machinery was better than ever before. Chemicals were widely used. Insecticides that were more effective than the relatively simple chemicals of the past helped the farmers produce more. Truck farming spread until Minnesota became one of the largest producers of sweet corn and peas for canning and freezing.

Sugar beets had long been grown in the Minnesota River Valley and nearby areas. Large new sugar factories were built in the Red River Valley and western Minnesota. Many thousands of acres that had been planted with other crops were now planted with sugar beets. Sugar beets are not as easy to grow as corn, and they require a lot of hand labor. Mexican-Americans came to Minnesota to work in the sugar beet fields. Housing these migrant workers became a problem for the sugar beet producer.

Another new crop was domestic sunflowers. These had been used for a long time to make a roasted product that people ate like candy. Now it was found that sunflowers were an important source of cooking oil.

Great progress was made in poultry farming. Turkey production was up and Minnesota led the nation in the production of these large birds. Egg production was no longer the simple business of hens and eggs in the old-fashioned laying house. Hens were scientifically bred for maximum egg production. They were housed about six in a cage, and their eggs would drop through the bottom of the cage. The eggs were carried away on rolling belts to centrally located processing places, where they were graded and packed. The production of meat chickens improved; chickens grew to butchering age in an amazingly short time.

During the 70's there arose a period of general awareness concerning pollution. During this time much was done in Minnesota to insure that the air was not badly polluted from the smoke of industrial concerns. The federal government forced automobile manufacturers to add pollution control devices on the exhaust systems of cars, and to make cars that used unleaded gasoline. Many sewage disposal plants were rebuilt so that they would not pollute the rivers and lakes.

With the awareness of pollution came an awareness of ecology. In the past much land had been drained for farmland. Some of the drained land was productive, some was not. Many Minnesotans began to feel that too much land had been drained and the ground water systems were changing. A slow run-off indicated that the land was operating normally, but when land was drained, fast run-off occurred. This fast run-off caused serious floods.

In the hilly southeastern corner of the state many of the hills had been cleared and the land was farmed recklessly. In time, rain washed the topsoil away. Thousands of acres were abandoned. In other parts of the state, farmers began contour farming to reduce erosion.

Contour farming

The television industry grew in the 70's. Color television was introduced. Advertising on television increased. More people spent more hours in front of their sets, and educators criticized parents for allowing their children to watch television instead of reading or studying.

Another memorable change in the 70's was the emergence of the energy crisis. This affected every household in the state as fuel oil prices rose from less than thirty cents a gallon to around a dollar a gallon within ten years. Wood heaters and furnaces became popular and the supply of wood became a big business.

Every Minnesotan became familiar with the Watergate investigation of President Richard Nixon. Nixon resigned in the 70's; he is the only man in the history of the United States to resign the presidency. Nixon's successor, Gerald Ford, pardoned him. Another major event in national politics was the ending of one of the most unpopular wars in our nation's history, the Viet Nam War.

A long-time senator from Minnesota, Walter Mondale, became vice-president of the United States. In the decade of the 70's, the Republican and Democratic Farmer-Labor Parties both grew in popularity and in 1979, Republican Albert Quie became governor of our state. Hubert Humphrey taught at the University of Minnesota, was elected senator again, and died while in office from cancer. He may well be remembered as one of Minnesota's greatest figures.

Words to Know — Define these words and terms. You may need to use a dictionary or encyclopedia to find some of the answers.

Ecology

Insecticides

Pollution

Sugar beets

Names to Know — Identify these people.

Walter Mondale

Writing Activities

Write brief answers to the following questions:

1. What crops gained new importance in the 1970's?
2. What measures were taken during the 70's to reduce pollution?

DATA AND RESOURCE SECTION

Statistical Information

Minnesota became the 32nd state in 1858.

Name: Derived from Dakota Indian words meaning "Sky-tinted water".

Capital: St. Paul.

State Motto: L'Etoile du Nord (The Star of the North).

State Fish: Walleye.

State Flower: Showy pink and white Lady's-slipper.

State Bird: Loon.

State Tree: Norway or Red Pine.

State Song: "Hail Minnesota!"

Area: 84,068 square miles. Ranks 12th among all states in size. 4,059 square miles consist of water.

Length: 406 miles.

Width: 358 miles.

Highest Point: 2,301 feet above sea level at Eagle Mountain, south of Brule Lake in Cook County.

Lowest Point: 602 feet above sea level on shore of Lake Superior.

Average Mean Temperature: 44 degrees.

Summer Mean Temperature: 70 degrees.

Annual Precipitation: 24.71 inches.

Annual Snowfall: 42.3 inches.

Number of Lakes: 12,034 (ten acres or more).

Largest Lake: Red Lake (440 square miles).

Navigable Rivers: Mississippi, Minnesota, St. Croix, Rainy, St. Louis, Red Rivers.

Main River Systems: Mississippi, Minnesota, and Red Rivers.

Water flows in three directions — to Hudson Bay, to the Atlantic Ocean, and to the Gulf of Mexico.

Source of the Mississippi River: Itasca State Park.

Minnesota State Seal—What does it symbolize?

Minnesota State Flag

Minnesota State Fish—the Walleye

Minnesota State Flower—Showy Lady Slipper

Minnesota State Tree—the Norway Pine

Minnesota State Bird—the Loon

Population Statistics

Population of State: 4,077,148 (1980 census).
Population Growth: 7% (1970 to 1980).
Median Age of Population: 29.2 years.
Largest Cities: Minneapolis — 370,951. St. Paul — 270,230.

COUNTY POPULATION

County	1980 Census	County	1980 Census
Aitkin	13,404	Freeborn	36,329
Anoka	195,998	Goodhue	38,749
Becker	29,336	Grant	7,171
Beltrami	30,982	Hennepin	941,411
Benton	25,187	Houston	19,617
Big Stone	7,716	Hubbard	14,098
Blue Earth	52,314	Isanti	23,600
Brown	28,645	Itasca	43,006
Carlton	29,936	Jackson	13,690
Carver	37,046	Kanabec	12,161
Cass	21,050	Kandiyohi	36,763
Chippewa	14,941	Kittson	6,672
Chisago	25,717	Koochiching	17,571
Clay	49,327	Lac qui Parle	10,592
Clearwater	8,761	Lake	13,043
Cook	4,092	Lake of the Woods	37,764
Cottonwood	14,854	Le Sueur	23,434
Crow Wing	41,722	Lincoln	8,207
Dakota	194,111	Lyon	25,207
Dodge	14,773	McLeod	29,657
Douglas	27,839	Mahnomen	5,535
Faribault	19,714	Marshall	13,027
Fillmore	21,930	Martin	24,687

Meeker	20,594	Roseau	12,574
Mille Lacs	18,430	St. Louis	222,229
Morrison	29,311	Scott	43,784
Mower	40,390	Sherburne	29,908
Murray	11,507	Sibley	15,448
Nicollet	26,929	Stearns	108,161
Nobles	21,840	Steele	30,328
Norman	9,379	Stevens	11,322
Olmsted	91,971	Swift	12,920
Otter Tail	51,937	Todd	24,991
Pennington	15,258	Traverse	5,542
Pine	19,871	Wabasha	19,335
Pipestone	11,690	Wadena	14,192
Polk	34,844	Waseca	18,448
Pope	11,657	Washington	113,571
Ramsey	459,784	Watonwan	12,361
Red Lake	5,471	Wilkin	8,382
Redwood	19,341	Winona	46,256
Renville	20,401	Wright	58,962
Rice	46,087	Yellow Medicine	13,653
Rock	10,703		

Forest Products of Minnesota

The forests of Minnesota are a valuable natural resource. They provide a scenic and protective environment for both people and wildlife, and also provide cash crop products. The value of forest products harvested in the state exceeds $650 million annually.

INCOME FROM FOREST PRODUCTS (1977)

Pulpwood	$579,344,290
Lumber, ties, logs, bolts	26,200,020
Christmas trees	10,850,000
Posts, poles, piling	4,828,580
Fuelwood	8,728,500
Specialty wood products	13,531,300
By-products, mill residue	14,711,960

MINNESOTA PULP, PAPER, AND FIBERBOARD INDUSTRY

Mill and office employees	9,360
Payroll and fringe benefits	$ 171,438,830
Total value of products	$ 659,325,930

ACTIVE WOOD PULP MILLS IN MINNESOTA

Company	Location
Blandin Paper Co.	Grand Rapids
Hennepin Paper Co.	Little Falls
Boise Cascade Corp.	International Falls
Northwest Paper Co.	Cloquet
Superwood Corp.	Bemidji
St. Regis Paper Co.	Sartell
Superwood Corp.	Duluth
Hoerner Waldorf Corp.	St. Paul
Conwed Corp.	Cloquet

Source: U.S. Department of Agriculture; North Central Forest Experiment Station.

Agriculture in Minnesota

Minnesota ranks among the nation's top ten states in the production of major farm products. It ranks second in total crop tonnage, third in all acres harvested, and fifth in total cash farm income. Minnesota leads the nation in the production of sweet corn for processing, sugar beets, and turkeys.

Minnesota has been blessed with many favorable assets that have made agriculture a major contributor to the state's economy. These assets are:

The People:

Hard-working, industrious and with varied agricultural backgrounds.

Topography:

Elevations of the state range between 602 and 2,301 feet above sea level. The average elevation is approximately 1,200 feet. The various sections of the state may be described as follows:

Red River Valley — Nearly level.

North Central — Rolling, many lakes.

Central — Undulating to rolling, with many lakes.

Northeast — Rough and stony.

Southern — Undulating to rolling.

Southeastern — Gently rolling to steep.

Soil:

Minnesota, along with Iowa and Illinois, has the largest acreage of excellent soil in the nation. The soils of the state may be described as follows:

North Central and Northeastern — Light-colored, medium textured, with many peat and sandy areas.

Mississippi River area — Dark soil.

Red River area — Heavy, dark clay.

Balance of state — Dark prairie soils, mostly heavy loams with clay loam subsoil.

Climate:

The growing season in Minnesota varies from an average of 160 days in southeastern areas to an average of 90 days in the northeast. Average annual precipitation varies from 19 inches in northwestern Minnesota, to 32 inches in the southeast and northeast. About 60% of this moisture comes between May and September.

Temperatures vary about 10 degrees, on the average, between the northern and southern borders. January is the coldest month, and July is the hottest.

Land in Farms — 30.3 million acres.
Number of Farms — 104,000.
Average Size of Farms — 291 acres.
Cash Receipts from Farm Marketing — $5.8 billion.

ANIMALS ON FARMS

Cattle and calves	3,650,000
Milk cows	850,000
Hogs	4,100,000
Sheep and lambs	255,000
Chickens	11,920,000
Turkeys	22,238,000

CROP ACREAGE (1978)

	Acres
Corn	6,190,000
Wheat	2,776,000
Oats	1,830,000
Barley	1,050,000
Rye	98,000
Flax	142,000
Soybeans	4,060,000
Hay	3,060,000
Potatoes	78,000
Sugar Beets	263,000
Sunflowers	683,000

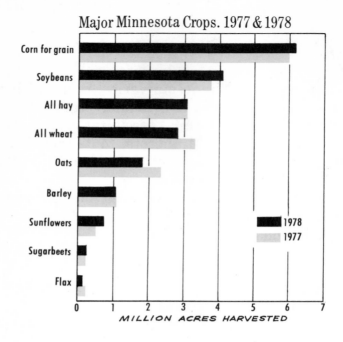

Major Minnesota Crops. 1977 & 1978

- Corn for grain
- Soybeans
- All hay
- All wheat
- Oats
- Barley
- Sunflowers
- Sugarbeets
- Flax

■ 1978
▨ 1977

0 1 2 3 4 5 6 7

MILLION ACRES HARVESTED

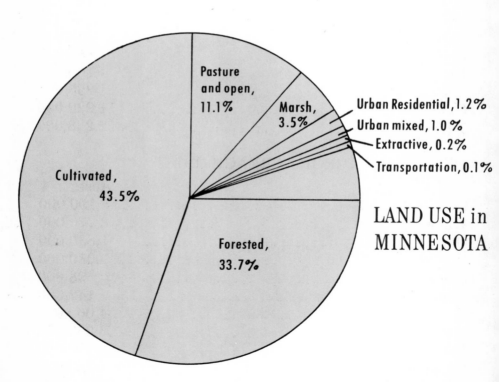

Pasture and open, 11.1%

Marsh, 3.5%

Urban Residential, 1.2%

Urban mixed, 1.0 %

Extractive, 0.2%

Transportation, 0.1%

Cultivated, 43.5%

Forested, 33.7%

LAND USE in MINNESOTA

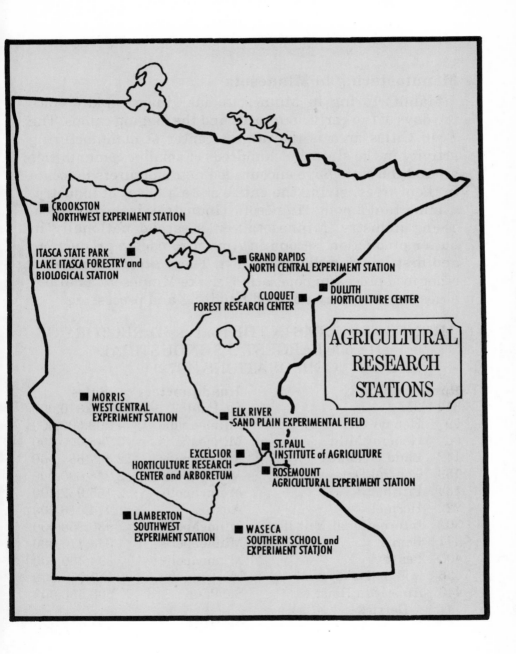

CROOKSTON
NORTHWEST EXPERIMENT STATION

ITASCA STATE PARK
LAKE ITASCA FORESTRY and
BIOLOGICAL STATION

GRAND RAPIDS
NORTH CENTRAL EXPERIMENT STATION

DULUTH
HORTICULTURE CENTER

CLOQUET
FOREST RESEARCH CENTER

AGRICULTURAL
RESEARCH
STATIONS

MORRIS
WEST CENTRAL
EXPERIMENT STATION

ELK RIVER
SAND PLAIN EXPERIMENTAL FIELD

ST. PAUL
INSTITUTE of AGRICULTURE

EXCELSIOR
HORTICULTURE RESEARCH
CENTER and ARBORETUM

ROSEMOUNT
AGRICULTURAL EXPERIMENT STATION

LAMBERTON
SOUTHWEST
EXPERIMENT STATION

WASECA
SOUTHERN SCHOOL and
EXPERIMENT STATION

Manufacturing in Minnesota

Manufacturing in Minnesota has grown rapidly since the days of the early flour mills and the logging camps. The Twin Cities area is the largest center of manufacturing activity in the state, but hundreds of smaller communities around the state have encouraged manufacturers to locate in their areas, giving the entire state a flavor of industry.

Important among Minnesota's industries is the food processing industry. Minnesota ranks second nationally in butter production, second in American cheese production, and first in dry milk production. These areas, along with other food processing operations make Minnesota a national leader in the area of food handling and processing.

MINNESOTA FIRMS IN THE FORTUNE DIRECTORY OF THE 500 LARGEST U.S. INDUSTRIAL CORPORATIONS (1979)

Rank	Company	Headquarters	Sales
51	3M	St. Paul	$5,440,370,000
79	Honeywell	Minneapolis	4,209,500,000
90	General Mills	Minneapolis	3,745,000,000
142	Land O' Lakes	Minneapolis	2,442,681,000
159	Control Data	Minneapolis	2,248,600,000
164	Pillsbury	Minneapolis	2,165,982,000
222	Hormel	Austin	1,414,016,000
302	International Multifoods	Minneapolis	930,968,000
377	Bemis	Minneapolis	648,475,000
400	Peavey	Minneapolis	594,430,000
436	Midland Cooperatives	Minneapolis	517,953,000
440	American Hoist & Derrick	St. Paul	508,556,000
467	Economics Laboratory	St. Paul	464,367,000

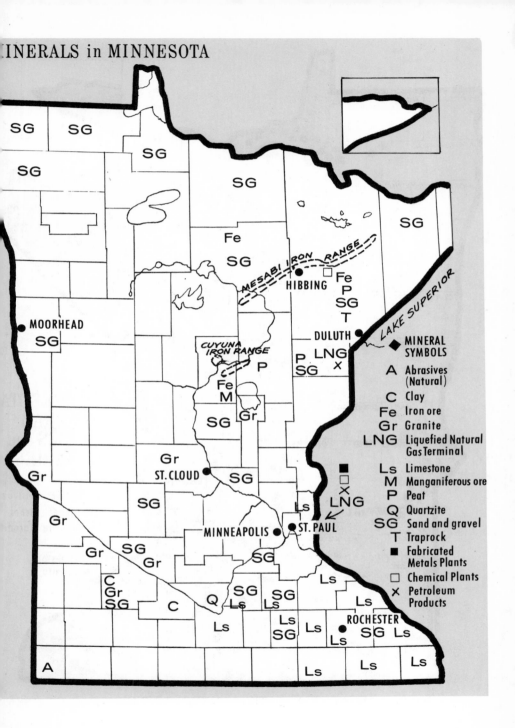

MINERALS in MINNESOTA

SG   SG

SG   SG

        SG

            SG

                SG

            Fe
            SG   MESABI IRON RANGE

                        HIBBING   Fe
                                   P
                                   SG
                                   T

MOORHEAD   DULUTH   LAKE SUPERIOR
SG   LNG   MINERAL
            CUYUNA   X   SYMBOLS
            IRON RANGE   P
                P   SG   A   Abrasives
            Fe   (Natural)
            M   C   Clay
                                        Fe   Iron ore
            SG   Gr   Gr   Granite
                                        LNG Liquefied Natural
                                             Gas Terminal
        Gr
        ST. CLOUD   SG   Ls   Limestone
                            X   M   Manganiferous ore
                            LNG   P   Peat
Gr   SG   Q   Quartzite
                            Ls   SG   Sand and gravel
Gr   St. PAUL   T   Traprock
        Gr   MINNEAPOLIS   ■   Fabricated
        Gr   Metals Plants
        C   SG   SG   Ls   □   Chemical Plants
        Gr   SG   X   Petroleum
        SG   Q   Ls SG   Ls   Products
                    Ls   Ls   ROCHESTER
                Ls   SG   Ls   SG   Ls
A   Ls   Ls   Ls

345

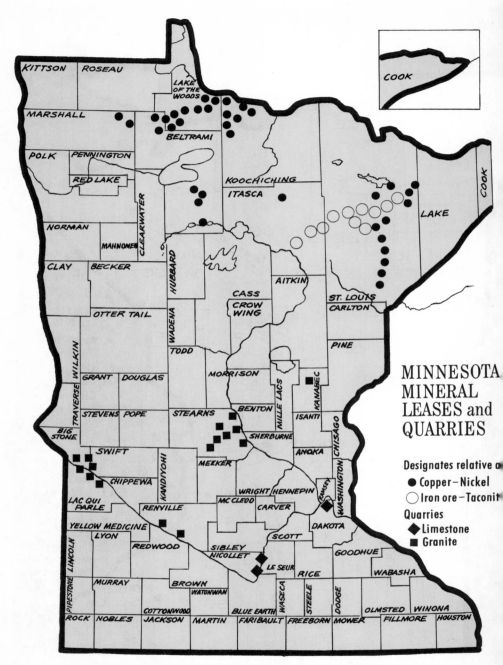

MINNESOTA MINERAL LEASES and QUARRIES

Designates relative a
- ● Copper–Nickel
- ○ Iron ore–Taconit
Quarries
- ◆ Limestone
- ■ Granite

KITTSON ROSEAU LAKE OF THE WOODS
MARSHALL BELTRAMI
POLK PENNINGTON
RED LAKE
KOOCHICHING ITASCA LAKE COOK
NORMAN CLEARWATER
MAHNOMEN HUBBARD
CLAY BECKER WADENA CASS CROW WING AITKIN ST. LOUIS CARLTON
OTTER TAIL TODD MORRISON PINE
WILKIN GRANT DOUGLAS MILLE LACS KANABEC
TRAVERSE STEVENS POPE STEARNS BENTON ISANTI CHISAGO
BIG STONE SWIFT SHERBURNE ANOKA WASHINGTON
CHIPPEWA KANDIYOHI MEEKER WRIGHT HENNEPIN RAMSEY
LAC QUI PARLE RENVILLE MC LEOD CARVER DAKOTA
YELLOW MEDICINE LYON REDWOOD SIBLEY NICOLLET SCOTT GOODHUE
PIPESTONE LINCOLN MURRAY BROWN WATONWAN LE SUER RICE WABASHA
ROCK NOBLES JACKSON MARTIN BLUE EARTH WASECA FARIBAULT STEELE FREEBORN DODGE MOWER OLMSTED WINONA FILLMORE HOUSTON

COOK

SOURCE: MINNESOTA STATE PLANNING AGENCY

Minnesota Taconite Plants

Company	Annual pellet capacity thousand long tons	Estimated investment thousand dollars	Employ- ment
Butler Taconite	2,650	66,000	600
Erie Mining Co.	10,500	350,000	2,900
Eveleth Mines	6,000	320,000	1,250
Hibbing Taconite Co.	8,100	350,000	1,050
Inland Steel Mining Co.	2,600	150,000	450
Minntac (United States Steel Corp.)	18,500	425,000	4,050
National Steel Pellet Plant . .	5,800	240,000	1,000
Reserve Mining Co.	10,800	350,000	3,000
TOTAL	64,950	2,251,000	14,525

Source: Minnesota Department of Natural Resources, U.S. Bureau of Mines.

TACONITE PLANTS in MINNESOTA

Mt. Iron
Chisholm
Nashwauk
Keewatin
Grand Rapids
Virginia
Eveleth
Ely
Babbit
Hoyt Lakes
Silver Bay
LAKE SUPERIOR
Duluth
53

1 Butler Taconite
2 National Steel
3 Hibbing Taconite
4 Minntac
5 Eveleth Taconite
6 Inland Steel
7 Erie Mining
8 Reserve Mining

Key:
■ -Taconite Plants

347

Iron ore is Minnesota's most important mineral, accounting for more than 90% of the total production value.
Value of Mineral Production: $2,062,468,000
Value of Iron Ore Production: $1,960,245,000

Transportation in Minnesota

Airports: 141 publicly owned airports and 16 privately owned public use airports in the state; 11 seaplane bases that are open to the public.

Major Airport: Minneapolis-St. Paul International.

Airlines: 10 airlines offer passenger/freight service.

Railroads: 8 Class I carriers; 7200 miles of track (subject to change in AMTRAK system).

Motor Freight: 2,750 carriers based in state.

Freight Center: Minnesota ranks 6th in nation.

Inland World Seaport: Duluth.

Major River Cargo Port: St. Paul.

AMTRAK INTERCITY RAIL PASSENGER ROUTES

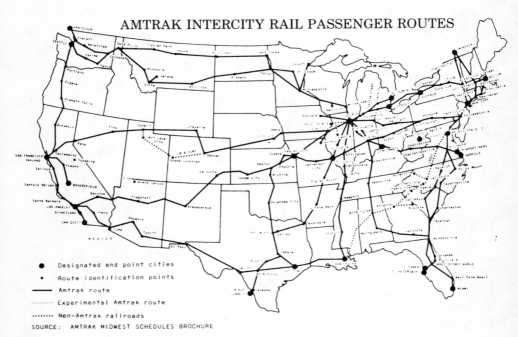

- ● Designated end point cities
- • Route identification points
- ─── Amtrak route
- ······· Experimental Amtrak route
- ········ Non-Amtrak railroads

SOURCE: AMTRAK MIDWEST SCHEDULES BROCHURE

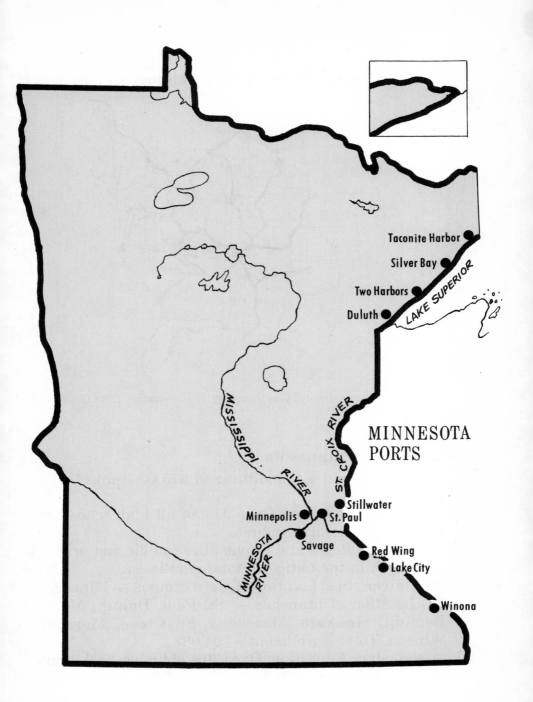

Taconite Harbor

Silver Bay

Two Harbors

Duluth

LAKE SUPERIOR

MISSISSIPPI

RIVER

ST. CROIX RIVER

MINNESOTA
PORTS

Stillwater

Minnepolis

St. Paul

MINNESOTA
RIVER

Savage

Red Wing

Lake City

Winona

Waterway Service from Minnesota

Source: Northern Natural Gas Company *Transportation Data Guide.*

Education in Minnesota

Per Pupil Annual Expenditure: $1,675.00; ranks 7th in nation.

High School Graduates: Over 90% of all high school students in Minnesota graduate.

Minnesota's colleges and universities (public and private) rank 18th in the nation in total enrollment.

State Universities: Location of main campus — Minneapolis. Location of branches — St. Paul, Duluth, Morris, Bemidji, Mankato, Moorhead, St. Cloud, Marshall, Winona. Total Enrollment — 94,082.

Post-secondary Education: Over 70% of high school graduates go on for some kind of post-secondary education.

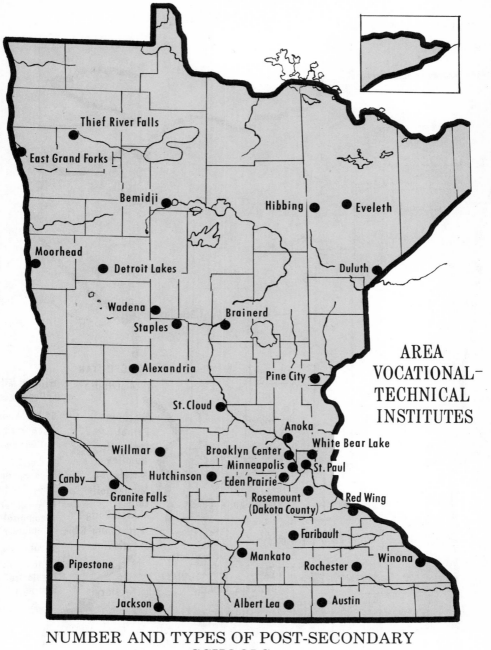

AREA
VOCATIONAL-
TECHNICAL
INSTITUTES

Thief River Falls
East Grand Forks
Bemidji
Hibbing
Eveleth
Moorhead
Detroit Lakes
Duluth
Wadena
Staples
Brainerd
Alexandria
Pine City
St. Cloud
Anoka
Willmar
Brooklyn Center
White Bear Lake
Minneapolis
St. Paul
Canby
Hutchinson
Eden Prairie
Granite Falls
Rosemount
(Dakota County)
Red Wing
Faribault
Pipestone
Mankato
Winona
Rochester
Jackson
Albert Lea
Austin

NUMBER AND TYPES OF POST-SECONDARY
SCHOOLS

Vocational-Technical Schools 33
State Colleges and Universities. 12
State Community Colleges 18
Private Junior Colleges 4
Private Colleges (4-year) 23

351

PRIVATE COLLEGES and PROFESSIONAL SCHOOLS

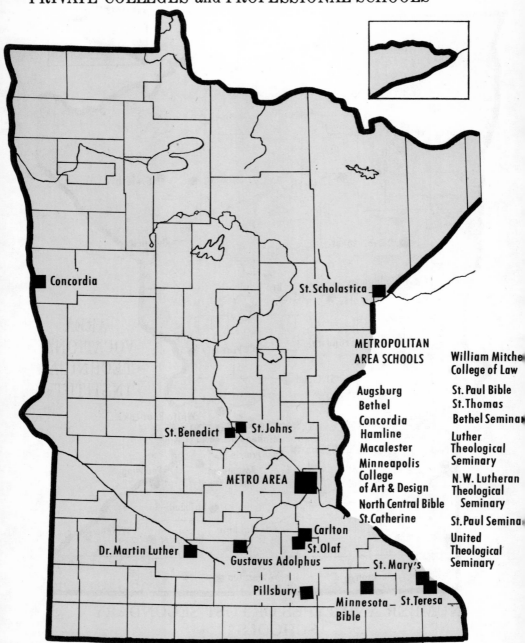

Concordia

St. Scholastica

**METROPOLITAN
AREA SCHOOLS**

Augsburg
Bethel
Concordia
Hamline
Macalester
Minneapolis
College
of Art & Design
North Central Bible
St. Catherine

William Mitchel
College of Law

St. Paul Bible
St. Thomas
Bethel Semina

Luther
Theological
Seminary

N.W. Lutheran
Theological
Seminary

St. Paul Semina

United
Theological
Seminary

St. Benedict   St. Johns

METRO AREA

Dr. Martin Luther

Gustavus Adolphus

Carlton
St. Olaf

St. Mary's

Pillsbury

Minnesota
Bible

St. Teresa

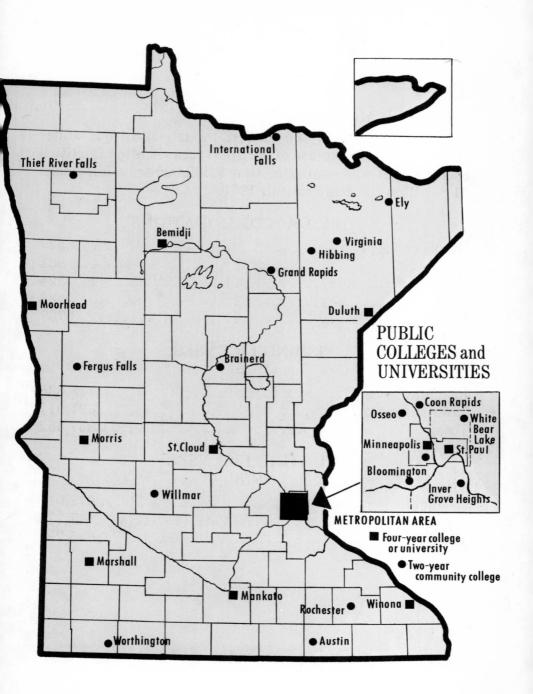

Thief River Falls

International
Falls

Ely

Bemidji

Virginia
Hibbing

Grand Rapids

Moorhead

Duluth

PUBLIC
COLLEGES and
UNIVERSITIES

Fergus Falls

Brainerd

Coon Rapids

Osseo

White
Bear
Lake

Minneapolis

St. Paul

Morris

St. Cloud

Bloomington

Inver
Grove Heights

Willmar

METROPOLITAN AREA

■ Four-year college
or university

Marshall

● Two-year
community college

Mankato

Rochester

Winona

Worthington

Austin

353

Tourism in Minnesota

Tourism is one of the largest industries in our state. Many tourists make use of our sport and vacation facilities each year. It was estimated that 8,398,000 travelers spent $1.8 billion in Minnesota in 1979.

TOURIST ACCOMMODATIONS

Resorts	2,527
Motels	884
Hotels	324
Other	32
Total	3,767

FISHING LICENSES
(1978)

Resident	715,635
Nonresident	321,917
Total	1,037,552

HUNTING LICENSES
(1978)

Resident	678,017
Nonresident	7,279
Total	685,296

MINNESOTA
STATE PARKS

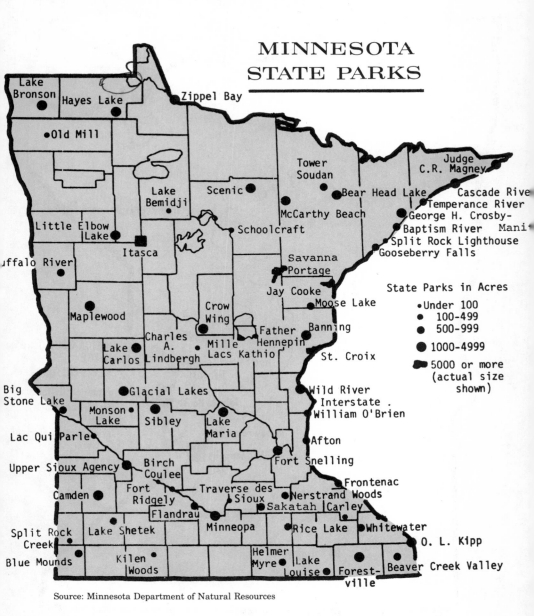

Lake Bronson
Hayes Lake
Zippel Bay
Old Mill
Tower Soudan
Judge C.R. Magney
Scenic
Bear Head Lake
Cascade River
Lake Bemidji
McCarthy Beach
Temperance River
George H. Crosby-
Little Elbow Lake
Schoolcraft
Baptism River   Mani†
Itasca
Split Rock Lighthouse
Gooseberry Falls
uffalo River
Savanna Portage
Jay Cooke
Moose Lake
Maplewood
Crow Wing
Father Hennepin
Banning
Charles A. Lindbergh
Mille Lacs Kathio
St. Croix
Lake Carlos
Big Stone Lake
Glacial Lakes
Wild River Interstate .
Monson Lake
Sibley
Lake Maria
William O'Brien
Lac Qui Parle
Afton
Upper Sioux Agency
Birch Coulee
Fort Snelling
Frontenac
Camden
Fort Ridgely
Traverse des Sioux
Nerstrand Woods
Flandrau
Sakatah
Carley
Split Rock Creek
Lake Shetek
Minneopa
Rice Lake
Whitewater
O. L. Kipp
Blue Mounds
Kilen Woods
Helmer Myre
Lake Louise
Forest-ville
Beaver Creek Valley

State Parks in Acres
• Under 100
• 100-499
● 500-999
⬤ 1000-4999
🦴 5000 or more (actual size shown)

Source: Minnesota Department of Natural Resources

355

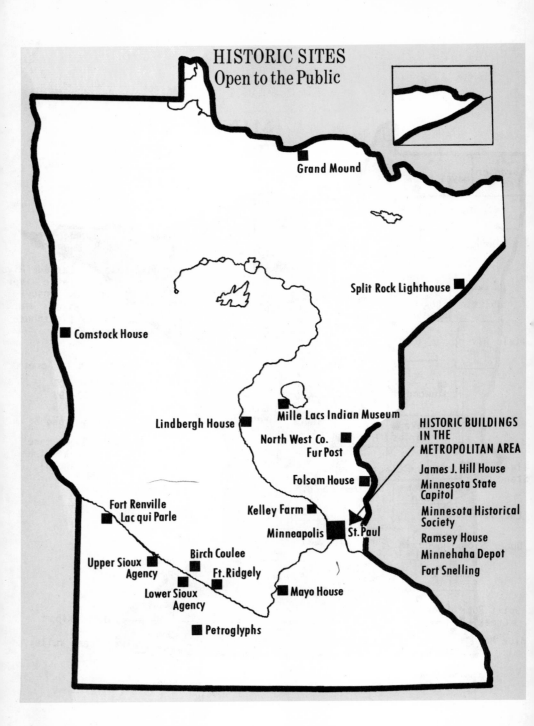

HISTORIC SITES
Open to the Public

Grand Mound

Split Rock Lighthouse

Comstock House

Mille Lacs Indian Museum

Lindbergh House

North West Co.
Fur Post

Folsom House

Fort Renville
Lac qui Parle

Kelley Farm

Minneapolis   St. Paul

Upper Sioux
Agency

Birch Coulee

Ft. Ridgely

Lower Sioux
Agency

Mayo House

Petroglyphs

HISTORIC BUILDINGS IN THE METROPOLITAN AREA

James J. Hill House
Minnesota State Capitol
Minnesota Historical Society
Ramsey House
Minnehaha Depot
Fort Snelling

Park	MAP INDEX	PICNIC GROUNDS	SWIMMING BEACH	TRAILS (F-Foot, H-Saddle, C-Cross Country Ski, S-Snowmobile)	INTERPRETATION	FISHING	CAMP GROUNDS (S-Semi-Modern, R-Rustic, E-Electricity)	SANITARY DUMPING STATIONS	BOATS OR CANOES	GROUP CAMP (P-Primitive, M-Modern)	PARK ENTRANCE SIGNED OFF OF TRUNK HIGHWAY
AFTON	7/26			FC	Under Development						
BANNING	K12 ♿			FCS	•		R		•		23
BAPTISM RIVER	O8			F	•						61
BEAR HEAD LAKE	M7 ♿	•	•	FS	•	•	SR	•	•	P	169
BEAVER CREEK VALLEY	O21	•		FC		•	SR		•	P	76
BIG STONE LAKE	B15	•		FS		•	R	•	•	P	7
BLUE MOUNDS	C6	•	•	FCS	•	•	S			P	75
BUFFALO RIVER	B10	•	•	FC	•	•	Si		•	P	10
CAMDEN	D18 ♿	•	•	FH CS	•	•	SRE			P	23
CARLEY	M19	•		FC		•	R			P	42
CASCADE RIVER	O7	•		FS	•		S			P	61
CHARLES A. LINDBERGH	G13	•		F		•	S	•		P	27/10
CROW WING	H12	•		FCS	•	•	S	•		P	371
FATHER HENNEPIN	J12	•	•	FS	•	•	S		•	P	27
FLANDRAU	G19	•	•	FH CS	•	•	SR	•		PM	15
FORESTVILLE	M21 ♿			FH CS	•	•	R	•		P	16
FORT RIDGELY	G18	•		FH CS	•		R			P	4
FORT SNELLING	X26 ♿♿			FC	•	•			•	P	5
FRANZ JEVNE	H4	•		F		•	R				11
FRONTENAC	M18 ♿	•		FCS	•	•	S			P	61
GEO. H. CROSBY MANITOU	O8	•		FC	•						1
GLACIAL LAKES	E14 ♿	•	•	FS		•	SR		•	P	29
GOOSEBERRY FALLS	N9	•		FCS	•	•	SR		•	P	61
HAYES LAKE	E4 ♿	•		FS		•	S			P	89
HELMER MYRE	J21 ♿	•		FS	•	•	S	•	•	P	16
INTERSTATE	L15	•		F		•	SE	•	•	P	8
ITASCA	F9 ♿ •	•		FCS	•	•	SE	•	•	PM	71/27
JAY COOKE	M11	•		FCS	•	•	S	•		P	39
JUDGE C. R. MAGNEY	R6	•		F	•	•	R			P	61
KILEN WOODS	F21	•		FCS	•	•	S			P	71/86
LAC QUI PARLE	D16	•	•	FHS	•	•	S		•	P	7
LAKE BEMIDJI	F7 ♿	•		FC	•	•	SE	•	•	P	71
LAKE BRONSON	B3 ♿	•	•	FS	•	•	SRE	•	•	P	59
LAKE CARLOS	E13	•	•	FH CS	•	•	SE	•	•	PM	29
LAKE LOUISE	L21 ♿	•		FH CS	•	•	S			P	14/56
LAKE MARIA	I15	•		FC	•				•	P	I-94 152
LAKE SHETEK	D19 ♿	•	•	FS	•	•	SRE	•	•	PM	30
LITTLE ELBOW LAKE	E8	•		F		•	R				113
MAPLEWOOD	D13	•	•	FH CS	•	•	S	•		P	108
McCARTHY BEACH	K7	•	•	FCS	•	•	S		•	P	169
MILLE LACS KATHIO	K13 ♿	•		FH CS	•	•	S	•		P	169/27
MINNEOPA	H19		•	FC	•		S			P	169
MONSON LAKE	L15	•		F		•	R			P	104/9
MOOSE LAKE	K11 ♿	•		FCS	•	•	R		•	P	35/73
NERSTRAND WOODS	K19 ♿	•	•	FCS	•		S	•		P	246
OLD MILL	B5 ♿	•	•	FCS	•	•	R			P	59
O. L. KIPP	O20	•		FC			R			P	90
RICE LAKE	K20 ♿	•	•	FC	•	•	S	•		P	14
ST. CROIX	L13	•	•	FH CS	•	•	SE	•	•	P	48
ST. CROIX WILD RIVER	K14 ♿	•		FH CS	•		S	•		P	95
SAKATAH LAKE	J19	•		FS	•	•	S	•		P	60
SAVANNA PORTAGE	J10	•	•	FCS	•	•	S	•	•	P	65
SCENIC	I8 ♿	•	•	FCS	•	•	S		•	P	169/38
SCHOOLCRAFT	I9	•		F	•		R			P	6/2
SIBLEY	F15 ♿	•	•	FH CS	•	•	SE	•		PM	9/71
SPLIT ROCK CREEK	B20	•	•	F	•	•	R			P	23
SPLIT ROCK LIGHTHOUSE	O9 ♿			F	•						61
TEMPERANCE RIVER	P7	•		FC	•		R			P	61
TOWER SOUDAN	M6	•		FS	•						169
TRAVERSE DES SIOUX	J19	•		FS	•		R				169
UPPER SIOUX AGENCY	L17	•		FCS	•	•				P	67/14
WHITEWATER	M20 ♿	•	•	FC	•	•	SR	•		PM	14/74
WILLIAM O'BRIEN	7-J K16 ♿	•	•	FC	•	•	S	•		P	95
ZIPPEL BAY	F3 ♿	•		FCS	•		R			P	11

△ WAYSIDE PARKS △

Park	MAP INDEX	PICNIC GROUNDS	SWIMMING BEACH	TRAILS	INTERPRETATION	FISHING	CAMP GROUNDS	SANITARY DUMPING STATIONS	BOATS OR CANOES	GROUP CAMP	PARK ENTRANCE SIGNED OFF OF TRUNK HIGHWAY
CARIBOU FALLS	O8	•		F							61
CROSS RIVER	P7	•		F							61
FLOOD BAY	N9	•									61
INSPIRATION PEAK	L12	•		F							78
JOHN A. LATSCH	N19	•		F	•		R				61
JOSEPH R. BROWN	L17	•									212
KODONCE RIVER	R8	•		F	•						61
MINNESOTA VALLEY LAWRENCE WAYSIDE	I18	•		FH CS	•		R				169
MINNESOTA VALLEY TRAIL SITE #2	I17			FHS	•						41
OLD CROSSING TREATY	C6	•		F	•						75
RAY BERGLUND	P7	•		F							61

NOTE: PERMIT REQUIRED FOR ALL VEHICLES ENTERING STATE PARKS. ANNUAL PERMIT—$5.00; OVERNIGHT PERMIT—$1.50; CAMPSITE FEE PER NIGHT—$4.00 SEMI MODERN, $3.00 RUSTIC. NO SEWER OR WATER HOOK-UPS. OVERNIGHT CAMPING IS NOT PERMITTED IN ROADSIDE AREAS UNLESS SO POSTED. FOR INFORMATION ON STATE PARKS, STATE TRAILS, AND CANOE AND BOATING ROUTES TELEPHONE (612) 296-4776.

FREE STATE PARK MOTOR VEHICLE PERMITS ARE AVAILABLE FOR PERSONAL CARS OF VISITORS 65 YEARS OF AGE AND OVER.

FOR INFORMATION ON SPECIFIC AREAS, HUNTING, FISHING, CAMPING OR BUSINESS OPPORTUNITIES IN MINNESOTA WRITE TO VISITOR INFORMATION CENTER, DEPT. M.H.M., 480 CEDAR STREET, ST. PAUL, MINNESOTA 55101.

VOYAGEURS NATIONAL PARK (under development). FOR INFORMATION WRITE TO: VOYAGEURS NATIONAL PARK, P.O. DRAWER 50, INTERNATIONAL FALLS, MINNESOTA 56649.

HISTORIC SITES IN MINNESOTA

Twin Cities Area
1. Old Fort Snelling
2. Old Mendota (Sibley House, Faribault House, Pilot Knob, St. Peter's Catholic Church)
3. Indian Mounds Park, Carver's Cave
4. The Chapel of St. Paul
5. Minnesota Capitol Sites
6. Falls of St. Anthony and the Stone Arch Bridge
7. Minnehaha Falls
8. Peter Gideon Homestead

Central Minnesota
1. Marine Millsite
2. Stillwater, First State Prison and Washington County Courthouse
3. Wm. Le Duc House
4. Wendelin Grimm Farm
5. Oliver Kelley Homestead
6. Fort Ripley — Old Crow Wing
7. Charles Lindbergh House

Southern Minnesota
1. Fort Beauharnois — Old Frontenac
2. Dr. William Mayo House — Mayo Clinic
3. Traverse des Sioux Treaty Site
4. Sioux Uprising Sites:
   Acton
   Lower Agency
   Upper Agency
   Fort Ridgely
   Redwood Ferry Ambush
   New Ulm
   Milford Monument
   Birch Coulee Battle
   Ruins of Joseph Brown House

Battle of Wood Lake

The Hanging of the Sioux

5. Lac qui Parle Mission

6. Pipestone Quarry

Northern Minnesota

1. Minnesota Man Site

2. The Grand Mound

3. Fort St. Charles — The Northwest Angle

4. Lake Itasca

5. Grand Portage — The Witch Tree

6. St. Louis River and Savanna Portages

7. Old Crossing Treaty Site

8. Duluth Ship Canal — Minnesota Point Lighthouse — Vermilion Trail

9. Soudan Mine

10. Mountain Iron Mine

11. Kensington Runestone

ORIGIN OF COUNTY NAMES

Aitkin — William Aitkin, fur trader.

Anoka — Indian name, "both sides."

Becker — George Becker, St. Paul lawyer.

Beltrami — Italian explorer of Minnesota.

Benton — Thomas Benton, promoter of Homestead Act.

Big Stone — Big Stone Lake (translated from Indian name).

Blue Earth — Blue Earth River.

Brown — Joseph R. Brown, early pioneer.

Carlton — Reuben C. Carlton, early settler.

Carver — Jonathan Carver, early explorer.

Cass — Lewis Cass, governor of Michigan Territory.

Chippewa — Chippewa Indians.

Chisago — Indian name, "large and beautiful."

Clay — U.S. Senator and statesman.

Clearwater — Clearwater River and Clearwater Lake.

Cook — Major Cook, soldier.

Cottonwood — Trees along Cottonwood River.

Crow Wing — Translation from Indian "Raven's Feather."

Dakota — Dakota Indians.

Dodge — Henry Dodge, governor of Wisconsin Territory.

Douglas — Stephen C. Douglas, statesman.

Faribault — Jean Baptiste Faribault, fur trader.

Fillmore — Millard Fillmore, U.S. President.

Freeborn — William Freeborn, member of territorial legislature.

Goodhue — James M. Goodhue, early newspaper publisher.

Grant — Ulysses S. Grant, U.S. President; Civil War General.

Hennepin — Father Hennepin, early explorer.

Houston — San Houston, Texas statesman and military leader.

Hubbard — Lucius Hubbard, ninth governor of Minnesota.

Isanti — Santee Tribe (Dakota).

Itasca — Lake Itasca.

Jackson — Henry Jackson, early St. Paul merchant.

Kanabec — Indian meaning for "snake" or "crooked."

Kandiyohi — Indian "where buffalo fish come."

Kittson — Norman Kittson, early fur trader.

Koochiching — Indian name for Rainy River or Rainy Lake.

Lac qui Parle — French-Indian translation, "lake that speaks."

Lake — Lake Superior.

Lake of the Woods — Lake of the Woods.

Le Sueur — Pierre Le Sueur, early explorer.

Lincoln — Abraham Lincoln, U.S. President.

Lyon — General Nathaniel Lyon.

Mahnomen — Indian name, "good berry" (wild rice).

Marshall — William R. Marshall, fifth governor of Minnesota.

Martin — Henry Martin, Mankato pioneer.

McLeod — Martin McLeod, early champion of education.

Meeker — Bradley B. Meeker, Minnesota Supreme Court Justice.

Mille Lacs — Mille Lacs Lake, French "one thousand lakes."

Morrison — Early fur-trading family.

Mower — John E. Mower, member territorial legislature.

Murray — William P. Murray, Minnesota politician.

Nicollet — Joseph Nicollet, early explorer.

Nobles — William E. Nobles, territorial legislature.

Norman — Scandinavian settlers.

Olmsted — David Olmsted, early St. Paul mayor.

Otter Tail — Otter Tail Lake.

Pennington — Edw. Pennington, president of Soo Line Railroad.

Pine — Pine trees.

Pipestone — Pipestone quarry.

Polk — James Polk, U.S. President.

Pope — General John Pope, explorer in Red River area.

Ramsey — Alexander Ramsey, first territorial governor.

Red Lake — Red River and Red Lake.

Redwood — Redwood River (where "red" bushes grew).

Renville — Joseph Renville, fur trader and explorer.

Rice — Henry M. Rice, early political leader.

Rock — Rock River.

Roseau — Roseau River, French-Indian "rush river."

St. Louis — Named by explorer Verendrye for Saint Louis.

Scott — General Winfield Scott, Mexican War leader.

Sherburne — Moses Sherburne of Territorial Supreme Court.

Sibley — Henry H. Sibley, first Minnesota governor.

Stearns — Charles T. Stearns, territorial legislature.

Steele — Franklin Steele, first sawmills at St. Anthony Falls.

Stevens — Major Isaac Stevens, railroad surveyor.

Swift — Henry A. Swift, 3rd Minnesota governor.

Todd — John B. Todd, Fort Ripley commander.

Traverse — Traverse Lake, French-Indian "lake that lies crosswise."

Wabasha — Chief of Dakota tribe.

Wadena — Indian "little round hill."

Waseca — Dakota word "rich" or "fertile."

Washington — George Washington, first U.S. President.

Watonwan — Watonwan River, Indian "where fish abound."

Wilkin — Colonel Alexander Wilkin, Civil War leader.

Winona — Indian maiden.

Wright — Silas Wright, New York statesman.

Yellow Medicine — Yellow Medicine River.

Sources for further information

County Historical Societies

Minnesota Historical Society, 690 Cedar, St. Paul, 55101

State of Minnesota, Documents Division, 117 University Ave., St. Paul (listing of publications)

Minnesota Dept. of Natural Resources, Centennial Bldg., St. Paul, 55101

Minnesota Dept. of Economic Development, 480 Cedar, St. Paul, 55101

International Institute of Minnesota, 1694 Como Ave., St. Paul, 55108

Iron Range Interpretive Center, Division of Iron Range Resources & Rehabilitation Board, Box 329, Chisolm, 55719

Minnesota Forest Industries Information Committee, 208 Phoenix Bldg., Duluth

Minnesota State Dept. of Education, Capitol Square Bldg., St. Paul, 55101

Minnesota Dept. of Transportation, Transportation Bldg., St. Paul

Minnesota Dept. of Agriculture, 270 Metro Square Bldg., 7th & Robert Streets, St. Paul, 55101

Tourist Information Office, 480 Cedar, St. Paul, 55101

Foreign Consulates located in Minnesota

CANADIAN CONSULATE — 15 South 5th Street, Minneapolis 55402

COLOMBIAN CONSULATE — 2218 West Lake of Isles Parkway, Minneapolis 55405

DANISH CONSULATE — 700 1st National Bank Building, Minneapolis 55402

FEDERAL REPUBLIC OF GERMANY — 1238 Baker Building, Minneapolis 55402

FINNISH CONSULATE — 404 Minnesota Federal Bank Building, Minneapolis 55402

MEXICAN CONSULATE — Suite 390, 386 N. Wabasha St., St. Paul

NORWEGIAN CONSULATE GENERAL — 800 Foshay Tower, Minneapolis 55402

SWEDISH CONSULATE GENERAL — 730 2nd Avenue South, Minneapolis 55402

Index

(Preceding the page number,
c stands for chart, m stands for map,
and p stands for photo or drawing.)

Mississippian Indians, 60-1
Mound Builders, 51-61
Mounds, locations of, 53-4, 285
Municipal government, 274-6, (c 274, c 275)

—N—

Natural resources, 40-3
New Ulm, 116, 161-2, 201, 293-4
Newspapers, 242-5
Nicknames (of state), 5
Northwest Fur Company, 86-93, 97
Norwegian exploration, 76

—O—

Ojibwa Indians, see Chippewa Indians
Olson, Floyd B., 193, 308-10, (p 308)

—P—

Parks, 46, 284, 286, 288, 290, 294-6, (m 355, c 357)
Parrant, Pierre, 95-7
Pembina, 90-1, 116
Pemmican, 116, 121
Perrot, 81
Pike, Zebulon, 92-3, 214
Plant life, 23, 30, (m 24)
Population, 17, 131-6, 337-8
Prehistoric cultures, 51-61, 292
Private education, 251-2, 257

—Q—

Quilting bees, 128-9

—R—

Radio, 247-8
Radisson, 78-80, (m 79)
Railroads, 121, 133, 186-9, 208-9, 218, 226-31, 319, 348, (m 229, m 348)
Ramsey, Alexander, 109-10, 119, 131, 150-1, (p 150)
Recreation, 42, 43-6, 282-96
Red River oxcarts, 220-3, (m 222)
Red River Valley, 23, 37, 39, 89-91, 121, 187, 220-3, 322

Red Wing, 71, 116, 131, 135, 201, 288, 311, 313
Roads, 213, 223-5, 232-3, 310, 319
Rolling mill system, 207

—S—

Saint Anthony, 115, 116, 120, 135, 169, 252
Saint Anthony Falls, 81, 94, 115, 205, 208
Saint Cloud, 201, 216, 305
Saint Croix River, 171-3, 175-6, 216-7, 219
Saint Lawrence Seaway, 220, 284, 320
Saint Paul, 83, 95-7, 116, 135, 147-9, 169, 275, 311, 313, 337
Saint Peter, 147-9, 294
Savage, 219, 311, 315
School district government, 277, (c 277)
Scott, Dred, 146
Sea, in ancient times, 30, (m 31)
Selkirk, Lord, 89-91
Sibley, Henry H., 97-9, 118-9, 150-2, 162-3, 223, (p 118)
Sioux Indians, 61, 63-7, 69-71, 80-1, 107-13, 158-64, 266-9, (c 267, c 268)
Sioux War of 1862, 113, 158-64
Size (of Minnesota), 17, 332
Slavery, 145-6, 152
Sod houses, 180-2
Sources for further information, 363
Stagecoach travel, 225-6, 242
State capital, 147-9
State government, 270-2, (c 271)
State symbols, 332-6
Statehood, 144-153
Steamboats, 133, 215-8, 242
Stillwater, 116, 117-9, 131, 135, 169, 241, 252
Street cars, 231-2, 305
Swisshelm, Jane, 145, 245

367